I'm Black, a Minister, and I'm Gay

Be Love

Benjamin Carlton (signature)

Benjamin Carlton

Copyright © 2021

All Rights Reserved

ISBN: 978-1-80128-345-8

Dedication

To my parents Gilda and Ricardo who did their best to raise a queer son in the hood

To my sister's Kandice and Ricquel who love me so dearly

To my cousin's Tianna, Justin, and Kierra who have my back

To my friend's Tim, Keven, Jonathan, Rebecca, Rosie, Tyler, and Chris who keep me grounded

To my friend Jae who drove me from Miami to Cali to pursue my dreams and my twins Brandon and Brian for the best coming out text thread ever

To my Florida A & M University FAMULY, y'all are my everything

To my Pastor Darrick McGhee and my Bible Based Church family for loving me no matter what

To my BMe Community for launching me into the world with love and grace

To my brothers of Alpha Phi Alpha Fraternity, Inc. who welcomed my queerness with open arms

To the many people who've had an encouraging word on my journey

To all the people looking for a word of affirmation

And especially to the little Ben who was always afraid to just be

This one's for you!

From the gorgeous tropical islands in the Gulf of Thailand and the Andaman Sea, to the glacier lagoons in the Land of Fire and Ice, to the Devil's Peak and Lion's Head of Table Mountain, I have traveled the world with computer in tow, writing this book. It is long overdue, but just in time.

My prayer is that your life is forever changed for the good of mankind.

Acknowledgment

To every warrior that has come before me.

To every soul that is in the fight with me.

To every heart that will rise after me.

I acknowledge you!

My hearts Sarah B. Evans, Vivian E. Henry, Lana Felton-Ghee and Benjamin C. Evans Sr.

I miss y'all everyday

About the Author

Benjamin Carlton is an actor, activist, and social entrepreneur from Philadelphia, Pa. He received his MBA from Florida Agricultural & Mechanical University before moving to Miami to pursue a career in accounting. In 2013, he co-founded the iconic BMe Community, a national movement of community builders that are led and inspired by Black people. BMe Community was founded on the principles of valuing all members of the human family, recognizing Black males as assets, and building more caring and prosperous communities together.

Under his leadership, BMe has influenced national policy, and committed millions of dollars to local community leaders around the nation. BMe's 400+ Fellows have raised over $400 million, earned 67 major national awards and helped over 3 million families secure educational, economic, human rights, health and wellness opportunities.

Benjamin has trained the world's leading authorities about asset-framing, storytelling, and narrative change. Some of these entities include the Bill & Melinda Gates Foundation, The Obama Administration, GM Financial, Friends of the Children, Comcast Universal, Focus Features, JP Morgan Chase, Deloitte, and Stanford Social Innovation Review.

In 2016, Benjamin decided to practice what he preached and came out as a gay minister on TheRoot.com. The TEDx speaker took his message of authenticity on the road and encourages his audiences to live their best authentic lives every day. He advocates for a better America and fights for the rights and fair treatment of youth and the Black and LGBTQIA+ communities.

Benjamin has been featured in a myriad of publications and platforms including, ABC, CBS, NBC, TBN, BBC London, FOX Soul, Vogue Magazine, The Miami Herald, and The Huffington Post.

Foreword

Isolation kills. Be it suicide, recidivism, or relapse into addiction, the first domino is typically a deep sense of feeling "alone" in the world. This kind of aloneness can grip high achievers, leaders, outwardly happy people and even ministers.

That's who Benjamin Carlton was when I met him in 2013. An accomplished, good-looking, charming 20-something who had a gift for speaking, creating laughter and making people feel welcomed in his presence. I quickly brought him on as co-founder and managing director of an ambitious fledging startup, called BMe Community, whose mission is to "build more caring and prosperous communities inspired by Black men".

In his heart Benjamin, like most of us, wanted nothing more than to love and be loved by people. That desire simultaneously gave his gifts a purpose and gave rise to probably the greatest challenge of his life. This talented, smart, capable young man was living a closeted life of isolation, and sometimes desperation, even when surrounded by others whom he loved and admired.

This is why his book is so important. Reading it will save lives. You will see yourself in its honesty. Just as importantly, reading it will breathe life into those of us who may not be suicidal but are slowly suffocating beneath everyday cynicism and fear of condemnation, rejection and disaffection for not being good enough, straight enough or ordinary enough to fit in with those around us.

How do you overcome that fear and take enough possession of yourself so that when the condemnation comes – and it will – rather than destroying you, it finally frees you?

I remember when Ben came out to me and our co-founder Sarah Multidor. The three of us were having an otherwise typical operations meeting, and I was recounting my admiration of my friend Susan Davis, the former founding head of BRAC-USA, who had just become a financial backer of BMe. Susan and I coached Social Entrepreneurship for NYU and it was her authenticity as an openly gay social innovator and leader that inspired the grad students to seek her guidance on sacred matters as they pursued their higher callings in life.

Ben took that moment to stop us and say, "There's something I've been working up the nerve to tell you two." In the uneasy pause that followed, a pang of fear shot through me that he might be breaking up the founding team by resigning from BMe! Then he broke the tension with the words "I'm gay, and I've decided to live my truth so that when I'm older like you and Susan, I can have that kind of confidence and joy in my life too." I'm sure that's not verbatim, but that is what he said.

Sarah and I leapt to cheer and embrace him for his powerful statement and step into freedom.

The thing is, freedom is never free, and Benjamin was about to pay the price in ways that I'm sure he hadn't anticipated. Shortly thereafter, for our groundbreaking #BlackMenLove campaign, Ben published his definitive article in The Root, "I'm Black, I'm a Minister, and I'm Gay."

In this naked, sincere piece, he outlined the first time he was made to feel that his very nature was dirty in childhood. He recounted his natural and uncontrollable attraction to men even in church and even during a time when he ministered against homosexuality as a sin. He told the story of a tormented man who did not want to offend his God, his family, his friends or his people and so lived a life of duplicity that affronted his soul, instead.

Even though the article plunged Benjamin into the middle of doctrinal feuds, hate mongering, and vicious social commentary, he emerged from those waters a new man. A stronger man. A Baptist baptized in the waters of his own truth. For the first time, he was a man who could legitimately Moses people through the wilderness of their own emancipation, if they were willing to be as vulnerable and as faithful as he.

Barely 30 years old, Ben was thrust onto national stages, receiving national honors and asked to speak on national issues, laws and incidents. And still BMe Community was a home for him. The men therein, several of whom were ministers of faiths that condemned homosexuality, saw "Brotha Ben" as their brother whom they love and admire – end of story. In BMe Community, we practice loving our family, our whole human family, and Brotha Ben in many ways embodies our beliefs.

We don't practice that hippie-dippy-think-happy-thoughts-and-avoid-conflict kind of love. We practice the other kind where you endure the ugliness of the world and put yourself in harm's way for children who are not your own, and you create light in dark places and build communities from chaos. And for the most part it is all done invisibly and thanklessly to the public eye.

Benjamin is co-founder of an inspired community of Black men who run nonprofits, businesses, communities, cities and movements. Black men who overcome all things to free themselves and others such as Shaka Senghor, NYT bestselling author of "Writing My Wrongs: Life, Death and Redemption in an American Prison"; Jason Wilson, critically acclaimed author of "Cry Like a Man: Fighting for Freedom from Emotional Incarceration" and Chris Wilson, artist, entrepreneur and author of "Masterplan: My Journey from Life in Prison to a Life of Purpose."

These men and over 200 like them are beyond fearless. They are all BMe Community Genius Fellows specifically because they have dedicated their lives to a better future for all of us and because their communities have vouched for their authenticity. It's a powerfully transformative group, and Ben often reminds me that "BMe Community gave me the courage to 'be me'."

So, it is my honor to introduce you to this imperfect, sincere, servant of God who has a different gospel than the one of judgment, condemnation, division and death. In BMe we believe in defining people, all people, by their aspirations and contributions before acknowledging any of their challenges. We call this "Asset-Framing", and it is like taking off the dirty lenses through which you've viewed the world and replacing them with clean, enhanced, lenses polarized to see people's promise and invest in them as assets. In this Gospel of Love & Power, Benjamin Carlton is a convert, a scholar and a minister on the rise. Please enjoy and embrace his testament.

Trabian Shorters is a retired tech entrepreneur, NYT bestselling author, founder of BMe Community and has been recognized as one of the world's leading social entrepreneurs for his pioneering work in Asset-Framing. www.BMeCommunity.org.

Contents

Dedication i
Acknowledgment ii
About the Author iii
Foreword iv
Introduction 1
Chapter 1: Born This Way 14
Chapter 2: Answering the Call 33
Chapter 3: I'm Not Gay No More 60
Chapter 4: It's Time 83
Chapter 5: Judgement Day 101
Chapter 6: Life After Death 115
Chapter 7: Overcoming Trauma 125
Chapter 8: Birth of Authenticity 138
Chapter 9: Coming Out, Again 149
Chapter 10: For the Bible Tells Me So 157
Chapter 11: Sexuality, Religion, and the Black Church 185
Chapter 12: Who Said That? 218
Chapter 13: Love Thy Neighbor 235
Chapter 14: Before the Atlantic Slave Trade 245
Chapter 15: Queer is the New Black 267
Chapter 16: Labels – Are They Needed? 296
Chapter 17: The Journey to Gender 311
Chapter 18: Black Rights is Gay Rights 324
Chapter 19: The Real Gay Agenda 344
Chapter 20: Love Wins; How to Live Free 354

"If I'm not Black enough and I'm not white enough and I'm not man enough, then tell me Tony, what the Hell am I?"

~ *MAHERSHALA ALI, as Don Shirley in Green Book*

Introduction

It was just after I had finished speaking to a group of young people about being their authentic selves and going after their wildest dreams that I had the most transformative encounter with a young man from Miami. During my speech about dreams, I slipped in my coming out story and told them that I became my best self once I became my truest self. As always, the room lit up with a multitude of facial expressions. Some you could tell that there was great interest in my story while others looked confused, especially the adults.

How could this man that I just greatly connected with, that I've grown to admire, that I just spent the last few moments laughing with, possibly be gay? And just like clockwork, after my speech there was a line of young people waiting to speak with me. Some of them with "coming out" stories of their own and others just plain old curious.

But there was one young man that particularly stood out on that day. He stood before me trembling with tears in his eyes, hardly able to speak a word. With his head down, eyes toward the ground, and hands clenched before him, he began to speak. "Mr. Benjamin", he said as one tear fell from his eye.

"Can I speak with you in private?" Considering there was a line of teens still waiting to speak with me I didn't want to cause a scene, so I said sure and motioned to one of the teachers to follow us out to the hallway. He was still hesitant to speak, I'm assuming because the teacher was standing behind him. I mouthed to her to give us some space and she walked down the hall.

Again, he started, "Mr. Benjamin", and the tears started to roll. "I'm like you". I asked him what does he mean, 'like me'? I knew what he meant, but I wanted him to say it.

What this young man said next shook me to my core. "I'm gay and my mom told me I'm going to Hell," and he began to weep, profusely. And then he began to repeat, "I don't want to go to Hell, I don't want to go to Hell."

Before I could get a word out, he started beating the wall and began grunting "I'm not gay. I'm not gay, it's just a phase." Stunned, I could not find the words to say. I was overwhelmed by his emotions. I began to hear my own voice in his voice. I began to see my tears in his tears. I began seeing the teenage version of me breaking down right before my eyes. So young, so bright, so full of life, but so crippled by the horrifying negativity that not only comes from the world but comes from home.

Overcome by relief and maybe even a little compunction he finally turned his eyes away from the floor, looked at me and said, "Please help me".

By this time, I was absolutely done. I had exhausted every ounce of inner restraint I had to keep from bursting out in tears. I needed a hug myself. My eyes filled with tears, the teacher's eyes filled with tears, he, looking depleted, seemed as if he did not fully comprehend what just happened. What were we to do? Where to go from here? I was perplexed because all my training told me not to get pulled into his emotions, not to get too attached to the story, not to get emotional myself. But I wanted to hug him and give him all the love he felt he was missing and reassure him that he was beautifully and wonderfully made, and he was not a mistake and there was nothing wrong with being gay. And most importantly that he wasn't going to Hell.

I took him by the hand, looked him in his eyes, and pointed to his heart and said my brother, my young king, you are not a mistake. You are here on purpose with a purpose and everything about you was made in the image of our Creator. I love you and there are millions of people all over the world who love you just for who you are. Not everybody understands people like us but God's love for us is no different from anybody else's. Know that your mother loves you and cares for you, she just doesn't understand you right now.

He immediately threw his arms around me and hugged me like I was what he'd been searching for his whole life.... a word of affirmation. After a little more dialogue, we prepared to go back into the room, I said wipe your eyes brother and we'll talk after I'm done with everyone else.

He responded, "You wipe your eyes first."

I'm writing this book for the millions of people who are struggling every day to accept who they are and need a word of affirmation. A word that says God loves you and wants you to win. I'm writing this book for the young Benjamin's of the world who wish that there was someone who looked like them, who believed in God like them, and who had a message of love and hope and not degradation and damnation. There is a lot of information in this book that I'm sure will ruffle a lot of feathers. But this is not a gotcha book nor am I trying to come against or attack anyone. I'm simply helping free some people from condemnation and judgement by laying out the truth, exploring misconceptions and shedding light on grey areas no one is quite sure about.

Too often we vilify the other, those whose opinions differ from ours. We jump into shouting matches without first gaining an understanding of the other's point of view. No matter how hard that pill may be to swallow there is always a reason someone thinks the way they do. And if you have love for them and they for you it is a journey worth exploring no matter how long it takes. In the end love will win.

I know my mother loves me but when I came out, she had some pretty harsh words to share. They cut deeply. I could feel them eating away at my core with every word she spoke. I was distraught, I felt lost even. How could this woman who birthed me, raised me, gave me the courage to be anything I wanted to be, now discard me like I never mattered?

I understand now that her response was based in fear and shame. Ingrained within most parents is a natural desire for their children to grow up "normal". And with society's prejudices I would imagine no parent wills for their child to be gay.

My mother feared how others would treat me, how people would judge her and our family, and how the life she imagined for me would never come to fruition. She dreamed of the day I would grow up, get married and give her grandchildren. In one statement, in one fell swoop, I took that dream away from her. I had time to cope with my new reality, rehearse what I would say and digest the realness of it all, while she in a matter of seconds was forced to face the death of the son she knew and had hoped for. Her response was real, her response was human.

In a perfect world my mother would have welcomed me with open arms. She would have hugged me and told me it's us against the world. But sadly, we don't live in a perfect world and there are so many misconceptions and negative stories about being gay. And this my friend is where healing begins, by removing what is false and replacing it with what is real.

In 2013, I joined a small team of social entrepreneurs in Miami to co-found BMe Community, a national network of leaders and innovators dedicated to building more caring and prosperous communities. Our work is based on Trabian Shorters' award-winning research on the principles of Asset Framing, which identifies people based on their aspirations and contributions not their deficits.

I got to travel the country inspiring all these amazing people to be themselves when all the while I wasn't being myself. So, in 2015 I broke the internet with an article on theroot.com entitled "I'm Black, I'm a Minister and I'm Gay." It had over 4 million views, hundreds of thousands of shares and tons of opinions - many of which are not worth sharing. On that day, I was judged by hundreds of thousands of people who had never met me. Never experienced my smile, my big boisterous laugh or witnessed the many tears I cried at night trying to rid myself of what I thought was my deficit.

In my work I've learned that their response to my vulnerability and their desire to "fix me" was motivated by one simple yet powerful mechanism, narrative.

The stories you tell become the life that you live. Everybody walks around with pre-scripted narratives about everything. Most of us live, act, and are because of the stories that we've been told. Whether it's through family, church, the media, or friends, people respond to one another based on narratives. Out of all the years people have fought to condemn homosexuals, there has never been any real evidence to support the notion that homosexuality is wrong other than the fear mongering narratives.

Surprisingly enough I used to be a condemner of homosexuals. I used to proudly stand before hundreds of people and say homosexuals are going to Hell. I strongly believed that homosexuality was a sin, and the gay agenda was going to destroy our Christian values. I even preached deliverance and pretended to be delivered from homosexuality because that is what we as ministers were supposed to do.

Was I harsh about it? Yes. Was I mean spirited when talking about it? Yes. Why? Because I was repeating a merciless pattern of hatred and ignorance that must be stopped. I was repeating what I had been told and quoting scriptures I had no understanding of. I had witnessed other great ministers of the gospel, who were secretly gay, judging and condemning homosexuals and receiving great applause and admiration and I fell right into the same trap. Why? Because it was the acceptable thing to do. It was orthodox.

The Path Forward: Dethroning Toxic Religion

The only way forward is to talk about it. It's a conversation most ministers and churches are not willing to have. Not because of the certainty of it all, but because of the uncertainty of it all.

Many can't even point to the direct scripture that says homosexuality is wrong. Most of us only know homosexuality is wrong because of what we've been told. The most common misconception being it's a choice. I'm a living witness, it's not. I, like so many others, have tirelessly tried to rid myself of my same sex attraction my whole life. Nothing worked. The worst of it all is the children and teens who are forced to stop their same sex attraction via abuse, conversion therapy, or even being forced to have sex with the opposite sex, and the list goes on.

It seems like out of all the "sins" listed in the Bible homosexuality is plastered as number one. Not because it is number one but because of the billions of dollars that have been placed behind telling the story of the great sin known as homosexuality.

When I travel around the world and speak about love and being free and I denounce the notion that homosexuality is an abomination, I always get the same type of questions and comments. How can you be a minister and contradict what the Bible says? Aren't you afraid to go to Hell? You are a false prophet. You are switching the Bible around to meet your needs. God created Adam and Eve, not Adam and Steve.

I don't get upset and neither am I offended because I used to ask those same questions. I generally respond with a few questions of my own, most of which go unanswered.

- *Do you agree with the horrifying acts of the Atlantic Slave Trade?* No, oh ok because in the Bible slavery was perfectly ok.[1]

- *Would you report a parent who beat their child in the face with a stone they found on the side of the road?* Yes, you would? But that means you'd be switching the Bible around to meet your needs because in the Bible that's what parents did when their child was being naughty.[2]

- *Would you agree if a judge encouraged a rape victim to marry her rapist simply because he had the right to?* You wouldn't!?!? But in the Bible that was the law.[3]

The next question I ask generally breeds anger and angst because it is a collective picture of what life was in ancient times.

- *Do you believe God is really as sexist, racist, abusive, and pro-slavery as the Bible reads? If so, will heaven be sexist, racist, abusive, and pro-slavery as well?*

Most people either don't have an answer or they stretch scripture to explain away something that is written very clearly. So, if you can stretch scripture for this, why can't I stretch scripture for that? My point is not to knock the Bible or discredit its validity but point out the stark contrast to life today versus life then. We can't base our entire lives on customs, traditions, and laws simply because they are in the Bible.

Practices like slavery, sexism, and community death sentences were common in antiquity. Biblical instruction that allowed for them in certain contexts wasn't necessarily God's approval. The Bible is our source of hope and inspiration, but it is also a history book. We must interpret instruction, who gave the instruction, the time in which they

---

[1] Exodus 21:1-11; 25:39-55; Deuteronomy 15:12-18
[2] Deuteronomy 21:18-21
[3] Deuteronomy 22:28-29

gave the instruction and whether it was God inspired or man-made. Stoning children to death is NOT God inspired. I believe anything anti-love is anti-God.

Most well-meaning Christians who believe homosexuality is wrong don't have a full understanding of the Bible in its totality. Why? Because most Christians don't read or know the Bible. At least 50% of Christians don't read the Bible while most of the other 50% only read their Bible 3 to 4 times a year. [4] This is what makes our fight for love and equality so frustrating and the reason the information in this book is so important. People who often use the Bible to discriminate don't understand the source in which they are using to condemn. Instead, they spend most of their time making sure other people are respecting a religion they don't know very much about themselves.

If you are reading this book in hopes of finding a scripture that supports homosexuality, stop reading right now. Because you won't. What you will find is irrefutable evidence that the Bible, though cherished and sacred, though the source of faith, though the story of God's love in flesh, contains ideas and ways of living that are not God inspired.

You see how I didn't use the term "lies". Most modern scholars of the Bible shy away from using the word lie, and for understandable reasons, it's a lot to take in. It normally turns people off immediately because how could the Bible contain any lies at all. Most scholars use a different term for the lies and forgeries and call such books and scriptures "pseudepigrapha."[5]

---

[4] American Bible Society, . (2015). State of the Bible 2015. https://americanbible.org/uploads/content/State_of_the_Bible_2015_report.pdf. Retrieved September 10, 2021, from https://americanbible.org/uploads/content/State_of_the_Bible_2015_report.pdf.

[5] Ehrman, B. D. (2011, May 26). *Who Wrote The Bible and Why It Matters*. HuffPost. https://www.huffpost.com/entry/the-bible-telling-lies-to_b_840301

The term used in seminary and universities simply means, "writing that is inscribed with a lie." The Bible is not a book that was written all at once. The stories you read were first told by word of mouth and then passed down from generation to generation. Then stories and books were written and translated and pieced together over thousands of years. To live by the letter alone without understanding is an effort in futility and practically impossible, and quite frankly would be illegal.

Love is the Principal Matter

Let me let it be known that I am a follower of Christ, I love the Lord and I am a believer of His word. My faith rest on the Great Command of the New Testament. Love.

Love is the one and only law in the New Testament. There were about 613 laws in the Old Testament, and only one in the New. Love is the basis for the entire Law (Matthew 22:35-40).

Love is what I see, and love is what I hear in my LGBTQIA+ communities. I hear story after story of children who have been adopted by same gender parents and they all couldn't be happier. I've seen love and family flourish in all my gay circles. We've seen gay leaders go on to make great change all around the world. We've worn clothes designed by gay people, sung songs written and performed by gay people, listened to sermons preached by gay people, and clapped to choir songs written and directed by gay people.

We've seen love, we've seen pure gay love and it is glorious.

With this book, I'm hoping to start a movement #imfreeforme with the tagline; I'm free for me be free for you. We have an opportunity to take this message of hope across the world and help others walk in their truth and freedom. With so many in America and around the world finally waking up to the fact that all the big bad scary stories about homosexuals aren't true, we have an amazing opportunity to shape the next generation. So often many people live for others and live under the spell of other people's opinions. Whether it be about what you wear, who you love, what profession you take, someone always has something to say. Yes, I know we are all born into families and cultures we didn't ask for. They are pre-existing norms over which we have no control. Some of them are wonderful ways of living and others not so much. We're taught to hate, to compare, we're taught to be prejudice, sexist, homophobic and the list could go on.

We allow these norms to control how we act, how we think, and how we interact with one another even if we find evidence to the contrary. For 29 years I pretended to live my life as a straight male knowing full well I was gay. I had adopted a narrative that was ingrained in me since I was a boy – and that was boys don't kiss boys. I allowed other people's judgements and opinions about who I should be to control my life. We may not have asked to be born into these circumstances, but we certainly don't have to adhere to them once we know better.

I opened the introduction with the story about the young man who was struggling internally with who he was with deep fears of spending an eternity in Hell. When he said, "I'm like you", I knew what he meant but I wanted him to say it. When I came out to my Aunt Dee Dee years ago, I spent most of the conversation beating around the bush. She did something that was so simple yet so powerful. She made me say it. She said say it out loud and be proud when you say it. And I started to cry and I smiled so proudly and said, "I am gay". From that day on I encourage people to say what and who they are out loud and proud. I want people to be free for themselves. Free to speak for themselves, free to live for themselves. Most thought that when marriage equality passed in 2015 in the United States Supreme Court that somehow the gays had arrived. Yes, this was a great victory in the fight for equality, but there are state laws that still heavily discriminate against the LGBTQIA+ community. There are gay people all over the world that are still persecuted and even killed in the name of God.

Today there are hundreds of youth who commit suicide simply because they were told they would burn in Hell for being gay. I'm writing this book because it's imperative for everyone to know what the Bible actually says about homosexuality.

Readers, especially those who are of the faith can expect to learn a little and even debate a little. Most will have some of their foundation shaken with pure fact. You will learn from my life story. You'll learn why and how I arrived at this point in my life, where I am absolutely sure, and why it was important for me to come out in such a public way.

This book not only gives meaning to those looking to be free from the bondage of judgement, but it frees many from having a judgmental mindset. It destroys the narrative that says God is a big bad wolf looking to punish you for the slightest thing you've done wrong. It crushes the notion that homosexuality is wrong, anti-God, and most assuredly will send you to Hell.

I want those who are in hiding to read my story and have enough courage to begin living in their truth. No, they don't have to come out like I did but at least begin walking in who they are with dignity.

There is no doubt in my mind that you reading this right now were created on purpose with a purpose. And that purpose is aligned with the truth of who you are. Until you bring your full self to the table the Universe cannot provide everything designed for you because you are not present to receive it.

My hope is that you walk away after reading this book with a great understanding of how to walk in your truth, live your truth, or help others live in their truth; no matter what the truth is. Because you can run from your truth, hide from your truth, even try to bury your truth, but at the end of the day, you are your truth.

> *"I'm beautiful in my way*
> *'Cause God makes no mistakes*
> *I'm on the right track, baby I was born this way"*
> *~ LADY GAGA: Born This Way*

Chapter 1: Born This Way

As a kid, I always had a special girlfriend or boyfriend, starting all the way back to preschool. I was a handsome little guy with a big head, gumby box fade, and a tail with the colors of the South African flag beaded on it. My mom kept me well dressed, and I was extremely nice. I made friends with practically everybody. I loved to smile and make others smile. That was my gift. When I arrived, I brightened up a room. Surprisingly enough, that remains true today. No matter where I am, I am bound to make a friend.

It was on the first day of preschool when I realized I had a type, yup, that early. All of us kids were on the playground running around when out of nowhere, I was pushed to the ground. It happened so fast I didn't even get a chance to see who did it. As I rolled over, there was a figure standing over me. But when the figure spoke, I was absolutely stupefied. She said, with the most fiendish voice, you stepped on my sneaker, and you better say sorry. Shaken up, I just started wondering how a girl could be so strong and why did she have to push me so hard. Before I could even apologize, she was whisked away by another group of kids playing tag, and I was left on the ground confused. Who is she? Why did she push me? Where did she go? I got up, ran after her, and made sure she knew just how sorry I was. But I'm not sure what good that did because, by the time the day was over, she would have pushed be four more times. When my mother came to pick me up from school, I was so excited to introduce her to my new girlfriend. She responded, you like snot-nosed little girls. I'm not sure if I didn't recognize it or if none of that mattered, but she did have a snotty nose, hair pulled back by two big braids and a gray sweatsuit. So yes, I guess I did like snot-nose roughneck little girls.

Now that I'm older, I realized I had a type, tomboys. The girls who played rough, played sports, and who quite frankly carried masculine energy. A tomboy is a girl who exhibits characteristics or behaviors considered typical of a boy, including wearing masculine clothing and engaging in games and activities that are physical in nature and are considered in many cultures to be unfeminine. Many of my adolescent girlfriends were tomboys who all played sports better than me. As a matter of fact, three of the girls I dated while in middle school are all masculine identifying lesbians today.

Do you think because I was drawn to their masculine energy and they were drawn to my feminine energy? Hhmmmm, something to ponder. My first encounter with a boy was in preschool as well. There was a fellow preschooler who used to take the van service home with me after school, and we were always the last two to be dropped off. Our van driver was old and moved really slow. And I'm not sure how, but he managed to hit every pothole known to man in Philadelphia. One day he hit a real huge pothole, and my guy friend fell over on top of me. We both laughed and made a game out of it. Whenever the driver hit a pothole, my friend would fall on top of me, or I would fall on top of him. This game went on for weeks. One day after a huge pothole, my friend fell on top of me but didn't get off. He looked me right in my eyes and didn't get up. Then he started to hump up and down. I wasn't quite sure what was going on, but I liked it. I smiled and began to hump him back. So, the "game" went from falling on top of each other when we hit a pothole to falling on top of each other for any reason. A wide turn, a stop at a light, a bug on the window, rain, any reason we could think of to get on top of one another.

I don't think we realized the magnitude of what we were doing. At least I know I certainly hadn't at that age seen a sexual act before. I didn't know the word sex until I was in middle school. We just liked each other, and I could not wait until the end of the day to get on the van. He got picked up before me. The back row was our meetup spot.

It wasn't until Kindergarten I realized humping boys was a big no-

no.

It was a normal day in class, and we were playing dress-up and role play. On some days, we played with the Hospital set up and pretended to be doctors with patients, and other days, we played with the McDonald's set and pretended to serve customers. It was normal for us to play families and claim this person as my wife or this person as my child. On this particular day we were playing house in the kitchen doing dishes, baking pretend cakes, and talking about nothing. I was pretending I was just coming in from work, and I had kissed one of the guys. He pushed me away and wiped his face, and said, 'you nasty.'

It was innocent, as most things are when you're 5. I didn't think anything of it. I had seen my dad kiss my mom many days when he came into the house, and us kids gave each other little pecks in most of our role playing. But when all the rest of the kids burst out with 'Oooohhh I'm telling' and 'You nnnaassstyyy', I knew I had done something wrong. I wasn't quite sure why it was wrong; I just knew it was wrong. Now that I'm older, I wonder if anyone went home and told their parents because nothing ever came of it. The drama of it all only lasted for the remainder of the day as some kid would tell another, 'Him kissed so and so.'

I was the type of kid that never liked to get in trouble, so I did everything I could to please everyone. From my parents, to my teachers, to my friends. So, when all the kids ridiculed me for kissing my guy friend, I felt really bothered. Was I the weird kid now? Did I have cooties? I honestly could not understand what the problem was and why they made fun of me.

But nonetheless, no one likes to be made fun of, so I never kissed another guy in that class again.

As I began to explore more of who I was, I began to push the envelope a little, and this time at home. Being braver, being bolder, forgetting that something wasn't quite right with boys kissing boys or boys acting like girls. During my preschool years, my family and I lived in a small apartment in the Northwest side of Philadelphia, now known as Uptown. My mom, dad, baby sister, and me. All of my family grew up near each other. I didn't need many friends because I always had my cousins. My maternal grandmother had 14 children, and my great-grandmother 11. Four of my aunts lived just blocks away. My great aunt lived just around the corner.

There was never a moment where I had time to just be on my own and discover myself. My cousins were always around. For instance, there was this girl I liked, and yes, she was a tomboy. She dared me to kiss the ground to prove I liked her. Like a dummy, I did, and she put a bug on top of my head. By the time I got home, the news had already been reported to my mom, and though I got in trouble for kissing the ground, she seemed more interested in the girl I had a crush on.

I'm pretty sure my mom recognized my feminine tendencies, and maybe that's why she was so interested in the girl I liked at age 6. Either way, she was about to get a dose of the real me in front of everybody.

It was like a scene right out of a TV-Sitcom or movie. It was a gathering at my mom's apartment, and we had a lot of family over. I don't know what possessed me to do this, but I went into my mom's room and put on my sister's patent leather wedge heels and came prancing out the bedroom into the party. The first thing I heard was, 'oooohhhh Gilda look at Ben-Ben.' I stood there smiling ear to ear with my hands on my hips. But that smile quickly turned to fear after I saw the look on everyone else's faces, especially my mom's.

It was a look I had never seen before. It was a sheer look of utter embarrassment and disgust and rage. Who was this lady? What was she about to do to me?

She stood there for a brief moment and just looked at me. I can only imagine what she was thinking. After her initial shock, she grabbed the first thing she could find, grabbed me by the hand, and spanked me back into the room. My mother never explained why she was spanking me. She just spanked me. Even still, after I got a spanking and was practically embarrassed in front of everyone, I still could not figure out what I did wrong. I just remember thinking I didn't even do anything.

My next incident forced her to have a conversation with me. It was at another gathering at my house with the normal crew, her sister's, and a few cousins. I don't know what caused me to always act out while everyone was over, but I just did. One of my guy friends was over, and we were in the backroom wrestling. He was a couple of years older than me, and I had a huge crush on him. I liked hanging around him. He would be the only reason why I did "guy things" around the neighborhood.

We got tired after about an hour of tussling and wrestling, and he rested on top of me after a wrestling move. I wasn't about to push him off me, so I did what I naturally knew how to do, I kissed him. He pushed off me and ran out of the room and went wailing to my mom. I heard him yell, 'Ben is being nasty he kissed me.' This he announced in front of everyone.

I was so scared I started to cry. Here was preschool all over again. But this time, my mother was going to beat my behind.

She came back into the room with that same look on her face. I just knew I was in for it. But this time, she didn't spank me. She sat me down, looked me in my eyes, and asked, what is wrong with you? I responded with a shoulder shrug and tears. Our conversation basically boiled down to boys don't kiss boys, and I had to stay in the room for the rest of the night.

Ever since that moment, she pushed extra hard for me to get involved in "guy things" and hang with the guys, none of which I had an interest in.

I was so stubborn and somewhat spoiled.

She sent me to basketball camp, and I acted a fool. My cousin's dad was the coach. He had us all stand in line and shoot the ball into the basket. I could never get the ball in the basket. I was short with a big head. I didn't hit my growth spurt until I was 8 years old. Even when I jumped, the ball didn't even get close. All my cousins made the basket and laughed at me when I didn't.

I was embarrassed and mad because I didn't even want to be there. My turn came up again, I threw the ball away from me and didn't even attempt to get it in the basket. The coach yelled at me in front of everyone and asked, 'what are you a girl or something?'

The room got so small as all eyes were on me. Tears welled up in my eyes. He yelled some more and made me go dribble the ball in the corner. I was so hurt, so embarrassed. How could he call me a girl in front of all the guys? Was I a girl? Did God make a mistake?

That was the first time I really internalized that something was different about me, and I wasn't like the other guys. I got teased at school, got in trouble at home, and now called a little girl at basketball camp. Who am I, and why can't I ever get it right? When he brought me home, he told my mom that I was not allowed to come back until I fixed my attitude. Needless to say, I never fixed my attitude.

All these life-altering experiences happened before I reached the age of 7. I learned to be ashamed of myself before I even really knew myself. Adults, well-meaning I'm sure, publicly defined me before I could even define myself. I was essentially told that who I am was wrong and I better act a certain way if I wanted to be accepted. No one, especially a young child should experience this coming from those who are supposed to make them feel safe and empowered.

I felt most of the times unsafe and unwanted and I did a darn good job of hiding it. There was so much hidden behind my smile and my will to make everyone else happy. I suspect now because I wasn't happy.

Make no mistake, I want everyone to know that my mother and my family weren't necessarily cruel, just misguided. My mother loved me and gave me the best care. Oddly enough the love of my family is how I survived. In the 80's and 90's, psychology said homosexuality was a mental illness, the AIDS epidemic had everyone believing all gays would die, and the church damned gays to Hell. How would you expect anyone to act when propaganda on all sides fed into their worst fears? I mean, you could literally be anything in the hood, an alcoholic, a teen mother, a thief, a whoremonger, a crackhead, but for heaven's sake JUST DON'T BE GAY! I knew exactly what I liked at a very early age. I knew I liked guys as soon as I started having interactions with them. There is no question or doubt in my mind as to whether I was born gay or not. Discredited doctrine and even popular consensus say the reason why people become gay is because of the lack of fatherly influence or some kind of sexual abuse.

The American Psychiatric Association notes that sexual abuse does not appear to be any more prevalent among children who grow up and identify as homosexual vs. children who grow up and identify as heterosexual.

I have never been sexually abused by a man, and my father was around the first six years of my life. I know plenty of gay people all over the world who have both parents and have never been sexually abused. I was born gay, and according to them, so were they.

Born A Sinner?

This next section is about to get really technical and nerdy concerning sin and science. If that's not your cup of tea feel free to move on to the next chapter. But at some point, you're going to want to come back to this section.

Some theologians and pastors have stopped arguing whether a person is born gay or not, and they point to the Bible and say we are all born into sin. They use Psalm 51:5 to support their viewpoint, which says. "Behold, I was shapen in iniquity; and in sin did my mother conceive me." Biblical Scholars use this scripture as a source for the Original Sin Doctrine, which is an important doctrine within the Roman Catholic Church. Original sin is an Augustine Christian doctrine that says that everyone is born sinful. This means that they are born with a built-in urge to do bad things and to disobey God, which ultimately explains how a person could be born gay. This is a huge stretch of scripture, considering this point is based on a hyperbole, an exaggerated statement, or claims not meant to be taken literally.

Without getting too much into the weeds. King David had a woman's husband killed so he could sleep with her. He intentionally sent him off to war to the frontlines, where he died. King David and the man's wife Bathsheba have a baby, and the baby died. God sent the Prophet Nathan to confront David about this huge transgression. David then writes Psalm 51, which is a Poetic Song to the Lord in repentance for what he has done. There he writes, "I was shapen in iniquity; and in sin did my mother conceive me." One could conclude that he was saying I was born into sin, while another could conclude that his mother conceived him while SHE was SIN-NING. No one is sure.

David's Psalm is full of hyperboles - Psalm 51:7-8 "Purge me with hyssop, and I shall be clean: wash me, and I shall be whiter than snow. Make me to hear joy and gladness; that the bones which thou hast broken may rejoice." David is not literally asking God to show up and physically give him a bath or unbreak his bones. He is asking God to forgive him and clean him up in the spirit. My interpretation is that David is so remorseful, not because he sinned but because his baby died, and he was being reprimanded by the prophet. He's basically saying I've been cursed by sin since before I was born, I've been surrounded by it since I came out of my mother's womb. My mother had me while she was surrounded in sin. Sounds more like an excuse than a statement of spiritual order.

The Bible does not mention King David's mother by name. We don't have much information on his mother other than she was a godly woman (Psalm 86:16). Some Biblical scholars believe David's sisters, Abigail and Zeruiah, may have been his half-sisters and that their father was not Jesse but Nahash. The Bible refers to Abigail as the daughter of Nahash (2 Samuel 17:25). So, was David's mother having an affair? Was this the sin David is referring to? These theories could explain why David was not accepted by his family, was smaller than his brothers, considered a stranger to his own mother's children (Psalm 69:8), and was left out when it was time to choose a King (1 Samuel 16:11).

Considering there are so many unknowns, we can't possibly use Psalm 51:5 to put a stamp on we are all born into sin. Thus, you can be born into sinful gayness.

Who Determines What Sin Is?

Most of us are born with the ability to activate our own free will and live on our own accord. We can think, do, and say what we want when we want. It is only when we encounter boundaries or rules placed on us by the laws of physics, the laws of the land, or the laws of our family that we explore what the church has deemed cardinal sins.

The church first called them the seven deadly sins. Pope Gregory the Great made up the list in the 6th century, and in the 14th century, Geoffrey Chaucer popularized them in his *Canterbury Tales.* The early church classified the seven deadly sins as cardinal sins or capital vices and taught that they could not be forgiven.

The Seven Deadly Sins Are

- Pride: The inordinate love of self. A super-confidence and high esteem in your own abilities also known as vanity.
- Envy: Resenting another person's good fortune or joy or the intense desire to have an item that someone else possesses.
- Lust: Is a strong passion or longing, especially for sexual desires.
- Wrath: Is strong anger and hate towards another person.
- Gluttony: Choosing to over-consume food or drink.
- Greed: The inordinate love of and desire for earthly possessions.
- Sloth: Is an excessive laziness or the failure to act and utilize one's talents.

I'm really surprised Pope Gregory the Great didn't add lying as a deadly sin, considering that's the most common behavior we come across. Maybe he was a liar and didn't want to call himself out.

The seven deadly sins don't actually appear in the Bible per se. A slightly different set of sins can be found in Proverbs 6:16-19, "These six things the Lord hates, yes, seven are an abomination to Him:

1. A proud look,
2. a lying tongue,
3. hands that shed innocent blood,
4. a heart that devises wicked plans,
5. feet that are swift in running to evil,
6. a false witness who speaks lies,
7. and one who sows discord among brethren."

Additionally, Galatians 5:19-21 mentions several more sins to be on our guard against: "Now the deeds of the flesh are evident, which are: immorality, impurity, sensuality, idolatry, sorcery, enmities, strife, jealousy, outbursts of anger, disputes, dissensions, factions, envying, drunkenness, carousing, and things like these, of which I forewarn you, just as I have forewarned you, that those who practice such things will not inherit the kingdom of God."

Notice how homosexuality is not listed but is considered by the church as one of the biggest "sins." Nonetheless, at some point or another, most people have dealt with one or more of all the sins listed. Furthermore, most people don't believe something as simple as jealousy or outburst of anger will keep you out of heaven. But yet there it is in plain sight.

Judge Ye Not!

We must be very careful what we repeat and believe simply because a preacher said it or because it's in the Bible. We willfully can become the voice of the oppressor. I believe we must, as sound-minded, loving, and caring human beings, raise questions with the Bible when something seems inconsistent with the character of God revealed in Jesus Christ.

Remember, sexual orientation is a pattern of desire, not of behavior or sexual acts per se. It is not a simple act of will or a performance. We fall in love with other human beings because we have gay, straight, or bisexual desires, not because we simply chose to do so. We were all born with different natural sexual desires, and we all deserve the right to live in peace about it.

People can be extremely cruel about someone else's life. I was born Black and gay, and feminine in an American hood. I was ridiculed at home, at school, at church, at the barbershop, and pretty much everywhere I went. I was the brunt of the jokes, the whisper of the gossip, the embarrassment of the sport, the one who didn't belong.

The most important thing I learned from my mother was how to be resilient. I don't know if she noticed the teasing and gossiping and indirectly gave me tools to combat it. Either way, I'm glad she did. I had an air of pride about myself that I still carry today. Can't nobody tell me nothing? I'm the smartest, most courageous, most brilliant man to walk this earth. Just kidding, but my external confidence is next to none. Though they teased me, and yes, it hurt like Hell, I always knew I was going to do something amazing with my life. I decided to take the high road and walk in love and spread love. The young me wanted to save the world and cure every broken heart. I didn't want anyone to feel what I felt.

Unfortunately, there are so many others who are not as fortunate. Suicide is the third leading cause of death among young people, resulting in about 4,400 deaths per year, according to the Centers for Disease Control.[6] Bully victims are between 2 to 9 times more likely to consider suicide than non-victims, according to studies by Yale University.[7] Gay teens are four times more likely than straight teens to

---

[6] Facts About Suicide. (n.d.). CDC. Retrieved September 10, 2021, from https://www.cdc.gov/suicide/facts/index.html
[7] *Bullying-suicide link explored in new study by researchers at Yale.* (2017, December 21). YaleNews. https://news.yale.edu/2008/07/16/bullying-suicide-link-explored-new-study-researchers-yale

attempt suicide.[8]

Only 37% of LGBT youth report being happy, while 67% of non-LGBT youth say they are happy. However, over 80% of LGBT youth believe they will be happy eventually, with nearly half believing that they will need to move away from their current town to find happiness.[9]

Hello! Sound like someone you know (vigorously waves hand in the air). I always knew I would be something great, hence happier, and I moved 2000 miles away from home as soon as I was able to.

It broke my heart when in 2018, 9-year-old Jamel Myles killed himself because he came out as gay. Jamel told his mom that he was ready to come out to his friends when he returned back to school after summer break. It took just four days for the bullies to convince him to kill himself. Madissen Paulsen and Sophia Leaf-Abrahamson, two 11-year-old schoolgirls who took their own lives within months of each other, were struggling with their sexuality while being bullied. We must advocate for the ending of the mistreatment of others because of the way they were born. And if truth be told, young people are not prone to suicide because they are gay. I was happy being gay. I liked my boyfriends. I was prone to sadness and depression because of the harmful rhetoric and rejection I heard from friends and family. If I can't be safe at home, I can't be safe anywhere. Rejection from those that are supposed to love you and protect you can make you feel like your life is worthless. Family and friend's acceptance is the cornerstone of any young person's development. It is important that we be there for them even when we don't understand or disagree. While you may disagree with who they are, it's never okay to make

---

[8] Child Mind Institute. (2021, July 23). *LGBT Teens, Bullying, and Suicide*. https://childmind.org/article/lgbt-teens-bullying-and-suicide/

[9] Human Rights Campaign. (2012). Growing up LGBT in America: HRC youth survey report & key findings.

them feel anything less than human for being who they are. For that reason, because of my lived experience, I encourage all young people to find love where love is being given. Pure love, safe love. Your teacher, your best friend, your neighbor, your pet, there is somebody out there that loves you. And if you can't find love, you love yourself. I remind them that they are never alone and that their life is valuable.

"If I speak with human eloquence and angelic ecstasy but don't love, I'm nothing but the creaking of a rusty gate. If I speak God's Word with power, revealing all his mysteries and making everything plain as day, and if I have faith that says to a mountain, "Jump," and it jumps, but I don't love, I'm nothing. If I give everything I own to the poor and even go to the stake to be burned as a martyr, but I don't love, I've gotten nowhere. So, no matter what I say, what I believe, and what I do, I'm bankrupt without love.

Love never gives up. Love cares more for others than for self. Love doesn't want what it doesn't have. Love doesn't strut, doesn't have a swelled head, doesn't force itself on others, isn't always "me first," doesn't fly off the handle, doesn't keep score of the sins of others, doesn't revel when others grovel, takes pleasure in the flowering of truth, puts up with anything, trusts God always, always looks for the best, never looks back, but keeps going to the end." - Corinthians 13:1-7

Being gay is natural, hating gay is a lifestyle choice –Author Unknown

Is There a Scientific Explanation?

The reasons behind why people are gay, straight, or bisexual have long been a source of public fascination. Scientists have been debating for years on whether there is biological support for a human being born gay. Year after year, scientists get closer and closer to discovering the infamous 'gay gene.' Because the topic is so taboo, not enough research dollars have been put behind its full discovery.

Scientists have known for some time that sexual orientation is partly heritable in men, thanks to studies of mixed families of gay and straight people[10]. These studies unfortunately do not include transgendered individuals, so views are confined to lesbian, gay, and bisexual people. In 1993, genetic variations in a region on the X chromosome in men were linked to whether they were heterosexual or homosexual[11], and in 1995, a region on chromosome 8 was identified. Both findings were confirmed in a study of gay and straight brothers in 2014.[12]

Study leader Alan Sanders of the NorthShore Research Institute in Evanston, Illinois, says the study erodes the notion that sexual orientation is a choice. He also says that biological understanding of homosexuality in women lags behind. Some researchers say this is partly because women who have sex with women tend to be more fluid in their sexual orientation. There have been studies suggesting that there is a genetic element to homosexuality in women, but more research has been done in men.

However, Sanders does not claim to have identified a single gene which 'causes' male homosexuality in humans and stresses that with complex human traits like sexual orientation, there are many influencing factors, both genetic and environmental. All of the scientific discoveries of recent make a forceful but by no means definitive case for scientific support of biological and genetic influences in determining sexual preference among males. Genes are

---

[10] Sanders, A. R. (2017, December 7). *Genome-Wide Association Study of Male Sexual. . .* Scientific Reports. https://www.nature.com/articles/s41598-017-15736-4

[11] Hamer, D. H., Hu, S., Magnuson, V. L., Hu, N., & Pattatucci, A. M. (1993). A linkage between DNA markers on the X chromosome and male sexual orientation. *Science*, 321-327.

[12] Coghlan, A. (n.d.). *Largest study of gay brothers homes in on "gay genes."* New Scientist. Retrieved September 10, 2021, from https://www.newscientist.com/article/dn26572-largest-study-of-gay-brothers-homes-in-on-gay-genes/

far from the whole story. Sex hormones in prenatal life are a contributing factor. For example, girls born with congenital adrenal hyperplasia (CAH), which results in naturally increased levels of male sex hormones, show relatively high rates of same-sex attractions as adults. Further evidence comes from genetic males who, through accidents or being born without penises, were subjected to sex change and raised as girls. As adults, these men are typically attracted to women. The fact that you cannot make a genetic male sexually attracted to another male by raising him as a girl makes any social theory of sexuality very weak. Genes could themselves nudge one towards a particular sexual orientation, or genes may simply interact with other environmental factors (such as sex hormones in the womb environment) to influence later sexual orientation.[13]

The brains of gay and heterosexual people also appear to be organized differently. For example, patterns of brain organization appear similar between gay men and heterosexual women and between lesbian women and heterosexual men. Gay men appear, on average, more "female typical" in brain pattern responses, and lesbian women are somewhat more "male typical." Differences in brain organization mean differences in psychology, and study after study show differences in cognition between heterosexual and gay people. Thus, gay differences are not just about who you fancy. They are reflected in our psychology and the ways we relate to others. The influence of biology runs throughout our sexual and gendered lives, and those differences that diversity is surely to be celebrated.[14] Though we can go back and forth on whether a person can be biologically or genetically gay, I know I was born just the way I am. I liked both girls

---

[13] Rahman, Q. (2018, February 14). *"Gay genes": science is on the right track, we're born this way. Let's deal with it.* The Guardian. https://www.theguardian.com/science/blog/2015/jul/24/gay-genes-science-is-on-the-right-track-were-born-this-way-lets-deal-with-it

[14] Rahman, Q. (2018, February 14). *"Gay genes": science is on the right track, we're born this way. Let's deal with it.* The Guardian. https://www.theguardian.com/science/blog/2015/jul/24/gay-genes-science-is-on-the-right-track-were-born-this-way-lets-deal-with-it

and boys but had a stronger attraction to boys. No one taught me, no one influenced me, no one harmed me. But that's not what's important because whether science proves it or not, I am who I am. What is important is disproving the use of science to discriminate and do harm to those in the LGBTQIA+ community.

Richard Horton, editor of The Lancet British medical journal, suggests that historians of homosexuality will judge much of twentieth century "science" harshly when they come to reflect on the prejudice, myth, and downright dishonesty that litter modern academic research on sexuality.[15] Horton outlines some of the commentaries of well-known scientists. Psychotherapist Sandor Feldman in 1956 said, "It is the consensus of many contemporary psychoanalytic workers that permanent homosexuals, like all perverts, are neurotics."[16] And respected criminologist Herbert Hendin said, "Homosexuality, crime, and drug and alcohol abuse appear to be barometers of social stress... Criminals help produce other criminals, drug abusers other drug abusers, and homosexuals other homosexuals.[17] Bernard Oliver, Jr., a psychiatrist specializing in sexual medicine, wrote in 1967 that Dr. Edmond Bergler feels that the homosexual's real enemy is not so much his perversion but [sic] ignorance of the possibility that he can be helped, plus his psychic masochism which leads him to shun treatment.[18] The notion of the homosexual as a deeply disturbed deviant in need of treatment was the orthodoxy until only recently.

In fact, in 2012, Dr. Robert Spitzer, the influential psychiatrist who helped remove homosexuality as a listed mental disorder in 1973

---

[15] Horton, R. H. (n.d.). A "gay Gene?" - Is Homosexuality Inherited? | Assault On Gay America | FRONTLINE | PBS. PBS. Retrieved September 10, 2021, from https://www.pbs.org/wgbh/pages/frontline/shows/assault/genetics/nyreview.html

[16] Lorand, S. E., & Balint, M. E. (1956). Perversions: Psychodynamics and therapy.

[17] LeVay, S. (1991). A difference in hypothalamic structure between heterosexual and homosexual men. Science, 1034-1037.

[18] A "gay Gene?" - Is Homosexuality Inherited? | Assault On Gay America | FRONTLINE | PBS. (n.d.). PBS. Retrieved September 10, 2021, from https://www.pbs.org/wgbh/pages/frontline/shows/assault/genetics/nyreview.html

apologized for a 2001 study that found so-called reparative therapy on gay people can turn them straight if they really want to do so. He concluded the study was flawed because it simply asked people who had gone through reparative therapy if they had changed their sexual orientation.[19] He admitted that he misinterpreted the data and caused sorrow and much pain to those who were in therapy, especially conversion therapy.

Despite your spiritual beliefs, the moment we are conceived, we are at the mercy of biology. Two-Hundred and fifty million sperm cells hurling toward an unsuspected egg with only one sperm being able to make it in. That one sperm and that one egg overcoming obstacles, defying all odds to create the perfect you. Some of us dark, some of us light, some of us tall, some of us short, some of us left-handed, some of us right-handed. Some of us gay, and some of us straight. And some of us in the wrong body. Did you know that 1 in every 1,000 births across the world, a human is born intersex? Yes, millions of people around the world since the beginning of time have been born both male and female. I wonder at what point in time will we get rid of heterosexual / cis gender, male / female, as the standard and except the true diversity of mankind.

Unfortunately, there hasn't been enough dedicated research and investment to scientifically understand why and how people are born gay, opposite their gender, or both genders. There also isn't enough data to make the claim that people cannot be born gay. The most accurate data that we can rely on are people's firsthand accounts. I was born gay. Period. Full stop. End of debate.

---

[19]Carey, B. (2012, May 19). Dr. Robert L. Spitzer, Noted Psychiatrist, Apologizes for Study on Gay 'Cure.' The New York Times. https://www.nytimes.com/2012/05/19/health/dr-robert-l-spitzer-noted-psychiatrist-apologizes-for-study-on-gay-cure.html

"Everybody has a calling. And your real job in life is to figure out as soon as possible what that is, who you were meant to be, and to begin to honor that in the best way possible for yourself."

~ OPRAH

Chapter 2: Answering the Call

Soon after kindergarten was over, my family moved from Northwest Philly to Northeast Philly. To say by this time that I'd experienced a whole lifetime's worth of woes would be an understatement. Don't get me wrong, I remember having a very happy childhood, but that's not to say that trauma didn't occur. It was just suppressed and ignored.

It wasn't until after a few therapy sessions as an adult I realized I experienced great trauma at a very early age. By the age of 6, I had gone through an identity crisis, been ridiculed for who I was, was spanked for expressing myself, survived a drive-by shooting, barely made it out of a high-speed police chase, and spent weeks in the hospital after my dad totaled the car during the chase. My parents also got into heated arguments because of my dad's stupidity. In fact, I had to have a few therapy sessions to overcome my fear of confrontation because of how bad I hated when they argued.

One evening my mother would not let my father in the apartment. He got so upset that he threw a brick through the window. My mother jumped up, my baby sister began to cry, and I was so scared I could not stop shaking.

When the police arrived, as soon as they opened the door, I vomited. The officer took me in the bathroom and began checking me out to make sure I wasn't abused or anything. All night I had a major headache, my body felt weird, and I could not go to sleep. One of the longest nights I've ever experienced as a child. They eventually got back together, and we moved on as if it never happened. Many may say what I experienced was no big deal. And therein lies the problem. It is a big deal. It's not normal. It has been my experience that because we normalize trauma, we don't allow our Black children to maintain the innocence of their childhood. We are made to face adult decisions and cope with adult problems well before we are adults.

Grown Too Soon

My coping mechanism for dealing with all that pain I hardly understood was to make sure others didn't have to endure that same pain. I went above and beyond to make sure others were loved and well taken care of. I am still that way today.

Sidenote: If you haven't experienced a few therapy sessions, it is something I highly recommend. You don't even have to be experiencing anything currently; just go talk to a professional, and I guarantee something will come up that will lead you in the direction of becoming whole.

Society pressures Black children to grow up fast and cope with problems well beyond their measure of understanding. This has been a pattern ingrained in our culture since Colonialism. When slave children were ripped out of the hands of their parents, they had no choice but to accept it. When Black kids watched as their fathers were lynched and burned, they had no choice but to accept. When Philando Castile's girlfriend's daughter watched him die at the hands of a police officer, she had no choice but to accept. She even chose to comfort her mother during the traumatic ordeal.

Children in most societies are considered to be in a distinct group with characteristics such as innocence and the need for protection. Research found that Black boys can be seen as responsible for their actions at an age when white boys still benefit from the assumption that children are essentially innocent. Research shows that overestimating age and culpability based on racial differences is linked to dehumanizing stereotypes. For Black children, this can mean they lose the protection afforded by assumed childhood innocence well before they become adults.[20]

According to Human Rights Campaign's 2018 LGBTQ Youth Report, 67% of queer youth hear their families make negative comments about queer people. Additionally, Black queer youth often face additional stress and adverse impacts on their health and well-being as a result of bias around their intersecting identities. Black queer youth who have rejecting families are eight times more likely to attempt suicide than those who do not have rejecting families, according to a study published in 2009 in the Journal Pediatrics. Trauma in poor and Black communities is hardly ever dealt with. We go through so much that it becomes our normal. We suppress the stress from our experiences that cause mental illness, thus ignoring the symptoms. We're taught to put on a mask, keep quiet and sometimes just pretend it never happened.

This behavior isn't new, especially for Black communities.

During slavery, any display of discomfort or displeasure often resulted in more beatings and abuse, which forced many slaves to hide their issues. During the Jim Crow era, many Blacks didn't trust White institutions because of racism and inadequate care.[21] Not to mention with being forced to endure the perils of racism and discrimination, who had time to deal with mental health?

Over time, Black communities dealt with trauma on their own, suppressed it, or normalized it. And because Black communities had to be careful and suspicious about who knew what, they kept everything to themselves. Many resorted to prayer. But who could blame them? Dealing with mental health was the least of their worries.

---

[20] Goff, P. A., Jackson, M. C., Di Leone, B. A. L., Culotta, C. M., & DiTomasso, N. A. (2014). The essence of innocence: consequences of dehumanizing Black children. *Journal of personality and social psychology, 106*(4), 526.

[21] Brandon, D. T., Isaac, L. A., & LaVeist, T. A. (2005). The legacy of Tuskegee and trust in medical care: is Tuskegee responsible for race differences in mistrust of medical care?. Journal of the National Medical Association, 97(7), 951.

Therapy Works

Unfortunately, the devaluing of mental health in Black communities today keeps people from dealing with their trauma. We have developed coping strategies that in the past kept us alive but currently no longer serve us. Therapy is thought of as something weak or crazy people do. How many times have we been told, "what goes on in this house stays in this house"? Trauma exposure is high in Black people who live in stressful urban environments. Posttraumatic stress disorder (PTSD) and depression are common outcomes of trauma exposure and are understudied in Black Communities.[22]

Through a therapy session, I realized the moment I stamped my biological father out of my life and the impact it had on who I was as a young boy and now grown man. And I tell these stories because they are all key to who I am today and why I accepted the call. Before we moved to Northeast Philly, my parents separated permanently, and this time neither had a say in the matter. My father was headed to prison. Charged for something dealing with drugs and arrested after taking his family on a high-speed police chase.

We were headed to a birthday party; I was sitting on my mom's lap in the front seat, and my two aunts and baby sister were in the back. When all of a sudden, my dad floored it and started driving at a very high speed. Everyone started screaming, except me. It was as if I was frozen in time. Everything slowed down while at the same time sped up. My dad, at one point, looked so cool driving with one hand weaving through traffic, but my mom looked petrified. I was so confused.

The blaring sound of police sirens and horns from oncoming drivers snapped me right out of it. But yet I still sat back quietly as my

---

[22] Alim, T. N., Graves, E., Mellman, T. A., Aigbogun, N., Gray, E., Lawson, W., & Charney, D. S. (2006). Trauma exposure, posttraumatic stress disorder and depression in an African-American primary care population. Journal of the National Medical Association, 98(10), 1630.

mom buried me into her chest. I believe I was honestly scared stiff. My mom and aunts pleaded with him to pull over and let us out, but with every yell and cry, he sped even faster. We ran lights, swerved into oncoming traffic, and were yanked around like rag dolls on a roller coaster.

The chase ended abruptly when we t-boned a car as my dad ran his last light. My dad got out of the smoking car and ran. My mom was screaming to the top of her lungs, and blood was everywhere. My aunts yelled at my mom to let them out because the smoke began to fill the car. I still remember the smell. My mother kept screaming, "my eye, my eye." She thought her eye was gone, but it was just blood covering her eye. My aunts kept saying Gilda, just open your eyes.

A police officer came and opened the door and grabbed us out. I was so sleepy, and the officer kept saying, don't fall asleep. I kept pushing myself off of him because I thought his uniform was hurting my body, but it wasn't him. It was me. My chest had caved in slightly when I hit the dashboard. The last time I would see my dad would be him being put in the back of a police car. What was he thinking? Why was he running from the police? Did he really just hop out of a smoking car and abandon his family? *(Sign me up for a couple more therapy sessions, doc.)*

I was in the hospital for weeks. Every day my family was lined up in the hall to see me. My greatest memory was seeing my two grandmothers together, my Nana, Sarah B., and my Mauma, Vivian Elizabeth. My uncle Dave brought me a big giant life-sized stuffed Lion, my favorite animal. I rode that Lion all up and down the hospital hallways. I was filled with so much love I didn't want it to stop. Who could cause this great joy to end? Who could stop me from feeling so good right now?

Daddy Issues

My dad....

I didn't know what happened to him, and quite frankly, I wasn't concerned. I asked my Pop-Pop, Ben Sr., what happened to my dad, and he told me not to worry about him right now.

At that moment, I stop worrying about him for a very long time. Since I could not stop him from emotionally hurting me, I could, in my little head, stop him from existing.

I was the man of the house now, and I needed to take care of my mom and baby sister Kandice, who today is my best friend.

The recovery phase of trauma is how we cope with danger once it is over. The best functioning persons learn from the traumatic experiences, become more confident about managing future threats and challenges, and gain improved coping skills. They function better after recovery than they did before the trauma, and they have found a way to use the traumatic experience to make their lives more meaningful and purposeful.[23] At the time, my thinking was this guy, who happens to be my father, keeps hurting us. That has to stop. I would never treat my family this way. I must now look out for them and anyone else who's dealing with pain. What I missed was, and was probably too young the catch, I never took care of myself. My immediate concern was my mom and my sister.

We get so busy taking care of other people that we miss taking care of ourselves and dealing with our own pain. Focusing on yourself can sometimes be seen as a bad thing in the Black community. And that's because we have not historically been taught that it is okay to focus on ourselves. We are not allowed to be victims. We always must be strong.

---

[23] Smith, W. H. (2010). The impact of racial trauma on African Americans. African American men and boys advisory board.

And because we don't have mechanisms for dealing, we fall deep on the opposite side of coping with trauma.

Poor recovery from trauma takes many forms, but generally, persons live as if the trauma is ever-present. They remain vigilant and sensitive to possible dangers. They have intense emotional responses to small threats. They avoid situations, people, and events that trigger re-experiencing danger, or they are numb and do not accurately perceive dangers and real threats. One way to remain numb is to recreate dangerous situations that re-trigger numbness. (For example, a sexually abused teen becomes promiscuous.) Another way is to avoid relationships and situations that trigger strong emotions. (For example, a sexually abused teen avoids dating and intimacy.) And finally, people numb themselves with food, alcohol, drugs, helping others, work, and exercise.[24] I've been criticized heavily about how I dealt with my father. But as Dr. Maya Angelou famously said, "When someone shows you who they are believe them the first time." Many times, we run back to our abusers simply because of the title they have in our lives. Father or not, no one is permitted to continuously bring pain into my life.

For those who experience traumatic events and recover usually have high-quality relationships that help them develop strong coping abilities. I had my mother and my family. We never really dealt with the trauma from the accident or my father's absence. We just moved on, and my mom did the best she could to fill that void. I was fortunate enough not to have those incidents greatly affect me.... Or so I thought.

I Want to Be President

My mom did the best she could with two kids to raise. She had us on a strict routine. I came home from school, did my homework, played

---

[24] Smith, W. H. (2010). The impact of racial trauma on African Americans. *African American men and boys advisory board.*

outside for a bit, ate dinner, watched one hour of television, and off to bed. There were no exceptions to the rules. I would often get in trouble for sneaking and turning the television on late at night. My big, boisterous laugh would always get me caught. My late-night shows were 'All in the Family, 'The Jefferson's, and 'I Love Lucy.' I would laugh and laugh all night until my mom came storming in with a belt or until the Star-Spangled Banner came on as the American flag waved me to sleep. Tuesday nights and Friday nights were my favorite nights to watch TV because my favorite shows came on. Full House on Tuesdays and Family Matters on Fridays. Plus, on Fridays, we got to order take-out. Most times, it was Chinese or a Chicken Cheese Steak, Cheese Fries, and Pizza.

On one Tuesday night, as my show was ending, I believe it was "Hanging with Mr. Cooper," it was interrupted. And the old guy who normally did the news appeared and started talking. I sat and waited because I thought my show would come back on. But it didn't.

Suddenly on the screen appeared a bunch of old white people in suits sitting in a huge auditorium. Everyone was smiling and seemed very happy. Who were all these people? What happened to my show? And why were they smiling so much?

Everyone being so happy is what made me stick around and watch. It was like a basketball game, except there was no basketball court. It was past my bedtime by just a few minutes, and my mom didn't make me go to bed. More reason to stick around and watch.

The room got quiet, and in walks, this man with the most beautiful blue striped tie and a big ol' smile just like mine, and everyone stood up and started cheering for him. The smiles got bigger, the handshakes a lot harder, and the hugs more frequent. I was so amazed. When he finally made it to the front of the auditorium, everyone was still clapping and cheering.

I asked my mom who that white man was, and she said that he was the President of the United States, George H.W. Bush. From then on, you could not tell me I wasn't going to be President of the United States. I even wrote in my journal before I went to bed that I was going to become the President. As I got older, it turned into becoming the first Black President. As you may already know that ship has sailed, but maybe I can become the first openly gay Black President. Either way, seeing President Bush that night deliver the State of the Union address lit a fire in me. I wanted to be the leader of everything. Line leader, council leader, class leader. There was nothing I could not do. My passion for people, now merged with my excitement for leadership, ultimately led me to answer the call.

The Call

I love people, I love serving people, and I particularly love making people smile. Any leadership role in school that involved helping other people, I jumped at the opportunity. I started out as a school safety. I would get to school early with my orange strap across my chest with my little silver badge and would help students cross the street. I became an adored student leader by the teachers and administration.

My first major speech was in the first grade on behalf of my school, Clara Barton Elementary. The school was receiving an award and my principal, Dr. William Lee, selected me to receive the award. I didn't have any dress shoes to wear to the ceremony. My mom stuffed my feet into my old penny loafers, and off we went. I was excited because my Nana was picking us up that day and taking us to the event at Temple University. She drove a 1965 Willow Green Chevy Nova Sedan that made a funny sound as she drove. You could hear her before you saw her. She had a handmade blanket to cover the back seat because of the holes in the chair, and you could see the ground outside from the holes on the floor. But everybody loved her and that car. When we arrived, the auditorium was filled to capacity. Thousands of people were in attendance. And to my little eyes, it looked like millions. I guess everyone started getting nervous because they all started giving me pep talks, including Dr. Lee. Everyone kept asking was I nervous. I don't think I had the energy to focus on my nerves because my feet hurt so bad.

As we walked in, my family went to their seats, and Dr. Lee and I went to the stage. I immediately thought about President George H.W. Bush. This must be what it felt like to be at the front of that beautiful auditorium. As I looked out into the sea of people, I could not spot my family. It took me a few minutes to find them, but once I did, I could not stop smiling and waving. They called on my school, and Dr. Lee took the podium and introduced me. After I gave my speech, everyone started clapping and cheering. That is a moment and a feeling I will never forget. The next stop was the White House.

They gave me the award to hold, and we took a picture with the representatives from Temple. When Dr. Lee asked for the award, my mom had to pry it from my little hands because I surely thought it was mine to keep. Though I didn't walk away with the actual award, I took home an experience of a lifetime. Added to my passion for service was a passion for public speaking. After that, I started doing the morning announcements and ran for the student council. I served in office every year I was in school. While in middle school, I was appointed to the teacher's advisory board, I was the only student representative on the board. While on the board, I would give the student perspective for the administration to take into consideration when making decisions about the students. Which meant I had to meet with students from all grades to try to figure out what they wanted. Some of the students were not so happy about me having so much favor with the teachers.

My First Encounter with Racism

The new neighborhood we moved into was majority white but over the years grew more diverse. Before moving there, I hadn't had any White friends. It was kind of strange because while playing games, they would always reference our skin color or say things like 'you people.' I hadn't heard of the word nigger until I beat one of my white friends in a game, and he called me a nigger and ran off. I was in the first grade.

I asked my mom what a nigger was, and she said the next time they call you nigger call them "poor white trash." And that was the start of the racial war for me because I did just that and got into a fight. And from then on, it became us against them. The Black kids against whites. We played together occasionally, but even when we did, there was always an air of suspicion and an unlit fuse that if sparked at any moment, all Hell would break loose.

Being a Black leader at school didn't sit well with some of the white kids either.

We were just about to go on spring break, and someone had to take the class hamsters home to watch. The selection boiled down to this white kid and me. I believe the teacher put our names in a hat and I won. I was so excited. I wanted to be a Zoologist as well, so taking care of those hamsters was a dream come true. It was three of them, a male and two females.

I wore a big ol 'smile for the rest of the day. After school, this middle schooler called me over to the fence that divided the elementary and middle school. I thought, wow news travels fast I'm already making friends with the cool kids. I had to climb some rocks to get to the fence, and by the time I got to the top, he threw a big rock at my head, spit on me, and called me a stupid nigger. News did travel fast; he was the older brother of the kid who I beat out to watch the hamsters over the break.

I was stuck between a rock and a hard place, literally. I could not safely be gay or safely be Black.

Where Do I Fit?

I never really fit in with guys. I mainly hung out with my girl cousins, and unbeknownst to me, I had very feminine mannerisms. My older cousins could not be bothered with me because I was also a tattletale, and cousins my age were annoyed by me because I was bossy. No one taught me how to be cool or told me that being the teacher's pet would not sit well with the other students. So, I spent most of my days trying to figure out where I fit in.

My family and friends would try to get me to play sports, but it all ended badly.

"You throw like a girl." "He's fruity." "He's gay." And why on God's green earth did someone invent a medicine called Ben Gay? That's all I would hear on the playground "Ben gay, Ben gay, Ben gay." I couldn't win even if I wanted to. It was brutal. I was told I could not hang with my girl cousins, forced to go play with the guys, and be ripped a part in front of everyone, all the while not being able to express any of this to anyone.

I used to suck my thumb; I believe now because it was my only security. One of my uncles at a house party in front of everyone said, take your damn thumb out of your mouth. Only girls suck on things. Literally, everyone stopped and focused in on our interaction, from the adults to the children. "Do you want to be a girl?", he continued. I didn't know what to say or what to do. My eyes just weld up with tears, and I went and sat in a corner. My mom asked me later what was wrong. I told her I was just tired.

I eventually got tired of the teasing and tried my best to fit in and make my mom proud to have me as a son. But I knew I couldn't play sports, so how else was I going to fit in? What would make my mom happy? I got it. She loves my good grades. I'll be a nerd. Now granted in the grand scheme of things, becoming a nerd didn't stop the teasing, but it changed the subject. I would rather be teased for being a nerd then teased for being gay. In fact, I got teased more for being gay from my Black community than being Black from my white community. I didn't feel accepted anywhere. I always felt like I was putting on a show. There was one cousin who I could be myself around. His name was Gary. He had feminine tendencies as well. Whenever we hung out, it was as if we could, for lack of better words, let our hair down (all pun intended). I wasn't alone anymore. He didn't judge me, and I didn't judge him. I loved him. He was my friend.

During one of our annual family barbeques in the park, there was an animal hiding in the girl's bathroom. Gary and I wanted to go see the animal but could not go into the girl's bathroom. So, we started talking and joking about dressing up as women to sneak in to see the animal. Someone overheard our conversation and told my mom. She confronted me at the park and asked what the Hell was I talking about dressing up as a woman.

Of course, I denied the whole thing. But because I got in trouble for having "girl talk" with Gary, I began to treat him differently. I began slowly distancing myself from him that very day. Gary passed away in 2009 from heart disease, but I have never been able to forgive myself. Even as I write this, tears are welling up in my eyes. I allowed other people's opinions about our friendship to change how I treated him. I even joined in on gossip sessions about him behind his back. For shame.

Look at that, the bullied becoming the bully. Hurt people hurting people. Gary didn't deserve that. He deserved better than that. I should have been defending him like I wanted others to defend me. He was nothing but good to me and showed me love. I was scared, and I was weak and still had not healed from all my trauma.

Gary was much stronger than I. He loved everybody and lit up any room he walked in. I wish I could share just one more laugh with him. I've never verbally said this before, and I mean it from the bottom of my heart, Gary, if you're watching, I love you, and I'm sorry.

I grew very tired of defending my manhood and my Blackness. I really didn't have anywhere else to run anymore.

Who Could Help Me?

By the time I was nearing the end of elementary school, my mother had met someone by the name of Ricardo Rolle, and they had my baby sister Ricquel. Yes, I now had a male figure in the household, but we didn't get along too well. I was the man of the house. Who are you, and what authority do you come in? We pretty much bumped heads until I left for college. Great guy, great father, and great husband. I just didn't appreciate all those things until I left for college.

While I was in middle school, his sister, my Auntie Janice, was visiting us from Miami and wanted to attend a church. Since we didn't go, my mom asked my Aunt Lana Felton-Ghee to take her to church. I wanted to go as well. Maybe God could help me out. I didn't have any church clothes. So, I went in my school uniform. I had such a great time that I had joined that day. True Light Fellowship Church became my first church home. I attended faithfully every Sunday. Somehow someway I would make it to my aunt's house so that I could get to church on time. And during the week, while my auntie Janice was visiting, she would have prayer in the room with her daughters, and they would all catch the Holy Ghost and start speaking in tongues. I was fascinated by this power that I could not feel myself, but I saw it impacting the lives of my cousins. I used to see people act like this when I visited BM. Oakley COGIC with my aunt Myra and aunt Blanche but never had I seen it up close and personal. I'm not sure why I thought church would be a safe haven for gays, but I did. One Sunday,

I'M BLACK, I'M A MINISTER, AND I'M GAY

I was sitting in church with my Aunt Lana and my cousins, and the pastor began preaching against sin. One by one, he started listing them - liars, cheaters, deceivers, drunkards' murderers, fornicators. By this time, my head already started nodding, and my eyes were closing until he mentioned people who lust with their eyes.

Wait a minute, I lust with my eyes all the time. Then he said the last thing I expected to hear that Sunday morning, homosexuality was a sin and if you did not repent and turn away from your sins you would spend an eternity in Hell. I was absolutely mortified. I felt a chill come over my body. I felt like everyone was looking at me, or somehow, they found out. Who told him, and why did he have to say it in front of everyone? (Meanwhile, no one was looking at me.)

Insurmountable fear came over me that day. I remained quiet and to myself for the rest of the day. I skipped church the following weekend because I just could not stomach going back, and I hadn't yet digested the concept of me burning in Hell if I didn't get rid of these homosexual thoughts and feelings. So, I prayed to God and asked him to take away these feelings, and I committed to serving Him faithfully. I promised God that I would live for Him, spread His gospel, and serve in His church if He promised to deliver me from homosexuality. I think I took my commitment a tad overboard as I became Mr. Holier-Than-Thou. But I couldn't help it. I was traumatized. I had just been told a week ago I would spend an eternity in Hell. My teenage thinking told me if I did everything else right, God would spare me. Many of my friends at church also went to the same school as me, World Communications Charter School. And if you asked any of them, I was the same at church as I was at school, Mr. Holier-Than-Thou. However, I could not say the same for many of them. My commitment to God was so strong that I started impacting my entire family. My mother first started sending my sisters to church with me, and then eventually, she started coming.

Ricardo dropped us off and picked us up every Sunday. One Saturday night service Ricardo arrived early to pick us up. He came in and sat in the back. We had a visiting college choir on tour, which was ministering that night and by the time they were through Ricardo was upfront dedicating his life to the Lord. So now, my entire family joined me at church. And since my mom and her sisters did everything together, my aunts joined us at church as well. In my eyes, I was doing alright. I had influenced my entire family to give their lives back to the service of the Lord.

Ministry

We all became very active in ministry. The choir, the praise team, the mission's department, the youth department, and we especially loved the mime ministry. K & K Mime ministry, twin brothers who became the Godfathers of Gospel Mime, made miming in church very popular. They literally revolutionized worship and arts ministries around the world. K & K Mime Ministry brought the lyrics of Gospel songs to life through creative depiction with the use of expressive choreographed movement and dramatic storylines. Who I am today has much to do with their pioneering. The public response to their ministry varied. When they first started choreographing moves to gospel music in white face and gloves, many ministries shunned them and called them blasphemous. But others embraced their ministry as a fresh and new way of relaying the Love of God.

Despite opposition and rejection, Keith and Karl committed themselves to carrying out the call on their lives. Those brothers took what was untraditional and made it traditional. What people said was Ungodly now became the anointed of God. Humans are fickle like that. It takes us a moment to overcome our fears or takes some time for our fears to become mainstream. In 1996 they ministered, for the first time, on BET'S Bobby Jones Gospel, and the rest is history. Mime ministries began popping up in churches all over the world.

At True Light, our mime ministry was founded by two women, a mother and daughter, and for years the ministry was made up of majority women and me.

Being a part of this mime ministry connected me to the power of God that I experienced at my house when my Auntie Janice would pray with her daughters. We traveled all over the city of Philadelphia and to many places around the country, witnessing the healing Power of God. There was something special about this ministry that literally changed lives. And while I was criticized for being one of the only males in the ministry, I didn't let that bother me because I was experiencing the Power of God. People who were literally on the verge of suicide would give testimony after we ministered of how they had been so moved to keep fighting and keep living.

There was a woman who was being beaten by her husband and at her wit's end. Right in the middle of our performance, she just burst out screaming and crying uncontrollably. Afterward, she said while we were ministering, she heard the voice of the Lord say if she left, she would live. Often, we would mime right before the preacher took the podium, and the Power of God would be so heavy that the preacher would not be able to stand to preach. I carried this anointing and this light from the Holy Spirit everywhere I went. People would speak of my demeanor and my character all in the same way, and I knew this had everything to do with the anointing of God that I received from participating in this mime ministry.

Leadership Influences

God surrounded me with some powerful individuals. My mom who did the best she could to raise a queer son in the hood and gave him all the confidence he would need to be anything he wanted to be. My Pop-Pop purchased a warehouse for $25 in the '80s and turned it into a multi-million-dollar business. My Aunt Lana pretty much ran the city. And a host of teachers and mentors who believed in me.

My 6th-grade teacher Mrs. Harris told me something that I will never let go. She would always have these moments where she would name an institution or a place, and we had to name all of the occupations associated. With every place she named I would always name the number one spot. Police station - commissioner, city - Mayor, school - principal, IBM – CEO. She said Benjamin, "no matter where you end up you will always land at the top, never forget that."

With their influence matched with the anointing God placed on my life, I knew I was bound to do great things.

My Aunt Lana was a big deal in the City of Philadelphia. She influenced city policy for nearly 30 years, from Mayor William Green in 1980 to Mayor John Street in 2008. She advised the campaign of Mayor Wilson Goode, the city's first Black Mayor, and founded the city-wide 4th of July Celebration, the largest Independence Day celebration in American history. She was so proud of the opportunities and jobs she brought in for so many.

She's worked with President Barack Obama, Michelle Obama, President George W. Bush, President Bill Clinton, Vice President Al Gore, South African President Nelson Mandela, Jesse Jackson, Secretary of State Colin Powell, UN Secretary-General Kofi Annan, Justice Sandra Day O'Connor, Afghan President Hamid Karzai, Oprah, Will Smith, Whoopi Goldberg, Julius Irving, Allen Iverson, Bill Cosby, Patti Labelle, Eve, and the list could go on. She broke barriers and advanced Black leadership in the city. And I was there on the sidelines to witness it all. She trained me and groomed me for success. She hired me to work for her in 1999 during John Street's first run for Mayor. I was with her at events, tailing along, running errands, and taking notes. She even sent me to high-level meetings on her behalf. Years after my time in the city, I ran into one of the former staff members of the City Representatives Office, and she said sometimes I would just sit there and think I can't believe I am taking instructions from a 15-year-old.

Some Mondays my aunt let me attend the mayor's cabinet meetings with her and take notes. I even had the opportunity to lead some projects and events. People would be amazed when they finally met me and realized the person they have been communicating with was a teenager. She would often say, Benjamin, you have a chance to make something out of yourself. Don't screw it up following behind what everybody else is doing. She was just as hard on me as she was generous. I got cussed out many of days.

I thought I was the mayor working around her. I traded the traditional book bag for a briefcase. I would take all her old Nextel's and two-ways and reactivate them. You could not tell me that I wasn't somebody already. I was living the high life witnessing history, all the while I was denying myself, struggling internally to suppress my homosexual desires. It got harder as I grew older. And became a lot harder to hide.

My Slip Was Showing

The Philadelphia Airport had opened a new international terminal, and my aunt's firm Lana Felton-Ghee and Associates, was running the celebration. There was a fashion show segment, and I had no idea the models were naked backstage. I walked into the space, and my eyes nearly fell out of my socket. A room full of tall, chiseled, beautiful men. My heart began beating so fast. I froze, not knowing what to do. Everyone was too busy moving to pay me any mind. So, I just kept looking. I think my aunt caught me because I heard her calling my name, but I could not snap out of it.

She just looked at me but never said anything. The pressure was always on for me to walk uprightly. I was the ideal candidate for parents. Everyone wanted me to date their daughter. Though I was sometimes teased for being soft, I had plenty of girlfriends throughout high school. Many accounted my softness to just being a church boy. As my charade got more comfortable, I began to fool myself. I thought maybe this is how life will be. I will always have to fight these feelings and keep them down. I thought that until I fell in love with a guy at age 15.

My First Love

He was two years older than me. I had no clue he was gay. But I suspect he knew I was. I will not mention where we met or how because he's now happily married with three beautiful children. We have no pictures together, so no need in trying to look us up on social media.

He was a ladies' man. All the girls loved him. All the girls wanted him; he was so fine. I think I wanted to be him. He was so popular and cool. He had his own car, and his mom traveled a lot for work, so he always had the place to himself. He took me under his wing and would give me pointers on being cool and teach me how to treat a lady. He was just a nice guy. He was basically teaching me how to be a man, who knew that he was grooming me to be his man.

Whenever we had our alone time, we were very passionate together. The thrill of it all is what excited me the most. All the girls wanted him, but I had him. Publicly we lived separate lives, people didn't even know we were close friends, and we liked it that way. After some time of being serious, he would get very jealous of my relationship with my girlfriend, which is something I never really understood because he went out with so many girls. I didn't feel guilty about being with him and having a girlfriend because, in my messed-up world, this relationship wasn't real.

I honestly thought it was just a plaything. I thought it was just fun and sex and nothing else. But one day, during one of his jealous rages, he told me he loved me, and he cried and held me. He was a masculine, tough guy, so for him to cry, it was serious. That was all she wrote for me. I fell in love hard and quickly; it was nothing I would not do for this guy. I had already experienced my first love with a girl, but it wasn't the same as this. I couldn't explain the feeling; I just knew it wasn't the same. It's something about falling in love that changes your perspective on life. For a minute, I forgot that being a homosexual would send me to Hell. I got so comfortable I started buying gay magazines and hiding them in our basement. Being with him unleashed those feelings so heavily that I couldn't control them. I would be out of my mind when I wasn't with him. Sometimes weeks would go by before we saw each other because we had to meet in secret. One time we had driven outside of the city limit and found a dark spot to make out.

Someone must have reported a suspicious car because the police pulled up behind us. You could have made an entire pitcher of lemonade from the sweat beads that were falling from my face. I was so scared, but he played it cool. He told the officer that I had just broken up with my girlfriend and needed some space to talk. I've always been an actor, so it didn't take me long to jump into character. I just recalled the story of when I really did break up with a girl and put on a really sad face. The officer told us it wasn't safe to sit where we were, and we should find somewhere else to talk.

I'm not sure why but that brought us closer together. This was very new to us. We fooled around with guys before but never in a relationship. He professed his love for me, and I professed my love for him.

He believed in God as well. Every so often, we would have a conversation about God and about life. He told me he wouldn't be this way forever and said we'd grow out of it. I'd oftentimes get sad because

I did not want to grow out of him. I knew in my heart of hearts that it would never work, but somehow, I held on to the love we had for one another.

He went off to college a couple of years before I did. We stayed in touch as much as we could but eventually would lose touch. For me, to travel to him would have been too much, and when he was home, he didn't have much time, and I had got busy with my own social life. He was my first love, my first gay relationship, and my heart still melts thinking about the good times we had. I've run into him a few times. Once I saw him with his wife, and I just kept walking. I guess he did eventually grow out of it.... Or did he?

The Jig Is Up

Because I was so active with another man, I had urges and feelings I couldn't control. At my Aunt Lana's house, my Uncle Jimmy had a computer in the third-floor library. I would often go up there while no one was home or late at night and visit gay porn sites. I'd wipe the computer history afterward.

One summer night, I was lying on the sun porch watching a movie. School had just let out a few weeks prior. My uncle walked in, turned off the TV, and said we need to talk. I was thinking we never talk so this must be important, maybe somebody died. I had no idea he was about to drop a bombshell on my summer.

He said, "what's up with this gay porn business on my computer." I froze. I literally could not move. I felt the same feeling I did when my dad threw the brick through the window. I was almost arrested in time. As I stared at him with almost nothing to say, tears began to fall. I immediately went to blaming not having a dad. He said he didn't have a dad either, and that didn't mean anything. He closed by saying he didn't understand it and it wasn't his place to try to figure it out, but he would have to tell my aunt. Nothing changed in our relationship; I was just banned from using the computer. My aunt never said anything to me about it, nor did she treat me any different. I heard she spoke about it with someone behind my back, but my mother handled that. I found out my dear ol' mom handled a lot of things without me knowing it. Weeks would go by before anybody would say anything to me. I was thinking maybe he didn't tell anybody. Every summer, my mom worked at the church's summer camp. And all my siblings and cousins attended. It was the summer hangout spot as all of us older cousins and other older youth from the church would stop in and visit. One day during her lunch break, my mom called me into a room and said we need to talk. I guess she needed some time to stomach what my uncle had told her. I honestly had forgotten all about it.

When we got in the room, before she even started speaking, tears begin to fall. I thought again, oh my goodness, somebody died. My family had experienced great loss over the past three years during that time. Mauma Vivian died, and my mom's sister Roxanne died just a few months later. She said your Uncle Jimmy told me about what you were looking at on his computer. My heart dropped, and I froze. Thank goodness none of these freezing moments were heart attacks, or else I'd be dead. Are you gay? She continued. Or this is a phase, isn't it? She basically answered the question for me and gave me the easiest way out of the conversation. I'm not sure if she did that to make it easier on herself or if she really didn't want to accept the fact that her son was gay. I started crying, and I said, no, I think this is a phase. What was I supposed to say? I think I was still confused myself. But moreover, I could see that this was hurting her, and I wanted it to stop. I vowed never to hurt my mother or sisters or cause them pain.

I don't remember the rest of the conversation. I do remember us laughing a lot. That's one thing I noticed about my family, whenever we have to face a difficult situation or have a hard conversation, we make light of it and make a joke. Laughing and joking is our coping mechanism. When I eulogized my Aunt Lana and my Pop-Pop, it was basically a comedic sermon because we laughed the entire time.

Looking back, I wish I would have said yes, mom, I'm gay, and it's about time we had this conversation. But hell, I wasn't ready to face her or the ridicule that would come from my friends, family, or the church. There was one youth leader who announced at a gathering that she didn't want any youth coming out around her. I'm not sure why she made the announcement, and it got very awkward right after. A few older youths were rumored to have been gay. They left the church, and everyone gossiped about them so badly. During one service, a feminine man was visiting the church, and the pastor preached on homosexuals so bad. I didn't want any of that drama.

My mom's relationship with me didn't change. She, just like my uncle, banned me from using the computer. We never spoke of it again. But that conversation put me back on the path of getting rid of all these homosexual feelings. Here I was again disappointing my mom, letting her down, embarrassing her. So, I went on a fast and ask the Lord to heal me of my evil ways. I cried many days, pleading with God. I began to spend so much time at church. I even joined the adult Bible school during the week. Nothing worked.

That same year was my first time preaching a sermon. Every year the church would have a youth retreat in the mountains. We would spend days in prayer and praise. My first sermon was all about love, loving God, loving your neighbor, and loving yourself. Looking back, the essence of that sermon is who I am today. My focus was on love, the benefits of love, the blessings of love. That sermon laid the foundation for my ministry today.

My church had a huge connection with Benny Hinn Ministries. Benny Hinn is an international televangelist who specializes in healings and miracles. Whenever Benny Hinn was close to town, we would go and take part in these huge services. I received the gift of tongues at his crusade at Madison Square Garden. I had never experienced the Power of God on that level before. People were being healed left and right. Entire sections of the stadium just falling out under the unction of the Holy Spirit. He became my mentor and didn't even know it. I purchased a lot of his sermons and watched him on television. His book, *Good Morning Holy Spirit,* really changed my prayer life. He always spoke about spending hours and hours in prayer and communion with the Lord. And I started doing just that.

The day after I preached my sermon at the youth retreat, I was due to lead praise and worship the next morning, and I woke up three hours before everyone else and went into the sanctuary and had alone time with the Lord. I prayed for hours and hours for the Spirit of the Lord to visit us in a mighty way and to move in the lives of all the young people. I repented over and over for my sins and asked God to free me from the spirit of homosexuality. People begin to arrive, and the adults referenced the presence of the Lord already being in the sanctuary. I was nervous because I felt something magical was about to happen. As I began to lead devotion, the Spirit of the Lord came in a mighty way. I begin to speak things I never heard before, quote scriptures I didn't remember reading, and prophesy over people's lives.

Young people were screaming and falling out and crying out to the Lord. I couldn't believe what I was seeing. I felt a warm presence over my body and had tingles in my hands and feet. Every time I wanted to give the mic up, the youth leaders would say, keep going, keep going. This experience was reminiscent of what I experienced at the Benny Hinn Crusade.

I knew it was serious when I saw my best friend Timothy Daniel in the back crying. This guy never took anything seriously. I became close friends with him after I took his sister out on our 8th-grade dance. We all went to the same school and church. He was so annoying. He laughed at her the whole time we were taking pictures at the house. I wanted to beat him up.

I'm not sure the exact moment when we became close friends. It just happened and happened fast. We went nearly everywhere together. Me, my girlfriend, him, and his sister. He was the total opposite of me. He played too much, and I was always so serious. While I was driving, he would sit behind me and cover my eyes as a joke. So not funny.

I spent a lot of my tweenhood over their house. His mom became my de facto Godmother. She was also one of the youth pastors. The one thing I appreciated most about him was he didn't care what anyone else said about me. Some of his friends urged him not to be my friend because they thought I was gay. He said he didn't care, and that was none of his business. For that, he will always be my friend. But since I knew this guy pretty well, I knew that it could only be the true Power of God to get him emotionally involved in service.

After the service was over and everybody went to eat, I went back to my cabin and cried and cried and cried. My goodness, that experience was so beautiful. How could you use me in such a mighty way, and I'm such a sinful person? How could you use me as you did and let me be gay? How could you hear everybody else's prayer and not hear mine? How could you heal their hurt but not heal mine? Don't you want to deliver me? Isn't that thy will? What have I done to deserve this?

No answer. Not a single reply. Simply, silence.

"For many are called, but few are chosen." - Matthew 22:14

"The speed of the human mind is remarkable. So is its inability to face the obvious."

~ SIMON MAWER

Chapter 3: I'm Not Gay No More

Ever felt abandoned by God?

I know I have.

For years, I prayed the same prayer and received the same answer. Nothing. Day and night, I pleaded with the Lord to take these homosexual desires away, and He didn't. I honestly did not know what else to do. I was too scared to reach out for prayer and too proud to admit that I needed help. And besides, who was I going to turn to? Certainly not my family and darn sure not the church.

If you can't take your problems to the church, where the hell else could you go? (Said in my Bella Noche voice)

This left the door of exploration wide open. I had already engaged in sexual activities with guys during high school, but I had to jump through so many hoops to do so. Now the playing field was even wider as I stepped foot onto the campus of Florida A & M University (FAMU) as a freshman in 2003. Two-thousand miles away from home. Free to be who I want and go wherever I pleased.

You want to know where I went?... Church. (Insert eye-roll)

The Lord had a hold on me that I just could not shake. I was so tempted to go hang out at the clubs and go to wild parties just like everyone else, but I was drawn to the work of the Lord. I joined the world renowned FAMU Gospel Choir and started touring the city and visiting various churches. I joined the United Methodist Campus Ministries and started volunteering with them during the week. Palmetto North Apartments was the name of my first real dorm. Each unit had a furnished living room, dining room, and full kitchen. They had two bedrooms with two beds in each room. During the summer of 2003, I visited FAMU for the TOPS program (no pun intended), a weeklong orientation for incoming students. They had us staying in Paddyfoote, which at first glance looks like urban housing projects. My first night there, I saw a roach. I went to step on it, and it flew up and nearly hit me in the face. Us city folk were accustomed to roaches, but when they attempted to fly up and defend themselves, it was time to go. I knew I could not stay there in the fall and put in an immediate request for better accommodations.

Luckily, there was space in Palmetto North Apartments for the fall semester. My roommates were three beautiful chocolate guys who were extremely nice. I could see I was going to enjoy my first semester. My sleep mate was on the football team. Girls were in and out of our dorm more than schoolbooks were.

My roommates often wondered why I never had girls in and out of my bed. One roommate was so adamant about me getting laid that he brought two girls home and said, you can have this one. She was gorgeous and was ready to get down. Needless to say, he enjoyed two girls that night. An attractive young man not getting his freak on was unheard of. Something had to be wrong. Like always, people just attributed it to me being a church boy. If you lived with me, you woke up to gospel music and went to sleep to gospel music.

The FAMU Gospel Choir was an amazing experience and really opened me up to so much. Meeting people from all over the world with all types of religious backgrounds. I just knew I was in holy-roller mecca.

The choir, formed in 1957, opened up for famed gospel artists such as James Cleveland, Jessie Dixon, Edwin Hawkins, Yolanda Adams, Vickie Winans, Shirley Caesar, and headlined many others. The choir has been nominated for three Stellar Awards and has been publicized as one of the best collegiate gospel choirs in the nation. The choir hit the national stage on TV when they opened for BET's Bobby Jones

Gospel and made a recording with gospel legend Twinkie Clark that earned top rankings in the nation.

The choir was still pretty popular when I joined. We traveled the state and country delivering the gospel FAMU style. We were often imitated but never duplicated. We turned churches upside down. So many people were not used to seeing young people with such zeal for God. We were talented and, above all, anointed. We could have been a mini church ourselves with the number of preachers, prophets, evangelists, and psalmists we had in the choir.

I made so many good friends in that choir and also a few friends who helped me experience some first. There was a tall, beautiful guy who always made sure he sat next to me in rehearsal. He would subtly brush my leg or accidentally hit my hand. One day we were talking about schoolwork, and he offered to help me with a paper I was writing. He came over to my dorm and kept asking about my roommates. I thought that was strange but brushed it off. I was focused on getting this paper done. I told him they were all in class, and that was all he needed to hear.

He started to get more touchy-feely, and his gaze grew stronger as we continued speaking. Me still being clueless, kept talking about my assignment. Well, while I began pulling out the library books, he sat on my bed and pulled out "his book."

Me being young, dumb, and naive, I really thought he was coming over to help me with my assignment. I was still very immature when it came to stuff like this. Every guy that I messed with in the past was older and always took the lead.

I stood there, not knowing what to do. My heart was beating so fast. He said, you know what time it is, get over here. I dropped my books and just sat on the bed next to him. I was so nervous. He clearly could see I was ill-at-ease, so he took my head, gave me a kiss, and then put my head to work.

He was a junior and experienced at this. There was no need for small talk or time to play the "are you gay" game. He said he already knew when he first laid eyes on me the day I joined the choir. He said he knew he had to have me.

The next time I saw him in choir rehearsal, he didn't sit next to me. He barely even spoke. He didn't answer any of my calls or text. When I approached him, he kept the conversation small. How silly of me to think that I was special. That was probably the same spill he gave to all the young guys he preyed on. I eventually noticed how he fancied another freshman and sat next to him in rehearsal. Yes, my little feelings were hurt, but who was I going to tell? There were a few more guys who volunteered themselves to be my mentor and give me guidance. I figured they must have "laid eyes on me too," and I declined.

The choir was filled with people of all ages. Some weren't even registered students anymore and had been in the choir for years. This process of "inducting" freshmen happened in broad daylight. I could not keep what I was witnessing to myself any longer. I spoke with a few of my fellow freshman members about it, and they noticed the same thing too. A few of them had already been with upperclassmen themselves. You would have thought we were the host of Unsolved Mysteries the way we tried to piece this thing together. We started rating the upperclassmen, it became a game. They thought they were playing us, but we were actually playing them.

I had totally forgot about praying for the Lord to take these homosexual desires away. I was having too good of a time. My roommates would bring their girls overnight, and I would bring my guys over during the day. To my roommates, I was mister do-no-wrong, and I liked it like that. At campus ministries, I met another young man named Jonathan, who was on fire for God. He lived just one building down from me. The first time he invited me over to his dorm, I thought he was trying to make a pass at me. I never thought he was gay; I was just used to being invited over to dorms for sex. When he pulled out his Bible and said, let's have prayer and a quick bible study, I was somewhat relieved and inspired. He had a strong desire for the Lord and walked around with a smile just as big as his faith. He would encourage me in downtimes and pick me up in prayer just when I needed it. He would walk around campus with me leaning on my shoulder. Jonathan was very touchy-feely and like to get up close and personal. He's still that way today, just a big lovable guy. He became my bestie on campus. He's the one who said we needed to find a real church to join.

During a fall concert at a pretty popular church in town, the Gospel Choir was a featured guest. I was there singing with the choir and also covering the event as a reporter for the university's newspaper, The FAMUAN. I asked the concert organizer if I could interview the pastor.

As I walked into the office, there sat a man dressed in urban wear and a fitted cap. He didn't look a day over 22. The people surrounding him were treating him with the same respect others treated my senior pastor with back at home. During our interview, I asked him what the service was all about. He said it wasn't about the choirs nor the good singing. It was about invoking the Presence of the Lord to make way for the change that was about to happen in our lives. He said we were going to be given the power to live right in church and on campus.

This is it!

I found my new pastor and church home. I could not wait to tell Jonathan. The concert was nothing short of amazing. I never heard a choir sing like that in my entire life. I never experienced an entire church where hundreds of young people were bursting out in praise, running around the room, dancing, and shouting. This was definitely going to be my church home. Many of the members of the church were also members of the gospel choir, so I joined already knowing a lot of the people.

Jonathan was just as excited to join as I was. We were welcomed into a community of extremely talented young people who were on fire for the Lord. Each and every service was like a WWF wrestling match. You walked in one way, came out another. You mainly sweated out your hair, and your clothes were in disarray, but your Spirit was lifted. And it's not that we always had a high time in the Lord. The air conditioner was always broken.

One evening our church was having some sort of revival. After the preached word, tons of young people filled the altar speaking in tongues, crying out to the Lord. The pastor called up other ministers in the room and asked them to pray for people.

This service was reminiscent of the missions trips I used to take with True Light Fellowship as a teenager. I would witness the mothers pray for people, and demons would manifest. People's eyes would change colors, and their voices would morph. The mothers would get to slanging oil and speaking in tongues and rebuking those demons, and they would flee. The demonic is something I didn't play with. But this revival night proved to be very transformative. There was one young man who was at the altar. He started growling and shaking profusely. I already knew what was about to go down. The pastor called all the other pastors, and they surrounded the young man and began praying for him.

The pastor asked everyone to cover their spirits and get any children out of the room. According to the Bible, when someone is freed from a demon, the demon will leave that vessel and look for another to land in.[25] Before I could think about leaving, the ushers had blocked the doors. I did not want any demon coming to land on me. Several pastors held the young man because he was quite muscular and would not stop shaking and growling and twirling his head.

The pastor asked the young man what his name was. The young man said, "we are suicide." Everyone burst out in tongues. As the pastor begins to rebuke the demon, he must have noticed that the young man's demeanor was not changing. The pastor said, there is a lying demon in you, what is your name? The young man said, "my name is homosexuality."

I 'bout fainted where I stood. Lord Jesus, if the homosexual demon can do this to him and he is this strong, what more can he do to me? The pastor begins to rebuke the homosexual Spirit, the young man began to shake even more, and the pastors prayed even harder. You could see the literal moment when the young man received his deliverance, from that demon at least. The pastor announced that there was an anointing for deliverance at the altar. Before he could finish his sentence, I flew to that altar. I told this woman I want it to be delivered from homosexuality too.

There was no way the demon would embarrass me like that. Get out of me right now. Honey, you got to go in the Name of Jesus!

She prayed for me, but it wasn't the prayer I was expecting. I was expecting her to call down the fire from heaven to get this Spirit out of me. But she calmly prayed a prayer, laid hands on me, and said, today you are free.

I guess that was the proper thing to do because she didn't want everybody in my business. She looked at me and said, son do you believe you are delivered. And I said yes ma'am. I didn't feel anything

---

[25] Matthew 12: 43-45

different, but I believed if the Lord did it for that young man, he could do it for me too. There was a line of people waiting to be prayed for, so I guess she couldn't spend too much time with me. She said, son turn around and walk in your deliverance.

As I begin turning around to "walk in my deliverance," I caught the eye of this beautiful brother sitting in the third row. He looked at me and smiled, I almost smiled back, but then I thought, wait a minute, God, what happened to my deliverance?

I was so confused; I wasn't sure what just happened. I didn't fall out and shake, and no demon came out of me. I didn't feel any different. I actually had the same desires as I did before. When I got home, I went to Jonathan's dorm and told him all about it. Surprisingly enough, he wasn't shocked at all, he immediately went into celebration mode. He was very proud of me, and he was going to make sure I walked in my deliverance.

He prayed for me and with me every day. And I actually started to change a little bit. I stopped hanging with the gossip crew from the gospel choir, and I stopped having sex. I met with the pastor of the church and told him about my deliverance, and he celebrated as well. He said he would make sure that I stayed delivered, and he would become my covering.

I convinced myself that this was real, and I had finally gotten to a state of being delivered. The desires were still there, but this was the first time I wanted more of God than I wanted these desires. I was surrounded by people who celebrated my deliverance and did not judge me for my past. It wasn't even a factor in our relationships.

Why I couldn't leave it at that, I will never understand.

I always overdo it, my zeal gets the best of me. I felt like I had to come clean. I felt like all the people I had lied to, I needed to reconcile with.

The first person I called was my mom. I told her that I was finally delivered. She, of course, was overjoyed. She wasn't quite sure what it all meant, but she was just happy I was on the path of not wanting to be gay anymore.

The second person I called what's my girlfriend. I wish someone would have stopped me. It was one of the best / worst decisions I made at that time. It was good because I needed to get it all on the table, but it was terrible because it hurt her deeply. She immediately began to cry, and the phone hung up.

What had I done?

My first thought was very selfish. I could not understand why she wasn't happy for me. But I was approaching it as if she knew for a fact that I was gay in the first place. Also, not realizing that telling her meant all the years we were together was one big lie. Lord knows what else she was thinking.

I called my Godmother and told her, and she began to praise God. She always thought it was my struggle but wasn't sure. I explained everything that had just happened with my girlfriend. She called my girlfriend and tried to straighten it out and make sure she was okay.

My girlfriend and I were never the same. We actually broke up not too long after, and no one could understand why. I regret what I did and how I did it, but I was somewhat glad I did it. She needed to be free. Free from dealing with someone who wasn't sure about who or what he wanted. We were high school sweethearts trying to make it work thousands of miles away from each other. She deserved better.

It is my desire that all people get that understanding sooner than later. No one deserves to be strung along while you're trying to figure it out. If the opposite sex is not what you want, leave them alone. If you are unsure about what you want, don't date anybody. If you can't be faithful to that significant other, release them and let them go. This is how so many diseases are passed along because people are living double lives and placing the health of their significant other in danger. This scenario was portrayed so beautifully in Tyler Perry's "For Colored Girls," Janet Jackson, who plays Joanna, found out she has contracted HIV from her husband Carl, who was living a double life, played by Omari Hardwick.

I cried like a baby watching that scene because I understood her hurt, and I lived his plight of being an undercover gay. While everyone saw him as the villain, I related to his humanity. I related to his pain. There's nothing like not being able to live out your truth because of fear. There's nothing like being disgusted within yourself because you can't help who you are and what you like.

It's also nothing like finding out your significant other, the one you've entrusted your life with has been living another life. And not just any life but a gay life. Everything about that situation was unfair. Thousands go through it all the time. Because in the world that we live in, people are not allowed to be themselves.

Rick Clemons, author of *Frankly My Dear I'm Gay: A Late Bloomers Guide to Coming Out,* conducted a study of gay men who marry women. The Sampling: Men, ages 30 to 60. Baby boomers and Gen X'ers. Most tied the knot with their wives between the ages of 21 - 35 and between the years of 1973 - 2002. Their marriages lasted from 8 - 38 years.

Reasons They Chose to Get Married:

- I had great parents that I loved very much, and I didn't want to disappoint them, so I thought I could overcome my gay feelings by getting married and having kids.

- I truly believed that if I did all the right things, God would honor my obedience and 'make it work.'
- I got married because I wanted to achieve an ideal of normalcy that was based on convictions that were thrust upon me by my family and religion, not on the convictions that I ever carved out on my own.
- I wanted to do anything that might make me straight.
- I believed that IF I didn't get married, everyone would know or somehow find out that I was GAY!
- I married because I wasn't strong enough to stand up to family, religion, and society. I was born and raised by homophobic people and structures, and I was persuaded to be a homophobic gay man.

I related to these stories on so many levels. I was both delusional and heartbroken over my breakup. Everyone said when I moved away for college that our relationship would be over. I honestly didn't think it would. Call it young love or dumb love, I know now it wasn't a healthy kind of love.

Because families are so homophobic, young people dealing with gay love and gay issues have no one to talk to. We make stupid decisions and end up hurting people. If only parents were open enough to have these conversations with their children to guide them through real-life dating issues.

Pushing The Envelope

Because I didn't walk around with a strong cloud of shame over my life anymore, I got more comfortable with my expressive side. A lot of the gospel choir and members of my church dressed a tad flamboyant. What I would wear and buy-in Tallahassee I would never wear and buy in Philadelphia. It wouldn't have been allowed.

My friends back at home even notice my style of dress changed. I went from wearing baggy pants and baggy shirts to very fitted outfits with bright colors and flowers on them. I'm sure people talked, but at this point, I didn't care because I was free and delivered. I just knew the Lord was pleased with me, and that's all that mattered.

I wasn't really into my looks. I actually didn't think I was handsome at all. When I first got to college, I had this really thick mini afro; sometimes I combed it, sometimes I didn't. I really didn't care. But after I went home for Christmas break, I felt I needed a change. I was a new man. I was now delivered. So, I cut the afro off.

When I came back to town, some people didn't even recognize me. I started getting more looks from girls and guys. This brought all kinds of attention. Guys that wouldn't give me the light of day were now wanting to get to know me. The pressure was on, and for a minute, I was very strong. No one was going to steal my deliverance.

When I came back from winter break, I had a big fat bill on my dorm room door. I owed for last semester's housing bill and the current semester's bill. Because I was an out-of-state student, this bill was thousands of dollars. I had expended all of my financial aid and scholarships. To avoid the bill collector, I started staying at a friend's place who lived off-campus. That didn't work too long because all my classes had been dropped because of non-payment.

My roommate said campus housing came by to evict me, but I wasn't home. He piled all my clothes and belongings on my bed so they would not take his stuff by mistake. I was devastated. What was I going to do? Where was I going to go? I had too much of an ego to go back home. I was Lana Felton-Ghee's nephew. How could I return to Philadelphia a dropout?

Luckily, some of the members of the church allowed me to move in with them. There I was leaving school with three trash bags full of my first-year college experience. Every day I stood in line and pleaded with financial aid, and if you know anything about Historically Black Colleges & Universities (HBCU), you know that got me nowhere.

My friends helped me get a job, and I started paying them for allowing me to stay with them. I only told a few people back in Philly that I was not in school. It seemed like as soon as I start living for the Lord, all Hell broke loose. Though I seemed very happy on the outside, I was losing it on the inside. I was homeless and prideless. I was sleeping on someone's couch and living out of a plastic bag. Surely this is not the life of the called of God.

Why Hast Thou Forsaken Me?

Depression started creating voids and heavy moments of loneliness. And not too long after, I was back in the arms of another man trying to fill these voids. I wasn't telling anybody that I backslid. As far as they were concerned, I was delivered and living for the Lord. Years would go by before I got back into school.

During my off time from school, I started a non-profit performing arts center for children and youth, Rakad' Institute of the Arts. It was a very successful venture. We traveled all around the city, mesmerizing thousands. Our children started at age four and went all the way to middle school. These children truly had a love for the arts and a love for God. Every time they graced the stage, it was full of the anointing of the Lord.

My passion for school also dwindled because I started making good money. The Florida Department of Elder Affairs made me director of an Alzheimer's outreach program. The program's mission was to educate Black families about the impacts of Alzheimer's disease and to provide resources for caregivers. I traveled the state and country working with families. I got a chance to meet my childhood idol George H.W. Bush at a Points of Light conference, and our outreach efforts were recognized by the George W. Bush White House. Your boy was in his early 20's making $43,000 a year with a big title. I was not interested in going back to school. Life was good. But something was missing from the picture. A girlfriend. You would think I would have learned my lesson from the last girlfriend. Nope. I just had to have the picture-perfect life.

One of my mentors taught me all about the steps you take in dating. You become friends, get to know one another, be truthful and honest, and the list goes on. I was courting this girl, and things seemed to be going well. We became really good friends. She was fun to be around, and though others thought we weren't a right fit, I was happy.

As we became better acquainted, I felt I could trust her, and I told her about my past. We had long conversations about my deliverance, and after some time, I felt she was okay with it.

Did I still mess around with guys? What do you think? SMH.

A Deeper Walk

I started advancing in ministry. Taking ministerial classes and speaking at engagements. My development in ministry was becoming noticeable. In the fall of 2004, Prophetess Tiny Lucas preached at our church for an anniversary service. She was amazing, and prophecy was on point. I had just finished miming "Walk into Your Season" by Donald Lawrence. She was laying hands and prophesying to people all night. While praying for someone, she stopped dead in the middle and asked where the dancer is. Everybody pointed to me.

"I have a special word from the Lord for you and I have to save it until the end." I thought, oh Lord, I'm in trouble. She knows all my business.

When she got to me, she said, because of your dedication to ministry and the Lord and because of the way you serve your pastor, the Lord is going to bless you tremendously.

The whole time she was talking, I was just praying she didn't say anything about me sleeping with these men.

"You are the apple of God's eye; you are His prized possession. I see you writing books, I see the White House, I see you influencing national policy, I see you advising the President of the United States. I see you leading massive amounts of men to the Lord." As she spoke, I could actually visualize what she was saying.

"I see your face on a poster outside of a conference room and hundreds and hundreds of men are on their face crying out to the Lord."

This lady whom I had never met just laid out my dreams as if we were best friends. I was a tad salty though, because she should have seen me as President LOL. But I digress.

I took what she said and ran with it. I immediately started penning a book about my deliverance, and I thought it was time that I work on how I was going to tell the masses that I was delivered. I wanted to be that shining light, that beacon of hope, for anyone else struggling with homosexuality.

But pause, I wasn't delivered.

I was absolutely delusional, I was bewitched.

I witnessed tons of pastors and ministers proclaim their deliverance from whatever issue but secretly still deal with the same issue. I was swept into a culture of hypocrisy where it was okay to stand up and condemn people for the very thing that you were doing.

I knew preachers from all over the country that were being caught up in scandal because the very thing that they judged and condemned people on was the very thing they were caught doing. It is said what preachers preach against the most is what they struggle with the most.

And it was no secret either. It was as if ministers had a secret pact. You don't tell my secret, and I won't tell yours. It's shameful because we'd all been indoctrinated into a culture of falsehoods, witchcraft, and deception. How dare we condemn another for something that we are doing? How dare we stand on the gospel and lie each and every Sunday?

And I'm not just talking about homosexuality. I'm talking about lying, infidelity, stealing, molestations, abuse, gluttony, gossiping, and the list could go on.

Here are a few examples of well-known outspoken preachers being caught in their hypocrisy:

- Bernard Law in the 1990s covered up the sexual abuse of priests for years.

- Colorado mega-church founder Ted Haggard who preached heavily against the LGBTQIA+ movement, was caught having an affair with a gay prostitute.

- Bishop Eddie Long was accused by several young boys of sexual abuse and using church resources to take part in the abuse.

- Famed television evangelist Jimmy Swaggart made a shocking, on-camera confession. He admitted to "moral indiscretions" and "incidents of moral failure" as tears streamed down his face on live television.

- Jim Bakker, founder of Praise the Lord Ministries, had had an affair with a former church secretary. Additionally, he was indicted on federal charges of mail and wire fraud and conspiracy to defraud the public of $150 Million.

- Peter Popoff was one of the bolder frauds in televangelist history. He claimed to be able to diagnose (and cure) any of his churchgoers' hidden diseases just by asking the heavens for help. He was later revealed to be wearing a wire, through which his wife would feed him the information.

- The Rev. O. Jermaine Simmons Sr., pastor of the popular Jacob Chapel Baptist Church in Tallahassee, was almost shot to death by his parishioner, who came home to find the pastor in bed with his wife.

- Pastor Chris Hill, formerly of The Potter's House Church of Denver, was forced to resign in April 2017 over an alleged adultery scandal involving a parishioner whose wedding he presided over.

- Bill Gothard is famous for his homeschooling ministry, known as the Gothard Institute of Basic Life Principles. He promoted extreme submission of women and ordered them to dress modestly. More than 30 women accused Gothard of molestation and assault, including underage girls.

- Doug Phillips was President of an extreme Christian-right group called Visit Forum Ministries. Phillips argued that women must be completely submissive to their husbands and fathers. Daughters should not even have a say in who they marry, and women should have as many children as possible. In 2013, Phillips was forced to resign after being publicly accused of sexual abuse and assault against a woman he met when she was only 15 years old.

- Michael Hintz was a youth counselor at the First Assembly of God Church in Des Moines, Iowa. During the 2004 presidential election, he supported George W. Bush, telling voters that he would fight against abortion and porn. But that same year,

Hintz was fired for having sex with a minor. He got off with no jail time, and 10 years after he was convicted, his name was removed from the sex offender list.

- Authorities in Orlando had barely finished identifying the 49 people shot to death at a local gay bar in June 2016 when Kenneth Adkins, a Georgia-based preacher and anti-gay activist, jumped into the fray. "Dear Gays, Go sit down somewhere," he wrote in a Twitter message the day after the attack on the Pulse nightclub. "I know y'all want some special attention," Adkins said. "Yall are sinners who need Jesus." He said homosexuals got "what they deserve." A jury in Brunswick, Ga., found Adkins guilty of molesting a 15-year-old boy and girl at his church.

Sidenote: If hearing these stories discourages you from building a connection with God, shame on you. Though humans may represent God, they are not God. And that is the fallacy of man, putting our hope and trust in another fallible man.

Enough is enough. Someone has to stand up for the people who are being verbally abused Sunday after Sunday by another human who is far from perfect. I myself have sat in services and cheered as the pastor damned people to Hell, shamed women who were pregnant out of wedlock, shamed teens who had made mistakes, and shamed men who were feminine.

Enough is enough. This way of teaching has got to stop. It is the kindness of God that causes people to repent[26]. Not our judgments and public damnations. When are people going to wake up and stop sitting under abuse Sunday after Sunday?

Silly me would scream amen to the top of my lungs when the

---

[26] Romans 2:4

preacher said the gays are going to Hell. No one told me this was wrong. No one told me that this was psychological abuse. No one told me that this was not of God. Beloved, I am here to tell you. The days of sitting in a service and allowing another human being to beat you up for being human are over. Go find you a place where you can receive a word of love and power and life. If the message you are receiving week by week is contrary to the love of God, run! I was so delusional during that time it pains me to think of it today. I thought I was doing God's service. I thought that if I spoke the word of God and still did right in the public eye, somehow God would have mercy on me. The Lord sees me out here doing his work. Surely, he'll spare me on the day of judgment. How delusional! I also unconsciously pointed the finger at others so the finger would not be pointed at me.

Preachers, humans even for that matter, have created rules and regulations for people to live by that are unattainable. Does that mean living for God is unattainable? Absolutely not! But trying to live by human standards is absolutely unattainable because they are more than likely unreasonable.

The Hebrew meaning for pastor in the Bible literally means to tend a flock. It is often translated into the English words "feed" or "shepherd." The Hebrew meaning for minister in the Bible literally means to serve.

Our jobs are to literally teach and serve. Not condemn, not judge, and especially not manipulate. If the Lord Himself is not imposing, who are we to impose on people's lives.

This leads me to this point. Stop telling pastors all your business. Your pastors are not your therapist! If you think it just stays with the pastor more times than not, you are mistaken. Two, you can talk to God just like they can. You already know what's right and wrong. I understand sometimes you need a little bit of guidance and advice. But if you are using them for every single issue, you don't need a pastor. You need a professional life coach! The reason why so many sincere pastors are committing suicide is that they are becoming human dump trucks, and people are just dumping their mess on them. Most pastors are not properly trained to counsel anyone. Even therapists need a therapist.

No human but Christ is designed to take on all your burdens and all your cares. The Bible says cast your cares on Christ, not cast all your cares on your pastor.[27] I'm not advising that you suffer in silence, but if your pastor is not a trained therapist. Go find a therapist.

So sorry about that rant. But pastors being able to manipulate people just doesn't happen all on its own. Somebody had to give up their own willpower so that another human can control them. I know people who have disowned their own loved ones because a pastor told them to. I know people who have thrown out their own child because the church told them to do it. Sad.

That's where I went wrong. I gave my life up to the opinions of judgmental people. I was so eager to convince people that deliverance was real, I was willing to lie. Because I became an expert in my deception, I got louder, and I got bolder.

I preached on it, posted about it, supported anti-LGBTQIA+ causes, cursed gays to Hell. I was literally a walking contradiction. Because I had not healed from my own trauma, I incited and replicated my pain.

Two people slowed me down, and they did it on social media.

Proposition 8, known informally as Prop 8, was a California ballot proposition and a state constitutional amendment passed in the November 2008 California state elections. The proposition was created by opponents of same-sex marriage. I weighed in on Facebook

---

[27] 1 Peter 5:7

and said, let the will of the people be done vote yes on Prop 8.

A friend from my old neighborhood in Philly commented and said something like, really dude do I need to remind you why you sound stupid?

This friend and I hadn't spoken in years prior to his comment. I actually forgot about him. That's how long ago it was, and for good reason. One summer, when I was a pre-teen, I stayed at his house for about a week. His brother and I had been experimenting with each other for years. During the summer, everyone was always out, and it was just the guys at the house. He would be off somewhere, not paying me and his brother any mind. My friend wanted to watch some porn, and that turned into us rubbing on each other.

In walks his brother. He drops everything that was in his hands. Everybody just freezes. The porn was still going, and moans started getting louder. It was a very awkward moment.

He screamed would y'all put some clothes on!

I didn't even know where my clothes were. We both were so scared. I could not stop shaking. After we got dressed, we just sat on the bed, not knowing what to do. His brother came back in and just said, what the Hell. We promised not to do it anymore and explained it was an experiment. Luckily, he didn't tell his parents because we could have got in big trouble. That was the last time I would speak to any of them until Facebook.

When I checked out his brother's page, to my surprise, he was gay. I immediately blocked him, and he sent me a pretty nasty note from another person's page. I felt so bad because he was so right. How dare me a gay stop other gays from expressing their love.

The other comment came in the form of a text from a guy who I had just slept with not too long before I posted about Prop 8. The text read, if I were to post all your text to me under your post, do you think your followers would still listen to you? I was so scared because I wasn't sure if he was serious or not. What does it look like you getting out of my bed to go post on social media about how same-sex marriage ain't right? Doesn't that make you a hypocritical preacher? I had no words. I just immediately deleted the Prop 8 post.

Those words would haunt me for two years. What would happen if all the people I slept with decided to come forward? Would everyone in the community still respect me? Is my labor in vain? Am I going to go to Hell?

"God is a Spirit: and they that worship him must worship him in spirit and in truth. "John 4:24

The individual has always had to struggle to keep from being overwhelmed by the tribe. If you try it, you will be lonely often and sometimes frightened. But no price is too high to pay for the privilege of owning yourself.

~ *FRIEDRICH NIETZSCHE*

Chapter 4: It's Time

Two years had passed since I was confronted about my hypocrisy on Facebook. During that time, I did a lot of thinking and made a lot of changes. It was something about the hidden parts of my life going public that shook me to my core. If there's one thing that I pride myself in, it's people's ability to trust me and to have faith in what I say. What would they think of me if they found out that I truly wasn't delivered and was still sleeping with men? What would they think of me if they found out that I've been cheating on my girlfriend with men? Who would I be then?

Shortly after I was almost outed on Facebook, I wanted to have a heart-to-heart with my boyfriend. I wanted to get his thoughts on how I should handle my childhood friend and the possibility of him outing me. I hadn't seen him in a while because we were both busy with work and school. I got to his house, and without even getting a few words out, we were in bed making love like it was our last time. Little did I know, it would be our last time.

After we lay there for a while, he dropped some news that would literally shift my entire mindset on life.

Ben, I can't do this anymore. I can't continue to live this lie. We can't continue to live like this. We've got to stop.

He was a devout Christian, just as I. We had gone through several of these let's stop and live right for God moments in the past. One day it would be me saying let's stop and the next him. But in just a few short moments of being around each other, we'd end up back in each other's arms. This time it was different. When I looked up at him, he was crying. And his voice was trembling.

I love you so much, and I'm afraid I can't stop. You're taking all of my heart, and I'm afraid when it's time for you to go, I won't be able to live with myself. I have to end this before I hurt myself.

Neither of us had planned to stay together forever. The same philosophy I had with my first boyfriend still lived with me and many of the other guys I dated. We'd eventually grow out of it. As I was now headed toward the age of 30, I think I was getting tired of that philosophy.

With this guy, it was different. I was really in love with him. I had imagined a future with him. I saw us hand in hand in every step of my imagined future. I had become so accustomed to dating both a girl and a guy at the same time that it didn't dawn on me that this would never work long-term.

My heart was shattered. I never really had my heart broken like this. As a matter of fact, I had never been in love like this. When we made love, it was beyond sex. I was one with him. I felt safest around him, and he was my everything. He healed me, he freed me, he made me, and now he broke me.

I got in my car and cried as if somebody had died. I couldn't stop. I dare not try to drive because I could hardly see. I sat there and cried uncontrollably. Suddenly there was a knock on the window. It was him. He wanted me to come back to the house with him. I could hardly move, so he sat in the car with me. He held my hand as I continued to cry, and I just kept apologizing to him for being so emotional. But I think those "I'm sorry's" were subliminal for whatever I thought I had done to cause him to break up with me. He could hardly stand to look at me without crying himself. He just looked out the window and kept saying, you know I love you so much.

I eventually calmed down, and we went back into the house and silently held each other the entire night. In the morning, he revealed that his mom was sick again, and she jokingly asked before she goes if he would give her some grandchildren. She had been sick before, and

I guess this time it was serious. He was a tad older than me, so I guess everyone was wondering where his wife and children were. We said our goodbyes and agreed it would be best if we didn't see each other for a while.

This unexpected blow set me on a path of discovering who I really was. I thought I was complete. I thought I had it made. Clearly, I was broken and living unhealthily. I really began to take a hard look at how I was living and realized it wasn't right at all. I was living a secret life that was filled with so much joy, and I couldn't share it with anyone. I was deceiving everyone around me, my girlfriend, my roommates, my family, my church. Who was I really?

My relationship with my girlfriend was rocky. She always had so many questions about my commitment and where my heart was. I could sense she felt I was pulling away, and that's because I was. I didn't have any more heart to give after it had been broken. The motivation that allowed me to live this charade was all burned up. I knew that I couldn't live this made-up life that everyone wanted me to live. I could get married, have children, get the house with the white picket fence, but I knew I could not love her the way that she deserved to be loved. And I did not want to get married and run the risk of hurting her.

Learning from other people's mistakes is something that I am very good at. I dealt with plenty of married men, many of whom were pastors, who were unhappy and miserable. At the time, I was very young and naive and didn't see the detriment of taking part in their infidelity. Most would get me with their sad sob stories of them being all alone and no one really there to understand them. And I felt for them and still do. There were a number of reasons why they all got married, and some were actually in love, but it wasn't who they truly were and what they really wanted. So instead of facing reality, they did just like I did and lived a double life. The only difference was I wasn't married, and I wasn't going to be.

I broke it off with my girlfriend and was so crushed inside because of the same reaction I had to my breakup I could see in her face. She knew something was wrong, but she didn't see this coming. No one did. As far as everyone else was concerned, we were already married.

I literally vowed that day never to date another soul until I figured out what the heck I wanted.

During this time, I was a member of a new church in town, Bible-Based Church, where Darrick McGhee was pastor and founder. When he started the ministry, he asked me to come on board as vice-chair of the board of directors. I joined the church and became a youth pastor. I knew Darrick for some time as we met years prior while he was deputy director of Legislative Affairs for the Florida Department of Elder Affairs. He today is my mentor and friend.

He knew about my struggle with homosexuality and never judged me. He trusted the God in me and always expected nothing but the best. Darrick is a motivator and is loved by so many young people. He has been a staple in the Tallahassee community for years and doesn't waiver from his commitment to people. He started this greatness decree that we would declare every Sunday, and I still live by it today.

"I believe and expect great things to happen in my life; because, my God, He is great, and greatness resides in me."

I learned a great deal serving under Darrick and will carry those life lessons for the rest of my life. The number one lesson I learned was that I am a human first above all, before any title, calling, or position.

Darrick served as my pastor up until I was preparing to leave Tallahassee. Graduation was quickly approaching, and I began to take stock of my life as I was about to hit another milestone. Moving to a brand-new city was exciting, and I didn't want to take any baggage with me. I grew tired of my own charade. I stopped dating, prayed every single day, and wanted so bad for God to heal me. Nothing was working. I literally tried everything humanly possible to rid myself of these homosexual desires. I was constantly on some type of food fast. I doused myself in holy oil, went to sleep with the Bible in my bed, and cut a lot of people out of my life. I even tried dressing in Black and white for six months with no sex in an attempt to be atoned by the Lord. Some may think that these methods were silly, but these are some of the things I was taught in my pursuit of deliverance.

For centuries doctors, therapists, and religious leaders have tried a wide variety of techniques from praying to surgery, to even exorcism, to convert gay people dealing with same-sex attractions.

There are so many schemes and scams to get people to walk in false deliverance, and it's shameful and harmful. Pray the gay away, beat the gay away, and let's not talk about conversion therapy. Some even go as far as raping a victim, claiming that the abuse would make them hate same-sex sex.

In Mississippi, Jeff White claimed that a local Baptist school teacher raped him as a means of a gay cure. He told the Washington Blade that the teacher would rape him because he was gay, and it would make him hate men and change. Jeff was sent to the school after coming out to his parents in the seventh grade. Raymond Bell, a pastor of the Cowboy Church of Virginia, made headlines with claims that sessions involving the stroking of horses could help cure certain addictions like homosexuality.

I had never heard of these crazy therapy stories until I experienced them myself. Therapy was the last resort. Not conversion therapy in the traditional sense but something along these lines.

There were these ministries in Texas that specialized in uprooting spiritual strongholds. I went to a special session with a counselor, and we spent the entire day traveling through my past, uprooting certain moments and repeating chants over and over. Although I had already paid for the session, the counselor made sure he referenced the tip jar multiple times towards the end of the day. To no surprise of my own, when I got back to my hotel, I was still gay.

A group of us from Tallahassee tried those counseling sessions for different reasons. They came at the recommendation from a church we all started attending in Dallas/Ft. Worth. The pastor, who claimed to be a doctor, ran the ministry from a beautiful home that was also used as a healing center. I guess our sessions weren't working because she told a couple of my friends, I could not be a part of the ministry any longer because I refused to be delivered. At this point in my life, I was tired of lying. So, when she asked are the feelings were still there, I told the truth. One of the men in her ministry confessed to her that he lusted for me, and somehow it became my fault because I brought "that spirit" into the ministry.

I wish I knew then what I know now because I would have let everybody have it. From the fake doctor all the way down to my friends who took me to that ratchet place. The sideshow and all of the antics were getting played. It should not be this hard-to-get God to do something that He wants done anyway. I'd been serving in ministry since the age of 14. I prayed for people, counseled people, and helped people walk into their healing, and yet God still hadn't delivered me. I was sick of it. I was tired of serving week after week, giving my all, and honestly not getting what I wanted in return.

How are you using me to do all these amazing things in ministry, yet you still haven't removed these homosexual desires from me? What have I done so wrong to deserve this treatment? When will I be able to settle down and start my family?

I had questions, so many questions, and I needed the Lord to answer me.

So, I went on strike. I told the Lord I would not serve another day in ministry until He answered me. It was a week before I was due to leave Tallahassee for Miami, and I called Pastor McGhee and told him that we needed to have a serious conversation. I told him everything.

I said I could not get rid of these homosexual desires, and the Lord has done nothing to help me. I'm so tired of seeing miracles and God move in other people's lives through my ministry, and there's no healing at the end of the day for me. So, I am stepping down from ministry until the Lord answers me. To my surprise, Pastor McGhee agreed with me. He said, my brother, you are allowed to ask God any question you want, but I strongly urge you to never leave God. No matter what you find on the other side of this inquest, don't you ever leave God. No truer words had ever been spoken in my desire for deliverance. I was always told to work through my problems, serve through my problems, and continue to keep coming to the church through my problems when none of that was working.

Three out of four of my roommates (Keven, Javar, Smith) had graduated that same school year, and we were all moving to Miami. I was about to kick off my accounting career with one of the top four accounting firms in the world. My trajectory for success was clearly painted. I was a favorite among company leadership and often used as an example during national convenings. I was making good money, driving a nice luxury car, and living just blocks from beautiful Miami beach. I could smell the ocean as my condo was only a few blocks away from the intercoastal. My office was on Brickell, and I would always sit at the window that faces Biscayne Bay. Dreamhouse, dream car, dream job, but something was missing.

Every day in a journal, I wrote to God morning and night. And in some capacity always had a question of when God would remove these desires. I missed my time in church, and I couldn't wait to get back to serving. I wanted to go back whole. I wanted to go back delivered, I wanted to go back without the shame and worry of someone trying to figure out whether I was gay or not. Still no answer.

Javar was already booed up by the time we got settled in Miami. The girl he was dating was the daughter of a popular Bishop in town. He coerced me to join them at service a few times, and I reluctantly went along. After a few services, I finally figured out what was missing, my time in service to the Lord. For The past 12 years, I spent two to three times a week at somebody's church. So, to get to Miami and go cold turkey was extremely hard. I didn't know what to do with all this free time.

Gospel Arena was extremely spirit-filled, just like all the other churches I attended. People were free to worship any way they want it. The main church was going through some renovations, and they were having services at the bottom of an apartment complex in the hood. I witnessed the bishop and his wife and members of the church give their all to that community. That was my type of ministry. During one of the services, the bishop began to prophesy to me. I don't quite remember what he said, but I remember the voice of the Lord saying this is it. Now all this time, during my inquiring, the Lord was silent. This was the first time He spoke in several months.

I joined the ministry just in the nick of time. I helped them transition and restructure some things before they moved back into the renovated church. They were also there for me when my grandfather, Ben Sr., died.

Of course, being young, single, Black, and successful made me a target for the ladies. I became very uncomfortable when approached by ladies because I was afraid that my rejection would automatically equal, he's gay. And the pressure was on because all of my former roommates were getting married and having children. I even officiated one of the marriages and served as a groomsman in the others. Everyone was pressuring me to get married. They would say things like your next or a handsome bachelor like you ain't snatched up yet what's wrong with you? A friend's sister even said to me, if I don't see you with a girl pretty soon, I know something's wrong with you. Well, I wasn't about to go down that path again. I was still sticking to my vows of not dating anyone seriously until I figured out what the heck I was going to do.

So, I just started getting real busy blaming my career for why my time was being occupied. I'd left the accounting firm and started my own consulting firm, Evans & Associates. I also jumped on board the founding team of the iconic BMe community, a national network of leaders and innovators dedicated to building more caring and prosperous communities. Together with Sarah Multidor and Trabian Shorters we forged a brotherhood of often unsung Black men from all walks of life who have dedicated their lives to the public good.

Our work is based on Trabian's research on the award-winning principles of Asset Framing, which identifies people based on their aspirations and contributions, not their deficits. We started by recognizing Black men's everyday contributions to the well-being of society and building America's future based upon positive values that we all share.

Trabian taught me that people only remember statistics that reinforce what they already wanted to believe, but meaningful stories and experiences have the power to change minds. I proudly traveled the country sharing that there are far more Black males in colleges than in prisons; Black men serve the United States in uniform at a higher rate than all other men, according to the US Army; The rate of business creation by Black males has been growing at nearly twice the national average for more than a decade, according to the US Census;

And Black men who live with their children or apart are the most likely to bathe, dress, diaper and interact with them more than any other racial group, according to the Center for Disease Control.

Walking in all this positivity and asset framing began to chip away at the negative narratives I had about homosexuality. Moreover, meeting phenomenal Black gay leaders who were making a significant change in communities began to inspire me as well.

One night our team went out for dinner, and Trabian, who probably doesn't even remember this, said something so simple yet powerful. We were talking about evil people in the world, and somehow Hell was brought into the conversation. Trabian said he didn't believe in all of that and his grandfather, who was a minister, taught him two principles that lead and guide his faith. Love God and love people, and you will be alright.

I sat there dumbfounded as I begin to think about how hard I was making religion to be, how hard I made religion for other people. I set up so many rules and regulations and ways of living that were pretty much the reasons why so many people were so disconnected from God. I and so many others made God unreachable, made His standard of living unlivable.

Those words lived within me the next several months. I just couldn't shake them. Love God and love people, and you will be alright. I started hearing sermons differently. I started treating people differently. All the years I spent judging people just came crashing down in one sentence. Love God and love people, you will be alright.

Here I was traveling the country inspiring all types of people to be themselves when all the while I wasn't myself.

When I came to that realization, I began to get depressed. I was fully functional on the outside but dying on the inside. My questions to God went from please take these feelings away from me to what kind of God would do this to people. Are you mad? Are you insane? Is this how you get off in heaven by torturing good-hearted people on earth? Answer me!

Still not one word on the matter.

The more and more I began to accept my reality, the more my reality became clear to me.

Meet one of my really good friends Shevrin Jones. We are alike in so many ways, handsome, successful, political, ministers, and adored by the community. We both attended Florida A & M University and were a part of Love & Faith Ministries. We also decided to take our talents to South Florida after our time in Tallahassee. He returned to South Florida years before me, began working in ministry, got married to a beautiful woman, and became a very active leader in his community. I looked up to him a great deal. I am where I am today in part because of my brother, who I call Shevy.

By the time I arrived in South Florida in 2012, Shevrin had been elected state representative and expanded a thriving youth program called the South Florida Youth Summit. He opened his rolodex and connected me with anyone he thought could help me advance my career. He also allowed me to join the board of his youth summit, and I eventually became board chair. While serving on the board, I became really good friends with a fellow board member Merdoche LaFrance. Together we planned the District 5 debate, which was my inaugural event as a political consultant in South Florida. That event put my name on the map and eventually led me to connect with Trabian and start BMe Community. So, I am forever indebted to Shevy.

It was at his birthday party in 2013 where I would receive a word that would tip me over the edge. Anyone who was anyone in South Florida was there. We had an amazing time. He then invited me to the after-party at an exclusive hotel on Hollywood beach. When I got there, it was a few of his closest friends, most of whom I already knew. There was one mutual friend of ours, Matthew Beatty, who I had no clue was close friends with Shevrin as well. When I walked into the suite and gave Matthew an odd look, Shevrin took me into the other room and said, let me update you.

We spoke about how his marriage ended and how he found his true love in Matthew. He warned me about trying to live for other people and how, in the end, it only hurts people. I know he was operating in the Spirit because he spoke to all of my insecurities at the moment without me even uttering a word. He said Ben, don't you do it, don't you go out here and get married to try to please the church, your family, or nobody else. Life is too short for you to live it unhappy.

I saw how happy my brother was, and I wanted that for me. I saw how happy Matthew made him, and it made me want to find that guy for me. To this day, they both inspire me with their love for themselves and dedication to community. Shevrin, an amazing activist, politician, and mentor, and Matthew, a powerhouse communications executive and mentor. Everyone loves them, and they love on everyone else. Had I not seen their example of a healthy homosexual relationship, I'm not sure how motivated I would have been to want that for myself.

At the time, Shevrin wasn't out yet, but he also wasn't hiding. The more I hung out with him, the more people would inquire about his sexuality. All those feelings of not wanting to be judged for being gay overcame me. I was very uneasy most of the time. I was a mess. I didn't know what to do.

My depression got so bad my face started breaking out. I thought it was some sort of bad sunburn. I went to the dermatologist, and he told me I needed to get a new job because what I was doing was stressing me out. I loved my job. I loved what I did. I knew exactly what this was, but there was nothing I could do about it. So, I went home and just wept.

Depression is a sneaky bastard. I had been depressed for a while and just didn't know it. Day in and day out, I was beating myself up for something that I could not change. Some days it would get me really good, and I'd be just solemn for the day, not realizing that I was depressed. Never had anyone to really talk to about it.

A few days after the dermatologist visit, depression hit me really good. I could not get out of bed. I called out of work because I just couldn't move. And that was so unlike me. I used to never miss work. I laid in the bed all morning. My dog kept coming to lay her head on my chest because I'm sure she sensed something was wrong.

Tossing and turning, sleep evaded me. Just as I was about to attempt to get up and feed my dog, I heard the voice of the Lord say just as clear as I could hear anybody talking to me today, "Get up and be who I called you to be, whoever is supposed to love you will love you and who ever doesn't just won't."

I immediately began to weep. I knew exactly what the Lord was telling me to do. Just be me. The whole time I thought God was ignoring me being silent. He was talking all the while.

He sent my childhood friend to check me on Facebook and let me know that this double life was not okay. He sent Pastor Darrick to let me know that it's okay to question God. He sent BMe Community to untrain me on all the negative ways I saw who I was and train me on celebrating my authenticity. He sent Trabian to let me know if you love God and love people, you will be alright. He sent Shevrin as a prime example of what a healthy, loving homosexual relationship looks like. And He sent hundreds of strong Black men like Malcolm Kenyatta, Curtis Lipscomb, and Akil Patterson, to the BMe Community to show me that it's okay to be exactly who I am. Isn't it funny how we ask God to speak to us or answer our prayers and then dictate to God how He should do it? I was expecting an audible answer or something supernatural. Have a bush start burning and talking to me like you did with Moses. Send a dove with a fig in its mouth as you did with Noah. Have the sky open up, and the voice of James Earl Jones give me my answer. Oh wait, that was The Lion King, but y'all get my point.

We sometimes miss out on what God and the Universe are trying to convey to us because we are so caught up in trying to be super deep, and the answers are right before us. Everything we need and every answer we are looking for has already been given. God knows our end before our beginning even started. We must learn how to tune into the Spirit and recognize what the Universe is doing right before our eyes. God didn't speak to me with one audible answer. He sent lots of answers over a period of time. God had to undo the toxicity planted in me by religious dogma and noxious societal norms. The only way was to show me a different path forward over time so that my mind could digest it all. Just like with most things in life, you can't just go from one extreme to the other. There must be a matured transition.

The only audible thing God said was to get up and be who I called you to be. Period. End of Story. After I heard that, I text the closest person to me, my sister Kandice. I said I'm ready to tell the family my truth. Without ever even saying I'm gay, she responded, "are you sure because once you go down this path there's no turning back and I don't want to have to curse anybody out." She's been my ride or die since birth. Often times, closeted people think no one knows. It's the ones closest to you that know you best.

I broke the news to my closest family and friends via text. Most if not all of the responses were, I was waiting for this. Everyone responded with so much joy I was overwhelmed. If I had known it was going to be this easy, I would have done it years ago. Ehhh Maybe.

I'M BLACK, I'M A MINISTER, AND I'M GAY

The next day I went to work and was filled with so much joy yet so much angst. I didn't know what to do with all of this newfound energy. During our weekly operations meeting, the Lord opened up the perfect opportunity for me to share with my colleagues. We were talking about a queer business leader and the impact she was having on communities across the country. I said I have an announcement. I'm sure I looked like I was about to poop my pants which probably made Sarah and Trabian very uneasy. They both had these very scared looks on their faces because they had no clue what I was about to say. I abruptly asked for the day off the day before, and now I have an odd unplanned announcement in a leadership meeting. They were the first people I was actually going to verbalize this to in person. I was so scared I almost didn't know what to say. I took a deep breath and said, guys, I'm tired of living this lie, and I want to walk in my truth. I'm gay.

There was a slight pause after, as I'm sure they were relieved that it wasn't I quit. They both embraced me and told me they loved me, and the tears began to fall.

After I composed myself, Trabian said, brother you are now free. And it dawned on me that for 26 years of my life, the real me had been locked up. The real me had been bound up by fear, people's opinions, social norms, stereotypes, taboos. I forsook authenticity for acceptance.

The stories you tell become the life that you live. Everybody walks around with pre-scripted narratives about everything. Most of us live, act, and are because of the stories that we've been told. Whether it's through family, church, the media, or friends, people respond to one another based on narratives. We're taught to hate, to compare, we're taught to be prejudice, sexist, homophobic, and the list could go on. Almost none of our prejudices are based on love and truth. They are based on fear. What a tragedy it would be to get to the end of life, never really having experienced true love because of fear and ignorance.

For 26 years, I lived my life as a straight male knowing full well, I was gay. I had adopted a narrative that was ingrained in me since I was a boy – and that was boys don't kiss boys. I allowed other people's judgments and opinions about who I should be to control my life. Well, I had had enough, and not just because I had a change of heart, but my secret was killing me literally. Hiding who I was, was detrimental to my health. Carrying around fear and stress was no good. I experienced a miracle. The deliverance I had been longing for all my life had finally come, but it wasn't in the form I was expecting. I asked the Lord to answer me, and He did. He gave me all the tools I needed to finally see myself as I really am - a facet of Him, a facet of His Love. There was a conscious awakening that could not be undone. I began to see myself, my life, my purpose through the lens of love and not through the blinders of fear. I once was lost, but now I'm found, was blind, but now I see.

Coming out to those closest to me was a walk in the park. Each conversation was a hard start, but it all ended in love and laughter. I hadn't told my mom or any of the rest of my family, for that matter, and I wasn't looking forward to it. But it had to be done. In order for me to live my life for me, I had to be honest with myself and those around me. Shortly after I finally accepted who I was, my skin went back to normal. The weight that I carried every day of my life was finally lifted. I began to see differently, hear differently, feel differently, connect with people differently. I was a brand-new man.

But who was this man? What did all this mean? What now?

Nothing real can be threatened. Nothing unreal exists. Herein lies the peace of God.

"For you created my inmost being;

I'M BLACK, I'M A MINISTER, AND I'M GAY

you knit me together in my mother's womb.

I praise you because I am fearfully and wonderfully made;

your works are wonderful,

I know that full well.

My frame was not hidden from you

when I was made in the secret place,

when I was woven together in the depths of the earth.

Your eyes saw my unformed body;

all the days ordained for me were written in your book

before one of them came to be.

How precious to me are your thoughts, God!

How vast is the sum of them!

Were I to count them,

they would outnumber the grains of sand—

when I awake, I am still with you."

Psalm 139:13-18

"We can disagree and still love each other, unless your disagreement is rooted in my oppression and denial of my humanity and right to exist."

~ ROBERT JONES JR.

Chapter 5: Judgement Day

Thanksgiving 2014 was quickly approaching; this would be the first time since I did a soft coming out that I would face my entire family on both sides. Though I wanted so badly for this not to be the typical Thanksgiving disrupter like you see in the movies, it was. You could have literally pulled the scenes right out of a Hollywood script. Tears, laughter, arguing, gossiping, bashing, drinking – as a matter of fact, I'm 'bout to sell this story to Shanda or Tyler, heck even Oprah.

The first people to find out was my dad's side of the family, the Evans'. I figured I'd go with the easiest bunch first, considering they weren't super religious, if religious at all. The first person I told was my Aunt Dee Dee. Little did I know she would be the perfect person. We went into the family room, and I said I needed to share something with her that I have been holding back for years. Still scared and ashamed to verbalize my story, I spent the whole conversation skirting around the issue. The entire time I kept telling myself to land the plane, but I didn't know how, so I just kept circling. I started to close with my depression story and how God gave me the green light to finally be me.

You would think she would have been totally confused, but by the look she was giving, I was confused. Why the hell is this lady smiling, I haven't said anything funny? She looked at me, smiled even bigger, and said, I want you to say it. At that moment, I saw my Nana, my late grandmother, in her face. My Nana was my favorite person in the whole wide world. She always made everything alright. She made the best fish and grits and sweet tea. She absolutely spoiled us and made me feel like I could be anything I wanted to be. She died when I was a teenager, and it broke my heart. So, to feel her presence at that moment was huge. A peace came over me. I wasn't alone. The Evans' all smile so big, and that was the first time I realized where we get it from, my late Pop-Pop and Nana.

My initial response was that of bewilderment. I did the confused puppy head tilt. She said I want you to say it, and I want you to say it proudly. My heart began to beat really fast, and my body got heavy. I finally grasped what she was doing. Tears immediately begin to fall, and I started breathing really heavily, and she held my hand and said Ben say it. As I shrugged my shoulders, smiled and in a very soft whisper, I said I'm gay. She gave me the biggest hug, and I cried like a baby. This is a moment I'll never forget. This was the first time I unapologetically, without shame, said, "I'm gay." This was the moment where I realized the power of proudly saying who you are.

The next person I told was my Aunt Carletta, and this time I closed my little spiel with a proud, I'm gay. She gave me a big hug and said, baby we've all been waiting for you. I was excited to hear her say that, but then I had a little pause like, wait what. You knew all this time and didn't say anything. Why are people so afraid to say something? I guess for the same reasons why people hide in the closet. It's the forbidden elephant in the room. My Aunt Dee Dee brought everybody into the living room and said Ben has an announcement. My sisters, who already knew, looked so nervous. My baby sister Ricquel came and held my hand. She's always been my emotional support. But by that time, I was okay and had mastered my little spiel. At the close of my proudly stated, I'm gay, my cousins rose to their feet, started applauding, gave me high fives, hugs, daps, and tears. My Grammy, who was crying, said I don't know what this all means, but nothing will change my love for you.

The best coming out Thanksgiving ever.

But now it was time to deal with my mom's side of the family, the Mills' and the Henry's. I wasn't sure how I was going to tell all of them. It's a lot of us. My great-grandmother Marion Mills had 11 children, and my grandmother Vivian Henry had 14 children. I have more cousins than I can count and probably even know. But the majority of us are really close. Normally the Henry's convened at my Aunt Lana's for Thanksgiving, but since her passing in 2013, we were all over the place.

As luck would have it, I didn't need to worry about convening everybody because, just like a typical big Black family, nothing is kept secret for long. One of my cousins who was driving up to Philadelphia from Washington DC was having a conversation on her car phone with my sister about how I should come out. I knew I needed some strategy for this side of my family, so I enlisted my siblings and my close cousins. I come from a very opinionated family who has no problem loudly offering their unsolicited view. I wasn't particularly emotionally strong enough just yet and knew their response would impact me greatly.

Taking the drive up with my cousin was her brother who was sleep, so she thought. Well, he wasn't asleep and heard every word. When she got off the phone, he confronted her, and of course, she had to spill the beans. And that was the start of my hard coming out to my mom's side of the family. Our cousin groups hang in age clusters. For some reason, people in my family like to get pregnant at the same time. He told his cousin cluster, and someone from that cluster told their mom, who happened to be one of my mom's nine sisters. My aunt then called all her sisters, save my mom, and told them. Nothing gets missed by them. We call them the Golden Girls.

My poor cousin was so remorseful. I assured her that it was okay and that the news would have eventually gotten out anyway. The day after Thanksgiving, I get a phone call from one of my aunts who had several of my other aunts on the phone. I thought, what in the party line is going on here. "Benjamin what is this we hear about you coming out" one said. "I know you feel better that the news is out," said another. "But you know this ain't right and you ought to know better as a minister," they all agreed.

They closed with, "when will you tell your mother because if you don't, we have to tell her?"

Today I am far from the man I was at that moment. Today, I would have had a few choice words for all of them that might have tarnished our close relationships. Until this day, I don't think they understand the magnitude of their actions. Forcing someone out of the closet is not your prerogative. It is an act of violence. But I wasn't to upset at the time, and I was too busy thinking about what I would tell my mother.

I hadn't planned on telling my mother until the last day I was in town so that I would not have to deal with her after I broke the news. I already knew her stance because she's verbalized it over the years. She was the last piece of the puzzle, or so I thought. I told them that I would be telling her real soon, and they wouldn't have to worry. They told me that if I didn't tell her the next day, they would. And I believe them. We really can't hold water in our family.

That evening I caught my mother and stepfather in their bedroom. I thought nothing else has gone as planned might as well get it over with now. My baby sister Ricquel was home, and I text her to join me. I'm not sure if someone told my mom already, but she had this look on her face that said the bad news is coming. My siblings and I get our dramatics from her.

I gave the same little spiel that I had mastered, but this time I nervously closed with I'm gay. This conversation was different because it wasn't our first. My mother knew that I struggled with my sexuality but also believed it was a phase, and I was delivered. Or at least that's what her hope was. But in my opinion, she probably knew since birth, right along with me. What baby gets excited when the doctor smacks their butt? Parents play dumb, but they be knowing.

Her immediate response was silence and then some tears. I

suspected she had some anticipation this day would come, and she was now living her worst nightmare. And I believe it wasn't the nightmare of me being gay, but it was everyone else finding out for sure that I was gay.

My close friends tried to prepare me for this day. Kandice even told me, don't get your hopes up. You know your mother. But still, the little Ben in me wanted his mother to finally accept him, and hold him, and say everything is going to be okay. It's us against the world. But that didn't happen.

She told me that I was going to get aids and was worried whether I would walk around in women's clothing. It took everything in me not to burst out in tears. I kept saying to myself, be strong, don't let nobody see you cry, be proud of who you are.

My stepfather was very supportive. He said you could finally be yourself. I've known for years; I was just waiting on you to have enough courage to be yourself. He even doubled down and said, your mother will be alright. She has to deal in her own way. I thought, well, he's sleeping on the couch tonight.

He closed with you live your life because it's the only one you have. Don't worry about your mother. She will eventually come around and she immediately replied, no I won't.

The conversation was extremely short. We don't like to display our emotions, so everyone kept it short to save face. She closed with you know better, and you know the Lord is not pleased. She looked down and never looked back up. I said goodbye and walked out.

Kandice was having a house party that night, and I and Ricquel headed over. I cried the whole way there. People prepared me for this, so why did it hurt so bad?

I called Shevrin, and he calmed me down. He told me that my mom still loves me, and I had to let her cope with the news I just broke. I understood what he was saying, but I didn't want to accept it. Mothers are supposed to be there for their children. Mothers are supposed to protect their children in their most vulnerable moments. One thing I think we children forget is that our mothers are humans too, with real beliefs and emotions that don't center around us.

By the time we got to my sisters, my eyes were bloodshot red from all the crying. I really wasn't in a party mood; I also didn't want to be a Debbie Downer. I put on a face to enjoy the party. Of course, everyone had questions about me coming out. While not wanting to distract me from the party, I became the center of the party.

My favorite cousin Richard pulled me into the kitchen and surprised me. He said I'm so proud of you. You are doing what so many others wish they could do. Hold your head up cousin, things will get better.

A Broken Heart

My immediate family is really close. There is not a day that goes by that we don't speak to one another. Prior to coming out, I spoke to my mother every day. The Sunday after Thanksgiving would be the first time I intentionally did not speak to my mother ever in life. It hurt so bad. I cried all day. I am a momma's boy. My mom is my everything. The day my dad got out of that smoking car and left us, I became, in my little head, the man of the house. She didn't treat me as such, but that was the source of our bond for me. I protected the house. I protected my sisters.

The next day after she processed the conversation, she sent me a really long note on Facebook that essentially said she will always love me but never accept this part about me. I responded, if you can't accept this part of me, then you can't accept me. And that was my last communique for several months.

The pain of parental rejection can leave a huge void in one's life. People resort to all types of vices and behaviors to try to fill the void or stop the pain. Drug use, reckless living, depression, alcohol, and irresponsible sex. Mines was sex. I went from bed to bed, trying to fill the empty hole in my heart. Somebody love me, somebody make me feel good. All I wanted was to feel loved, and I thought I could get that from all these men. The only thing I got was sent to the doctors for STDs. And even that became reckless. It didn't bother me. All I had to do was pop a pill or get a shot and wait seven days, and I was back at it again. Unfortunately, this reckless behavior followed me for years until, during a therapy session, I was finally able to face the pain of being rejected by my mother.

Both my mother and I are stubborn, and I have it bad because my dad is stubborn too. Once we say something, we stick to it, even if it hurts. For months I was so angry with my mom and had already started painting a life without her in it. This pained my sisters, and that hurt too, but I thought this is my life. They tried to smooth things over by telling me things my mom would say or ask. Things like: Is he dating? Does he have a boyfriend? Where's your brother? And they were right to do that. Her inquiry let me know she still loved me and was just being stubborn. I still wasn't speaking to her, though. Not until she took back everything she said.

The Public

I slowly rolled out the news publicly, testing different groups at different times. The first test group was a group of Black philanthropic executives that met for an executive planning retreat at the beginning of each year. I gave them my spiel and proudly closed with I'm gay. But I also shared the difficulties I was having with my mom, and they all replied, she'll come around. Each person was extremely proud and said they could sense something was freer about me. They could see it in my face and my demeanor. One even said there is a book coming from your story. Well, Van Jones, here it is.

The second test group was the entire BMe Community. At the close of our national conference, we hold space for the brothers and sisters among us to share their hearts. We lock arms and stand in a big circle until everyone is finished speaking. This session lasts for hours. But it is so healing. I gave them my spiel and proudly closed with I'm gay. But this time, I was so overwhelmed with emotion, the space was made for it. I was still hurting and didn't know how to cope. My impassioned speech opened up a ripple of emotions in the room. People crying, people cheering, people not knowing what to do with what they just heard. Because I was one of the last speakers, the room had no choice but to sit with the bomb I just dropped. I stood speaking for another couple of hours because there was a huge line of brothers waiting to hug me and tell me they loved me. This was exactly what I needed to face the world. Knowing that I had 200+, mostly straight identifying, brothers in my corner having my back. It was also then that I realized how important my story was. The majority of comments from the brothers centered around them being homophobic but not knowing how to not love me. From that short 5-minute speech, I helped people start their journey of overcoming homophobia.

With tears in his eyes, one brother embraced me and said I never thought I'd see the day when I really loved and admired and cared for a gay man. He hugged me tight and said, brother, I love you, I'm here for you, and most importantly, I'm proud of you. I cried for the rest of the day. This was one of the proudest moments of my life. To be loved and accepted by a group of people I once feared because of rejection.

God is funny like that. I always have been uncomfortable in male-dominated spaces. As soon as I showed up or got too comfortable, my feminine side appeared, and I got teased. I hated sports, the barbershop, the gym, the locker room, I even hated being in the same room with all my guy cousins. You would find me around the corner gossiping with my girl cousins. Knowing male-dominated spaces made me nervous. God calls me to co-found a Black male organization. Again, God was speaking in His own way. The third and final test group was leaders in my faith-based community. Saved the most difficult for last. They were my people. The faith-based community was the source of most of my homophobic rhetoric. At the time, I was serving in ministries all over the country. I was vice-chair of the board of directors for Bible Based Church in Tallahassee, FL. I served on the board of directors for a church in Raleigh, North Carolina, and served locally as an Elder in ministry at Gospel Arena in Miami. Now I know I told God I wasn't serving in ministry until He answered me, but I couldn't help myself. When a friend asks me to serve, and it's in service to the Lord, I'm there.

I met with each of the pastors, gave them my spiel, and proudly ended with I'm gay. The North Carolina pastor was extremely disappointed and denounced me before I could even finish the word Gay. He warned me that I was making a terrible decision and he could no longer be associated with me. He said that he would be praying for me and hoped that I would come to my senses. My pastors in Miami didn't quite know what to do with the information I gave them. They loved me and knew me as a strong-willed leader. They knew that I wouldn't just do anything on a whim. Though they did not accept what I was telling them, they didn't treat me any different. We are still close friends today, and whenever I'm in Miami, I visit the ministry, and they still affectionately call me Minister Ben.

My brother and friend Pastor Darrick was the best conversation of all. I even quoted him in my coming out story on theroot.com. He said he had a feeling this was coming. He explained that he didn't understand it and had no place to judge and said he would always be there for me. What made his response so special was this part. He said that I was his brother, and he wanted to be a part of my life no matter what. He said there is nothing I should be hiding from him, even a significant other. He said he needed to meet him to make sure he was good enough for me. I just sat on the phone and cried.

This was the type of love and support that I needed at the moment. This was real true brotherly agape love. Whenever I'm in Tallahassee, I see him and all my church family. The youth ministry, including the youth and parents, sent me a note sharing how much they loved me and supported me. I respect him and my church family so much. Pastor Darrick took so much flack for supporting me publicly. I told him he didn't have to, but he insisted. He said he was honored to stand up for his brother. He said I am your friend and brother first before anything.

Why did I feel the need to do all of that? I can hear some of you now saying he's doing too much. I stepped down from all those ministries because I didn't want them to have to sit me down once the news broke publicly. All the pastors were my friends, and I didn't want our friendship to come between their congregations and me. I also wanted to give them time to explain to their congregation what was about to happen. A responsible leader understands the ripple effects of their actions. I knew I had to soften the impact of what I was about to do.

I had to come out to the world.

I spent years condemning the LGBTQIA+ community, and now it was my time to build it up. Furthermore, I could not go from gays are going to Hell, to then posting me and a new boo on social media. There needed to be some explanation of the transformation. What caused my change of heart? How can you be a minister and be gay? I wanted to not only share my story but free so many of the other ministers who I knew struggled in the shadows of trying to be perfect for the church.

My coming-out sequence worked perfectly. I was finally ready to tell the world, and at BMe, we were preparing to launch a national storytelling campaign, #BlackMenLove. It was a series of articles shared in national outlets in partnership with BMe Community to remind readers of who, what, and how deeply Black men love. During our planning meeting, we were discussing potential topics and authors. Community, family, children, career, and Trabian said how about you write about who you love Benjamin.

Everyone was excited, and I think we all were a bit nervous at the same time. I enlisted the help of my friend Rebecca Fishman Lipsey to help craft my story. I wanted her to help me because she really humanizes stories in a way that makes them relatable to all. She took my thoughts and my feelings and toned down the aggression in my story. I was still mad at my mom and the others who rejected me. She said to stick to love. Be love. Spread love.

She then directed me to Tony Lima, who was the executive director of SAVE LGBT, South Florida's leading organization dedicated to protecting people who are lesbian, gay, bisexual, transgender, and queer against discrimination. Together along with team BMe, we drafted my coming-out story.

The title changed so many times, but I remember my Aunt Dee Dee saying, just say it, so I did. I'm Black, I'm a Minister, and I'm Gay was published on Friday, July 31, 2015, at 3 am.

The Release

When I got the notification that the article had been released, I had a panic attack. My body got really heavy, and I could hardly breathe. I texted Pastor Darrick and told him that I had a panic attack. He responded, what did you expect to happen. In other words, it's too late to chicken out now. Own your decision.

Only a few people had seen it at that point because it was the wee hours of the morning. I prepared a very nice long statement to attach to the article but then trashed it and wrote from my heart.

"I am beyond excited to share with the world my journey to freedom. I didn't come to this decision lightly... Me and the Lord started this conversation in 2012 and with His help I am able to walk in Love, Liberty, and the Pursuit of Happiness! It is my sincere hope that others on this same journey would find some relief in my story and those that don't understand would get understanding. Special thanks to my family and friends who have been supportive along the way! #Shalom #BlackMenLove"

The year 2015, on the Lord's Day of July 31, was my Ground Zero. I introduced myself to the world as a Black gay minister and child they let me have it. My social media lit up like fireworks, my text messages literally froze my phone, and the blog sites had a field day. To say I was overwhelmed would be an understatement. I was in way over my head, and I actually didn't think it would cause this much of a stir.

I made headlines, show producers were reaching out for interviews, I even made it to the blogs in Canada, the United Kingdom, and Africa. People were arguing back and forth online. Celebrities came to my defense on Twitter. Churches made statements and videos publicly denouncing me. My friends who were supporting me started losing friends. I even had a producer from BET reach out about creating a reality TV show. It was crazy. The worst of it all was all of the so-called friends that reached out and denounced our friendship. I was so hurt. My friend Felecia Hatcher said Ben put everything down. The good comments and the bad. Step away from your phone and the internet. So I created one last post and stepped away. Luckily, I was leaving the country right after.

"BIG THANKS to everyone for your love and support today! It was amazing and truly overwhelming - no, really, I've cried several times since my post this morning. The love and sentimental words really meant so much. I've learned that I am loved by many near and far - you've stood with me as the world, and even the "church" judged me and literally damned me to Hell. I have no intention of fighting with each individual person... I don't even want to change your ideology; it's pointless. My mission is to help the suffering, the lost, the confused, find hope and rest in my friend and Savior Jesus Christ, especially our young people. Because obviously most of these condemn... I mean, Christians don't want anything to do with those in the LGBT Community. It is my hope that one day I'll be able to make that statement null and void. Because we, as mature adults, should be able to have a real conversation about what the real scriptures say about homosexuality and stop making people feel less than because we were born different from you. I am so excited about my next post because it will address many of the scriptural concerns that my true friends brought up in love and answer questions about what's next.

Many of us claim to know the scriptures, but most really don't. You pick and choose which scriptures work for you and have no clue what they really mean. I have over 50 inboxes of strangers damning me to Hell and over 200 "Christians" calling me everything but a child of God on the Roots FB post. No wonder no one wants to come to church. And worse, when I asked most of the condemners who inboxed me whether they read my story or not, most said no! #ByeYall #iCant -
___-

The crazy thing is all I've ever heard was we want people to stop being on the DL stop creeping... well, when we do decide to come on out, this is the welcome reception we receive!!! NO-THANK-YOU. I'll take the love of the so-called "heathens." But overall, today was an amazing day. And I look forward to the many days ahead."

"After your death, you will be what you were before your birth."

~ ARTHUR SCHOPENHAUER

Chapter 6: Life After Death

The day after I came out to the world, I was on my way to South America with a co-hort of influential civic leaders from Miami. We were headed to Medellin, Columbia, with the Miami Foundation and Global Ties. While there, we explored urban transformation and exchanged ideas with government officials, businesspeople, and fellow civic leaders. We also had the opportunity to experience the very unique sights, sounds, and flavors of Medellin. On a personal note, I was also there to search for Pablo Escobar's buried fortunes, just kidding.

Getting away so quickly gave me time to gather my thoughts and remove myself from the hype. Many of our explorations kept me from being engaged online, and I sure wasn't taking any calls on my phone. I was handling business, but it was also a spiritual retreat. I was putting on a good game face for my fellow leaders, but at any moment, I was ready to crack. The pressure was too great. But it's something about when I get to the mountains or the water that gives me peace. Medellin is known for its springtime weather all year long. The environment was perfect for clearing my head. The air was so crisp. I could smell my oneness with the universe, hear the universe speaking through nature, and see God's hand even in the lives of those less fortunate.

There was a moment I had with some kids on the mountainside that caused my spirit to be at peace with my decision. We were touring an enrichment center that was equipped with the latest and greatest in technology. But right next to this beautiful center, people still lived in homes pieced together by whatever sheltering material was available. Some homes with cardboard, sheet metal, wood. No plumbing, no electricity, no flooring, but the homes were full of life and love.

As we exited, we ran into some kids playing with sticks, rocks, and a deflated kickball. They didn't have any shoes on, their clothes didn't match, but they were so happy. One of the kids threw the kickball at me. All of their faces lit up in anticipation of which direction I would throw the ball. I threw it straight up in the air so they would have to run towards me to get it. By the time they got to me, I caught the ball and held on to it. I secretly gave them each some money, and they all went running off without the ball. One little guy came back but with a new kid. He came back for the ball and wanted me to give the new kid some money too. I obliged, and off they went.

Two things happened at that moment. Those children were living in third-world conditions but had more happiness in them than I held in my pinky. Amid great poverty, life wasn't complicated for them. So why was I making life complicated for me? I had to forget who was not for me and who didn't agree with my decision. Secondly, that little boy was not satisfied with being blessed alone. He went back to get his friend to make sure he got blessed too. And here I was, blessed with being free from religious bondage, contemplating whether I made the right decision. I am blessed to be a blessing. And at that moment, the spirit said, you are free now go free someone else.

Forgiving Yourself

Our time on this earth is very limited, especially when we compare it to how old the earth actually is. We don't have time to hold onto anything that does not serve us, especially mistakes from the past. It is imperative that we do what we can to cope with the past and move beyond the mistakes we've made. I was a terrible human being. I degraded people who I deemed sinners and damned people to Hell. The first thing I had to do was forgive myself for repeating the merciless pattern of degradation. This was hard. For many people, the real challenge is not seeking redemption but rather learning to forgive themselves for all the wrong they have done.

One of the first things I wish I would have done prior to coming out was gone to therapy. It's been nearly seven years since I came out, and I am just getting to dealing with much of the emotional drama of living a closeted judgmental life.

From the moment we are born, the world tries to enforce its values on us. We come as a blank slate, and we get riddled with the opinions of society. In this process, we start to believe the tales we are told. The greater the repetition, and the earlier the exposure, the stronger the bond between a human and what they are told. For many people of the Black queer experience, it is a lifetime journey of torture and self-hatred.

I was a product of my environment. I believed and acted in ways that I learned. None of it was who I am at my core. There is a reason for every action and behavior. I have spent the last several years trying to make sense of everything and remain true to it all. Why did I act this way? Why was I so comfortable judging others? Why did I believe gay people were going to Hell?

When I started getting the answers to the 'whys,' forgiving myself became much easier. I was simply responding to my environment. It wasn't until I was exposed to new ways of thinking that I had the option to make a choice. And I chose light. I chose love. When the core of me was faced with change, I chose the right path. That's what made forgiving me easy.

You may ask yourself, why should I forgive myself? The answer is that the hardest parts of the journey happen in the mind. There is no torture equal to that which man commits on himself through misery, self-hatred, and self-loathing. Most of our problems happen in our imagination. All the world could sing your praises, but if you do not consider yourself valuable, they are worthless.

Forgiving yourself is the first step to realizing that you have value, that you can make mistakes, and that you are willing to atone for your wrongs and become a better person. The first step in this journey is to accept that you will make mistakes in your efforts to do the right thing. You may be cruel to yourself, or worse, someone else. It is a part of who you are; only God is perfect. By recognizing this, you can repent and then move forward with a clean heart.

A person who is weighed down by sin and regret is worn away by the burdens he carries. Be forgiving and do not judge yourself too harshly; the world already does that for you. No one taught us this. We are all learning as we go.

Forgive yourself as you forgive others. Try and think about the events in your life and how you feel about them. Let those feelings pass through you, do not hold onto them, or try to repress them; it will exacerbate things. As you slowly process little bits of your life, you will come to realize that many of the feelings that you have been clenching are just tiny moments in the grand scheme of things. By holding onto events, especially negative occurrences, we blindside ourselves to the blessings we do have.

Processing, accepting, and then moving on from the past will allow you to achieve a state of peace that no drug, music, or worldly entity can grant you. There is a high chance that you will encounter many unpleasant emotions, but this cleansing is necessary to remove your spiritual debris. Think of it as bathing your spirit; it washes off the dirt and purifies your soul.

Be Delivered from People's Opinions

During my exploration process, Pastor Darrick told me one thing that will stick with me for the rest of my life. He said the greatest deliverance you can have is from the opinions of people. If you start to chase after the opinions of everyone else, you will become an empty shell of who you really are. Those that seek approval from everyone end up pleasing no one. You have to be true to yourself and live a life such that it brings you content.

First, let me make one thing clear, everyone has an opinion. They may not tell you about it, or they may shove it in your face, but people will judge. It is in our nature to try to ascertain the quality of something by applying our rational minds. But this is where the key point lies, that the thoughts of people are subjective.

Everyone perceives things differently, and thus, through that lens, we have to evaluate people's opinions. People do not see the fullness of reality, they see what they want, and they ignore the rest. Sometimes it is simply more constructive to walk away from aggressive confrontations. There will be many times when you will be tempted to preach your path, that you are peaceful, that you love God. However, you have to present your case in front of God, not people; do not let their words carry you away from your own path.

Does this mean that you should ignore and run away from everything that you find unpleasant? No, that would be foolish. Merely realize that you cannot convert the entire world, no matter how right you are. Some people are simply stuck in their ways, while others are more open to discussion and rational thought. Instead of wasting efforts on stubborn people, try to interact with those that treat you with respect and keep an open mind. Chasing after the pipedream of becoming eternally popular or loved will turn you into a puppet dancing on the strings of everyone else. This is a hard pill I had to swallow. I wanted to be loved and adored by everyone. You shouldn't hold so much weight to what people say about you. I'm sure you even hold some unfavorable views about people and issues. The key is to respect these differences while still maintaining a sense of friendliness.

Many times, people will criticize you or even insult you because you are different. The key here is to learn the difference between constructive criticism and outright hatred and malice. In some instances, bitter words may be just what you need to improve yourself. In other cases, honeyed words might hide the intentions of someone trying to hate on you. You must look at each case critically and decide who you want to rely on.

An easy way to get started on this process is to learn about yourself, the topic, and the person offering their opinion. By learning about yourself, you will know where you are strong and where you fall short. Knowledge of the topic will allow you to discuss the specifics without being led astray; this is very important. Finally, understanding the person talking to you helps you identify their point of view.

Some people offer very good advice or criticism, while others will try to guilt-trip you or attempt to chip away at your character. They may give you bad advice in the hope you cause yourself harm. You must learn to distinguish between people of value and those that are best left ignored. Ultimately, the only thing that will matter in the end is God's word. For a surefire way to know if you are on the right path, use the Lord as a reference. If someone or something brings you closer to God, go for it. If it leads you astray, be wary and find better people.

The one thing for sure that every human being will have to face one day is death. And when that day comes, all the opinions of others and things you let weigh you down won't matter. At all! So, if it won't matter in your death, why are you letting it matter in your life? Be delivered from people's opinions and live your best life.

Accepting Your Truth

The first step in eliminating your stress is to accept yourself for who you are. You alone know your truth. Everyone else can only interpret your life from their own set of circumstances. We know the reality of who we are when we wash away the debris that the world throws on us. From the moment we are born, we are bombarded with messages and slogans that tell us who we are or what we should become. All these slogans by marketing teams have one single purpose, to sell you something. You might even get caught in the rhetoric and believe that you actually need what they offer to become a truer version of yourself.

The truth is, what you are is already present within your own self. You do not need a product or a service to reach the real you; you only need clarity of thought to see deep within. Behind every message is an intent. You must be very careful about accepting every narrative someone offers.

How can you trust people who see you as an abomination to tell you who you are? Either they want to sell you something, or they want you to abandon your true self to satisfy their ego-driven agenda. Accepting yourself also means accepting that not everyone is going to like you or accept your reality. You cannot change the mind of a person when they are on the defensive to protect their own position. It reminds me of an old saying that you cannot shake hands when one is clenched into a fist.

This is likely going to be the most challenging part of the process. It is very tempting to try and logically convince people of your thoughts and your validity as a person. I know people who have wasted their time and energy trying to get people to look at them through a humanistic lens. Some managed to succeed, but many only caused further harm and suffering. You must accept yourself and other people as they exist; there is no other way. It does not mean you have to fraternize with them; just know that they are not on your side.

Once you release yourself from this burden of trying to set things right, you will witness a massive shift in your personality. When you run into intolerant people, you will merely acknowledge their presence and then go about your own day. You have a limited amount of time and energy, and it is best to use it on things that bring you joy and peace. Acceptance is key; I cannot stress this enough. It may sound like I'm beating a dead horse here, but trust me, you need to engrave this lesson into your head.

You are who you are, and the sooner you realize this, the more you will minimize your stress. Accept reality and move on. Trust me; you will feel much better. And hey, you're going to have a kind of peace that most people do not find in their entire lives. Acceptance unlocks levels of peace and relaxation.

Surround Yourself with Like-Minded People

So, say you achieve a great level of acceptance, what about your tribe? You cannot just survive as an island; you need connections. This is where the power of modern technology and the global village truly make a difference. In major US cities there is a great level of community amongst queer groups. But what about the conservative and isolated parts of our nation and the world?

In the past, strong queer communities could only exist in places where our presence was significant enough to create a bump in the demographics. Now, with the internet, we can communicate with like-minded people across the globe. We are no longer subject to the limitations of physical meetings and interactions. There are different queer communities on the internet. Even a simple Google Search for "Queer support groups" will land you thousands of results.

When you find like-minded people, you will have an easier time expressing yourself and your pains. Those who have been in a similar situation as you will be able to sympathize with your plight. Nevertheless, this does not mean that you have to make yourself exclusive to queer communities. You should make friends and connect with people so long as they respect you and your choices. Remember, insular communities turn into echo chambers. If we started doing this, we would be no better than the bigoted people we try to stand against. Your goals should be to connect with people who can help you become a better person and find the true you that exists deep inside yourself. Sometimes that includes the hard decision of breaking away from people that do not value your existence. I had to cut a lot of people who peddled the love the sinner, hate the sin line to me. If you still think being gay is a sin, then you are not for me.

"No visible symptoms, no runny nose, just a head full of darkness. No fever or rash no fractures or sprains, just a longing for something unable to explain."

~ UNKNOWN

Chapter 7: Overcoming Trauma

Overcoming Traumatic Experiences

Being told every day in one form or another that your existence on this earth is worthless can really cause major psychological problems. Ever since I was shamed for kissing my guy friend in kindergarten, I have been on a journey of finding a point in my existence. Why would God make me this way? What am I here for? Why can't I be "normal"?

Those of us of the queer experience know quite well the experience of living in a world that does not understand us. Every day I felt attacked, every day I felt like I was living under a microscope. Is somebody going to see and point out my gay today? When first confronted with this type of trauma and shaming, we may react differently based on our temperament. Some get violent, some overcompensate, and others become isolated. It is common for people to feel a shock or a sense of disbelief when their personhood is attacked or called into question by someone else.

This type of trauma most times leads to a sense of isolation. Human beings are social animals, and when cut off from the community, we tend to suffer significant psychological and physical detriments. The strength of your feelings may surprise even you. You reach a point that you may have never considered before. Sometimes, it may even feel that you are standing against the entire world, like Atlas from the Greek myths, holding up the sky to keep your world from collapsing.

Overcoming and healing from these scars and traumatic experiences is an essential part of your journey to find peace and content. Your childhood, upbringing, and the environment you grew up in have a significant impact on your cognitive and psychological profile. What we may consider normal or regular may, in fact, be highly irregular and cruel. It is harder to recognize these things when you do not have a point of reference. For this very reason, children who grow up in abusive environments suffer from emotional immaturity.

For example, there was a very disturbing video of a young Black boy being abused by his older siblings for being gay. They shaved the word Gay on his head and filmed themselves beating him up and posted it on social media. I was so upset I wanted to jump through my phone screen. Without fail, Black Twitter jumped into action and found out everything about the boy and his siblings. Authorities were called, and people even showed up at their house. Everyone was ready to defend that young boy and even pull him out of that environment. After a few days of unrest, the young boy appeared on a Facebook live defending his siblings and asking people to stop harassing them. He began to make excuses in his young mind that defended their actions. My heart was so broken because so many of us, like him, make excuses for the abusive behavior we're subjected to, all in the name of family and love.

The first step to overcoming your pain and wounds is to recognize that they exist. Just because something was presented to you as being normal does not mean that it is so. Abusers will try and gaslight you to make you think they are acting in your favor or that your suffering is validated. It is a complete lie. Every human being has a right to basic decency and dignity, for we are made in God's image.

How will you know if you finally come across a standard that you can follow? The key is looking for inner peace and content. Try and look at how family and community are supposed to function. We, as humans, are here to help each other and support the collective. If a group does not act in this manner, then you are in the wrong place. Recognize that you are a human being who deserves empathy, support, and basic dignity.

Only when you start to value yourself as a person will you start to climb out of the hole left behind by trauma. Sometimes, it can mean leaving behind the toxic elements in your life that once acted as the "pillars" of your being. This includes family traditions, events, people, church, social gatherings, and the list could go on. What are you holding onto currently that does not serve your best interest?

It is better to ditch these toxic elements and embrace change. Do not let your fear of the unknown prevent you from taking a chance. Some may fear what they might find on the other side, but you're already suffering, so why not take a chance?

Forgive Others

Forgiving others is another important step in the process of healing. It is, perhaps, one of the most challenging aspects when you consider the core of what it means to forgive. Forgiving others is just as much about acceptance as it is about healing your own wounds. So long as you do not accept that the past happened, you will never be able to move on. In our minds, we see things as they should be, not as they are. This filtration process has us going over the past by reliving the trauma over and over again.

I'm sure that many people know the harrowing experience of constantly flashing back to the pain. At that moment, we think about all the wrong that has been done to us and why it should have gone differently. However, we cannot change the past, and reality does not conform to our desires. We can have a hand in changing things for the future, but the past has to be accepted. This does not mean that we see our trauma as valid. Instead, we should acknowledge that it happened.

At that moment, we realize that we are just as much a product of our environment as we are of our own free will. Forgiving others does not mean that you have to reconcile with them. We all know that kids can be cruel, but we start to develop a sense of morality as we grow up. Most know that experience of the childhood bullies growing up and then regretting their actions. As they mature, people start to see that their actions can cause pain to others, so they make amends.

For these people, it would be good for you to be the bigger person and forgive them for the acts they committed. Remember, they too might be suffering internally from the implications of their actions, and at that moment, you two become joined by the pain you share. Maybe you have been unkind to yourself in an attempt to relieve your pain. The same case applies. You need to accept that you made a mistake. It is a learning process, and any step to improvement is better than regressing into a stage of denial and hatred.

However, it is sad to say that others might not reach this stage and could even dig themselves further into their hole of intolerance. For these people, it is wise to forgive them from a distance and then move on with your life. The best revenge is a life that is well-lived. If you really think about it for a moment, you're shedding the emotional baggage that weighs you down. The intolerant people carry around their hate. The more they go through life, the more of this baggage they drag behind them. Can a life defined by hating others really be considered as a life lived well?

Trust me; when you reach this stage and shed all your emotional and psychological debris, you will know what I am talking about. When it first occurs, it's like a magical moment. You suddenly think to yourself, was I really worried about all that stuff and hurting myself? I feel so much better now that I have accepted my past and am eager to be present and move onto the future. There is no better feeling than being light and free from all that debris. When you reach this stage, you will start to pity the people lost in their hate, for they make victims of themselves through their actions and words.

Seek Therapy

Still, even with all these positive desires, goals, and ambitions, the path to healing can be arduous. You may find yourself in a tumultuous state as you try to resolve the pains of the past. When you grow up in an environment that oppresses you, you tend to close in on yourself. This isolation effectively cuts you off from different perspectives. It may be evident to some people, but others might be so lost in their pain that they consider it to be a normal part of their lives. This is one of the reasons that the cycle of abuse continues. The victim does not know how to exist outside of a setting filled with chaos and suffering. Thus, they end up recreating the same scenario just to feel at home in their suffering. Many of the things that you do to try and cope might, in fact, be leading you deeper into the hole. You cannot know what you do not know, and this is why outside help can be so beneficial.

A therapist or a similarly trained professional is well versed in the workings of the mind. They study these subjects and cases of people trying to fix their lives through erroneous methodologies. An outside and supportive voice can help you express your concerns while also showing you different ways to heal as a person. You have to be willing to reach out to that helping hand to get you out of the abyss.

There is no shame in seeking help. While it is always good to be self-reliant, assistance from others can help us reach heights that we never considered. Those who specialize in cases like identity crises or gender dysphoria are particularly well suited to helping the queer community. Just because you do not find the right person the first time does not mean that you should give up. Shop around for different people and go with the one that makes you feel the most comfortable. Therapy takes time, and sometimes it can bring up really painful memories. However, as you progress, you will find the process to be quite cathartic. Sometimes, venting out your pain can really bring you inner peace.

Identify Your Pain Points

The mind works through a complex series of associations between events and the stimuli that you encounter. These interconnections help you develop perspective and meaning, helping you make sense of events and how they relate to your being.

Mental associations can trigger flashbacks or recollections to previous memories when similar or linked stimuli are encountered in the future. Suppose that you have a favorite song or food you like to eat; the sensation can become even more potent when connected with a contextual event.[28] Think back to significant positive or negative events in your life. During such a time, your body continues to contextualize the stimuli and associate them with that event. Still today, Versace Blue Jeans Cologne sends me in because one of the first guys I fell in love with always wore that cologne. Thank goodness we had good times or I would be horribly triggered every time I smelled that cologne. When you encounter any smell, sound, sight, or event that is familiar to your own experience, it will trigger a recollection. Association is an integral part of your thought process because it allows humans to develop coherent links between events and experiences. That's why that familiar cologne or perfume smell can trigger you or a song can bring you happy feelings.

However, this association works both ways; it can bring you positive emotions, or it can leave you suffering through flashbacks. Many people know the positive side of this equation, but few know the harrowing experience of traumatic flashbacks.[29] Negative emotions and dangerous situations are often more strongly associated with stimuli; even the imprint they leave behind is stronger. This makes evolutionary sense, as the mechanism would help us avoid the same situation in the future. However, this tendency to hyper-focus on negative events can also cripple a person by having them relive an

---

[28] Ehlers, A., Hackmann, A., & Michael, T. (2004). Intrusive re-experiencing in post-traumatic stress disorder: Phenomenology, theory, and therapy. *Memory*, 12(4), 403-415.

[29] Butler, L. D., & Spiegel, D. (1997). Trauma and memory.

event over and over again. Things like phrases you heard, the way your abusers talked, the songs that were playing in the background, the smells surrounding you at the time, all of these can trigger flashbacks.

Abuse leaves a strong mark and the recollection of the events is just as vivid. A trigger is merely an associated subject that causes you to recall or relive your previous experiences. This can manifest in a number of ways. Some people may go catatonic; others will vividly recall their pain and may go through a surge of emotions.[30] Some might keep replaying the scenario over and over, leading to an even stronger association. In more extreme cases, the person may become violent and act aggressively because they enter a fight-or-flight mode. They may rationally know they are safe, but their emotional mind will continue to be influenced by that traumatic event. Any event, subject, or element that causes you to regress into that state of helplessness can be called your trigger. Given the complex nature of memory association, even smells may be able to drive you back into that dark hole. However, before that cascade of events takes place, you will be able to feel the onset of negative emotions slowly taking over you. In that brief moment, you have to practice mindfulness and recognize how your mind is being hijacked by the very mechanisms that are meant to keep it safe.[31]

It is helpful to keep a note or journal and list down the things that make you upset or cause painful recollections of past events. Your body will start giving off physiological signs associated with stress, indicating that the stimuli are causing you distress. Look out for things like a rapidly pounding heart, dizziness, an upset stomach, sweaty palms, and a feeling of dread and anxiety.

Once you identify your triggers, you will have to slowly overcome

---

[30] Van der Kolk, B. A. (1998). Trauma and memory. *Psychiatry and Clinical Neurosciences*, 52(S1), S52-S64.
[31] Jones, E., Vermaas, R. H., McCartney, H., Beech, C., Palmer, I., Hyams, K., & Wessely, S. (2003). Flashbacks and post-traumatic stress disorder: the genesis of a 20th-century diagnosis. *The British Journal of Psychiatry*, 182(2), 158-163.

them to live a normal life. Some might consider merely avoiding or escaping the triggers. This might work in the short term, but it will cripple your ability to deal with everyday situations. Given that triggers can come in any form, it might be entirely impossible to avoid them in some cases. Consider the example of crowds, smells, sounds, or sights. Instead of running away, you have to acknowledge your feelings.[32] It is alright to feel these things because your emotions are valid and what happened to you was true. You have to accept that circumstances in the past might have caused you pain, but those scenarios are not repeating at the moment.[33] For example, you might have had an overbearing mother who would continuously interrogate you on where you were and what you were doing. Suppose that a friend asks you where you are and what you are doing because they want to hang out with you.

Initially, you might get triggered into a state where you recall all the things your mother did. Your emotions will start flaring up, and you will think of your friend's inquiries under the same association as you did with your mother. It is here where you have to practice mindfulness. First, accept that your feelings are valid. Then, stop and think about why you are feeling this way. Yes, your mother was unjust and unkind, but is your friend trying to do the same to you? So, you go ahead and ask them for clarification, and you find out they just wanted to hang with you. Isn't that a relief?

Essentially, overcoming mental triggers is a process of retraining and relearning to contextualize stimuli and create new associations. The entire reason we have triggers is that some associations become so strong that our ability to change their context becomes impaired.[34]

---

[32] Ehlers, A., Clark, D. M., Hackmann, A., Grey, N., Liness, S., Wild, J., ... & McManus, F. (2010). Intensive cognitive therapy for PTSD: A feasibility study. *Behavioural and Cognitive Psychotherapy*, 38(4), 383-398.
[33] Center for Substance Abuse Treatment. (2014). Understanding the impact of trauma. In *Trauma-informed care in behavioral health services*. Substance Abuse and Mental Health Services Administration (US).
[34] Wu, R., Liu, L. L., Zhu, H., Su, W. J., Cao, Z. Y., Zhong, S. Y., ... & Jiang, C. L. (2019). Brief mindfulness meditation improves emotion processing. *Frontiers in neuroscience*, 13, 1074.

Give Yourself Grace

The time it takes to stabilize, recover, and reintegrate can vary from one person to another. In part, it depends on the nature of the trauma, the age of exposure, and the duration of the episode. The more significant the trauma, the greater the impact it leaves. Younger children are less capable of managing their emotions, and thus, would likely form strong associations that become the basis of their contextualization in the future.

Acute (short-term) trauma may leave a mark that does not have enough time to form strong associations. Chronic abuse and trauma (long-term) can lead the mind to see it as the default pattern. In such a case, the associations are powerful, and for some, will never truly heal.[35]

The point of healing is not to speed up the process because everyone is different. Our approach and understanding of the problem greatly dictate our ability to manage our pain and our path to recovery. Those who tend to face their problems and resolve them through regular effort will be much better off them those who merely think about it from time to time.

Still, there are no short answers to the inquiry of how long it would take a person to heal. At best, I can give you a framework from which you can derive your own answer.

Remember, just because you take longer to heal than someone else you may know does not make you less of a person. The other individual may have experienced a completely different set of circumstances, and it does not invalidate or reduce your own integrity. In the path to recovery, we are all on a journey to heal and grow. The path that is best

---

[35] Bremner, J. D. (1999). Acute and chronic responses to psychological trauma: Where do we go from here?. *American Journal of Psychiatry, 156*(3), 349-351.

for you is the one that helps you heal; speed is incidental.

Some people might be under the impression that therapy healing is like a magical pill, you go in there, and it just goes away. This could not be farther from the truth because therapy may just as well make you feel uncomfortable by having you face your problems. It is natural to feel that sometimes, therapy is making you feel even worse. However, this is merely your body reacting to your efforts in retraining and recontextualizing your triggers.[36]

There will be times when you might break down and regress, and that's okay. So long as you maintain an effort and continue to move forward, you will slowly begin to heal. Years of trauma and abuse cannot be taken away in a few weeks or even a few months. You have to slowly chip away at the problem one step at a time. Once you start the healing process and begin to feel better, consider it as a small victory.

The scale of your problems may make you feel like the entire thing is useless. This is why you should consider these small victory steps to healing as progress on your journey to become whole. When you know how far you have come, you will realize that your efforts are paying off, you are becoming a better person.

Once you have enough stability, you can start to become an anchor for others who have shared your pains. It can mean all the difference in the world to have someone by your side who knows everything you have been through; wouldn't you have appreciated such a person in your own time of pain?

Hurt People Hurt People

Abuse and trauma are cyclical elements that perpetuate themselves; the victim becomes the next oppressor. This leads to a

---

[36] Courtois, C. A. (2004). Complex trauma, complex reactions: Assessment and treatment. *Psychotherapy: Theory, research, practice, training*, 41(4), 412.

constant creation of new victims, who themselves go on to abuse other people, creating a chain of pain and suffering. Mind you, the victims themselves may not be aware of this cycle or may be unable to break away from their disturbed mental state. Look at me, I was an undercover gay telling gays they were going to burn in Hell. When a person suffers from abuse, their mindset settles into a mode of aggression and hostility as a means of guarding whatever personal ego remains after the event.[37]

Those who have been hurt in a relationship might seal themselves off emotionally, preventing them from creating a bond with others. In the future, they will be distant and might even become hostile. Their partner, in turn, might feel insecure and close themselves off, repeating the cycle. It's like a virus or disease that infects anyone who comes in contact. Only those who can mindfully manage their emotions, recognize the context, and control their associations can see the reality.

A child that is shunned and made an outsider might associate difference as something to be hated and despised. In a cruel twist of irony, they may end up bullying another vulnerable person as a means to feel secure about themselves. They end up making their victims an "other," thinking it might help them become part of the accepted circle. The best way to bring this to light is to put yourself in the shoes of another.[38]

Think about it from their perspective or turn the situation around. Would you like to be treated in such a manner? Are you taking the feelings and thoughts of the other person into consideration?

Be the kind of person you wished you had when you were being attacked, bullied, or abused by other people. What sort of support

---

[37] Ren, D., Wesselmann, E. D., & Williams, K. D. (2018). Hurt people hurt people: ostracism and aggression. *Current Opinion in Psychology, 19*, 34-38.
[38] Wood, C. W. (2008). *Hurt people hurt people*. Xulon Press.

would you have liked in your own time of need? Perhaps you needed someone to be there to help you or just lend you an ear to vent your feelings. You may not be able to change your past, but you can help other people avoid the same pains and trauma.

What happened in the past does not need to color the rest of your future. Accept what happened, recontextualize, retrain, and then move on; bitterness will only leave you trapped in that hole. Helping other people may just be what you need to climb out of the hole yourself; you could even support each other in your respective journeys. Break the cycle and cut off the perpetuation of abuse and pain.

"To find yourself, think for yourself."

~ SOCRATES

Chapter 8: Birth of Authenticity

After Trauma and Depression

When you start to climb out of your traumatic hole, you start to see the world from the surface again. While the initial stages of recovery might feel good, there is still quite a bit of debris left that must be dealt with. The challenge becomes integrating back into life without compromising the "real" version of you. While we can work all day to manage ourselves and our emotions, we cannot modify every single element of the outside world. And therein is where the clash begins.

The idea is well explored in the book *The Velvet Rage* by *Alan Downs*. When you grow up within a society or environment that actively and passively shuns your existence, you take on the same approach. The values within a person are instilled from their environment, and when the values clash with the inner world, the person starts to suffer a tug of war. This struggle is where you are pulled between what feels right and what society tells you is acceptable. This duality eventually becomes the source of so many problems.

Unfortunately, the outside world cannot be escaped, you need to interact with people. Even if you isolate yourself, you become someone who suffers from isolation and its detrimental effects. When you are told in Church, in school, and within society that "your kind" is a supposed enemy of something to be reviled, you start to believe the narrative. After all, we learn from the environment and apply those teachings to become a part of ourselves.

The trouble here lies in how the presentation of ideas can lead a person down a myopic path. Being designated an undesirable instills a condition of self-hate, a rebellion against the inner desires and wants of self. Ironically, this maladjustment only further amplifies the calls from the inner self as it lashes out against what it sees as a polar opposite of its existence. The internal and external are supposed to work in unison, but you absolutely suffer tremendously when the two clash. When the world is constantly telling you who you are has no place in society, it disturbs who you are at your core.

Everyone wants three things: security, to be heard, to be seen. Most people of the queer experience don't have any of these things. So, to become loved and desired, we seek to morph our beings into an image that is beloved by society or receives attention and awe. According to Alan Downs, it is one of the reasons why you find queer people dominating in all industries. We are working hard to be heard, be seen, and be accepted.

Domination behavior is a fabricated element, worn like a mask to receive acceptance and praise. Behind this charade, you can find the true hate within the individual that exists for self. By believing our supposed undesirable status, queer people leave behind our own identities.

Because of our innate desire to be accepted we adapt to the world that does not accept queer people for their true nature. In chasing validation from the outside world, the inner voices of peace and desires are silenced. The only thing that matters is the approval of other people. In silencing our inner voice, the queer community loses sight of any internal means of validating our actions or lifestyle. As everything is external, the inner self becomes a husk that cannot provide intrinsic motivation or drive.

Without having the inner self validate our existence, one can begin to recognize their acts as nothing more than a means to appease other people. In trying to please the people from which we seek validation, we end up becoming isolated from our own beings. We become someone that our inner self can't connect with. This leads to behaviors that attempt to fill that emptiness in the form of serial relationships or attempts to self-medicate via drugs and alcohol.

You act out, seek attention, while actively suppressing your true self. Eventually, the goal to become desirable starts to create impossible standards of wealth, looks, beauty, fame, reputation, and a host of other elements taken to their extremes. You don't just try to keep up with the Jones', you want to put the Jones' to bed. You want everybody to be keeping up with you. Such unrealistic standards further cause harm when one falls short of these supposed ultimate ideals, leading to a feeling of worthlessness and self-loathing.

Discovering The Real You

In order to truly become at peace with the real you and avoid chasing an end that will never become a reality, you must listen to your inner voice. To consider your external environment without any input from the inner being or vice versa is a recipe for disaster. You must maintain a balance between the two if you ever hope to achieve a greater sense of self. You are just as much a product of your environment as you are of your makeup. One taking precedence over the other leads to an uphill battle powered by narrow-mindedness.

This does not mean that you should validate or accept anything that comes your way. Think back to the previous example of how some people ignore the inner self in favor of society's opinion. Apply this same principle in reverse, and you will see how problems may arise. When you only think of the inner self, you ignore the rich and diverse world around you. One may even state that this obsession with the inner self and ignorance of the outer self is a function that leads to intolerance in the first place. People that may dislike queer people may, in fact, be so focused on themselves that they are unable to see the plight of "other".

If you were to apply a similar approach, you would end up in the same position. The names of the groups might change, but the framework would remain the same. Discovering your true self is a journey that will take you a lifetime. This does not mean that the goal is unachievable; instead, think of it as a process that never ends. Recall your childhood and the things you wanted, disliked, feared, or revered. Many of the matters in your childhood would likely seem like a small and minor element in your adult state. This is because you gained a broader perspective and grew as a person.

The person you were in the past, what you are today, and your future self will differ in their thinking. The idea that you can remain consistent in your life would be folly unless you isolated yourself to merely your inner being. You should be comfortable with the fact that your personality is not a fixed constant; you will grow with time. Start to learn how to best listen to your inner voice.

Your inner voice knows what you want and desire because it reflects the core nature of your being. At the same time, you should also consider the values presented by other people. These new and fresh perspectives will help you find other means to express your individuality. You may find that the values others espouse may be in line with what brings you peace and joy. Finding like-minded people is a good idea if you want to stay within a group that can empathize with your life.

Even those who disagree with you may help you develop into a better person. While this may seem counter-intuitive, it acts to provide a polarity between ideals. When you look at hateful and bigoted people, you will know in your heart that you do not wish to be like them; you want to be better and more tolerant. In this way, you end up becoming an inverse of the hatred that sought to destroy you in the first place.

Everyone says I will be an amazing father because of how I am with children and teens. I'm loving, caring, attentive, strict, all the things I did not receive from my biological father. Everything he wasn't for me I have become for some many young people. I'm thankful for our experiences because it made me a better man. It showed me everything not to be.

Your authentic self will help you validate and evaluate your life by using your core identity as a basis for comparison. Instead of one side pushing out the other, you will be able to incorporate elements of both in order to live in harmony. You don't have to include everything from the external into the internal. You take what brings you peace and makes you into a better person. The thoughts and ideas which act as poison to your identity should be discarded with a cautious note to avoid such things in the future.

Ask yourself the difficult questions. What do you feel? What do you want? If all the external factors pushing you to act in a certain manner were taken away, what would you do? If Hell was not a factor, who would you be? Would anything change? Do you wish you were freer to act out as you feel? Do you ever feel like you are putting up a façade to gain the approval of other people? How do people react when you let your guard down around them?

How Do I Know What I Really Like?

This is a really complex question, one which puzzles me from time to time. There is no universal answer that I can give you, merely what I have learned throughout my own experiences. Still, some of these frameworks and guidelines will help you get a better idea of what you love without getting lost in existential thought. Your own process may be unique, and your individual approach could differ from the one I present. That is completely fine; you should experiment and play around to see what gets you the best results. Because we spent most of our lives in hiding, trying to live up to others' expectations, we never got to experience the fullness of who we are. When we finally make the brave decision to come out of the closet, we are not only introducing the world to our true selves, but we are also being introduced to our true selves. There are so many things I did not partake in because I was afraid people would discover that I was gay. So now that I am truly free, how do I discover what the real me likes?

When we're younger, we often yearn for things based on a pure want that is less governed by the complicated decision-making process that adults use. Ask yourself, what is it that you craved as a child, and does it hold any merit for you now, in the present? Maybe you loved to paint and express yourself artistically. In that case, you could try to take part in a number of activities that take inspiration from the inner self. Art, dance, creating sculptures, writing poetry, painting, singing, and writing are just a few ways you can give form to your inner thoughts and feelings.[39]

The next method is a bit more practical, but you have to be honest in your evaluation. Suppose that all your monetary needs were fulfilled or that you didn't have to consider your expenses as a factor. What would you gravitate towards in such a scenario? Many times, we restrict our wants based on our ability to afford a certain item or service.[40] Is there a difference in your wants when money is eliminated from the equation? This may not work in all cases. For example, suppose you are enthusiastic about rare wines, vintage cigars, or sports carts. In that case, you will need a solid financial standing to make those dreams a reality. Still, you will know what you want, and then you can start to work your way to achieving that goal. It can help you create the drive necessary to undertake that project or business plan to make your dreams a reality. Remember, not every dream can be achieved; you have to stay within the realm of reality.[41] If the former

---

[39] James, S. (2015). Finding your passion: Work and the authentic self. *M/C Journal*, 18(1).
[40] Brooks, R. (2011). *Blowing Zen: Finding an authentic life*. Sentient Publications.
[41] Webb, L. (2012). *Discovering the authentic self: The concurrent processes of being and becoming* (Doctoral dissertation, Fielding Graduate University).

was possible, I'm sure many of us would have simply snapped our way into being accepted by society. Still, you should not become discouraged; instead, reassess your goals into a more achievable version.

Another method is to look up your heroes and the people that you value. By studying their hobbies and actions, you can find a list of things that you might also like. For example, do you have any friends or people you consider as role models? What do you like about them and why? Maybe you should try to develop similar capabilities, skills, talents, or qualities within yourself. It's not about becoming a clone. Instead, it's about taking on the useful and beneficial characteristics to help you on your own journey.

Finally, there is the idea of "just do it." With this mentality, you open yourself up to a whole world of experience that you might have otherwise missed. When using this mindset, you become receptive to the message and the knowledge everyone has to offer. You turn into a sponge, constantly taking in input and expanding your horizons. Based on all the information you collect; you can start to sort out the data and get a better idea of what you liked and disliked.[42] Each event or experience will impart an impression within your being. How you choose to interpret and perceive that is up to you. When you gain a sufficient amount of experience, you will start to develop a like or dislike for things based on your temperament. It is also one of the most constructive paths to discovering yourself. You may find yourself developing a taste for things that would have previously been glossed over or ignored.[43]

When you know what you want, you can filter out the noise of the world and hyper-focus on your goals. Still, you should remain open to

---

[42] Fierro, R. S. (2019). Authentic Self in Evaluation Consulting: Reflections after 10 Years. *New Directions for Evaluation*, 2019(164), 141-154.

[43] Hicks, E., & Hicks, J. (2004). *Ask, and it is given: Learning to manifest your desires.* Hay House, Inc.

further discussions and revisions. Think back to your tastes as a child and where you stand now. I can guarantee that who you are and what you like changed dramatically with the passing years. In the same way, what you like now is not going to hold true 10 or 20 years down the line. This is a process and a journey, not a static position. Keep learning and evolving.[44]

How Do I Discover My Authentic Self?

Living within a world of facades, social media, and the need to maintain our secrecy, we often wear a mask to hide our true selves. This holds true for us queer folk. I'm sure everyone knows the painful experience of suppressing our honest thoughts when we interact with people. You never know if the other person will accept your truth or if they will lash out and attack you for being different. I think this is truer for the queer community than any other group. We have so much historical data and personal experience to back up our reluctance to open up.[45]

Wearing a mask all the time, we start to lose sight of ourselves. Eventually, the mask can become permanently attached, and we cannot take it off even when we try. Have you ever had the feeling that you could not get in touch with your inner thoughts? I experienced this when a friend asked if I would attend his wig brunch and wear a wig. I wanted to answer from the bottom of my heart, but I could only stand there and scratch my head as to what my authentic self would reply. At that moment, I realized the danger of wearing a mask and suppressing myself to the extent of erasing my original identity.[46] I very much wanted to go and be supportive but then thought about how others would think about me in a wig.

---

[44] Clark, D. (2011). *Becoming: Get All Your Heart Desires!*. Lulu. com.
[45] Minus-Murrell, B. (2015). *Unbogus: Living the Authentic Life*. AuthorHouse.
[46] Kwon, Y. J., & Kwon, K. N. (2015). Consuming the objectified self: The quest for the authentic self. *Asian Social Science*, 11(2), 301.

So, the question then becomes, how do I know my authentic self? First thing first, we have to know authenticity to reach the goal. Your authentic self is the version that reflects your inner being without the masks or illusions that you create in your everyday life. When you take away all the things that prompt you to hide and blend into society, you end up with something that is unique to yourself.[47] Ask yourself, what would remain if we were to take everything away? What if you didn't have any reason to hide or suppress your feelings? What if you could say what you want without feeling embarrassed or fearing an attack on your person?[48] The question I really love to ask people is, what would your life look like if Hell wasn't a factor?

This exercise is likely going to be difficult. I know from personal experience that exploring the authentic self can be a painful experience, one that is full of emotional burdens. As we grow up, we are constantly pestered by society to "fit in". The traditions and the culture of our home enforce this behavior, turning deviants into pariahs or outcasts. We act and think like we are taught, and not in the ways that would be reflective of our true nature.[49]

To learn about your authentic self, you have to take a step back and out of your own being. This mindfulness exercise will take some practice, but you need to think on a meta-level. Focus on the present, what are you doing, and what is your reason for acting in this specific manner? What thoughts cross your mind as you go about your day and come across different people? Do you really mean to say and do these things? Or are you adapting to meet the expected standards of the environment?

As you keep up this observational exercise, you will start to pick up on the little things. Eventually, you will start seeing how your entire

---

[47] Allen-Young, M. (2019). # queer: Community, Communication, and Identity in the Digital Age.
[48] Costantino, A. (2011). *Without a Mask: Discovering Your Authentic Self.* John Hunt Publishing.
[49] Baumeister, R. F. (1997). The self and society. *Self and identity: Fundamental issues*, 191-217.

day is dictated by different things pulling you to act in equally unique ways. From this, you should start to ascertain what actions and thoughts are derived from a need to adapt and what is reflective of your core being.[50]

Think about your family and the environment in which you were raised. Do you really act out these traditions and cultural practices because you want to? Or do you merely desire to fit in? Is there a better way? Are there people and cultures out there who would better reflect the values that you carry deep inside? It would be wise to start learning about other people and how they live their lives. When you gain a broader perspective, you will gain a better appreciation for the value of each culture. At the same time, you will see how each culture can restrict its people into set boxes. Well, you don't want to be a part of the box; you are going to make your own box that fits your individual needs. Slowly start to gather all the elements that feel true to yourself, do not hold back in an attempt to blend in or hide.[51]

Once you develop a basic framework in line with your authentic self, you will learn how to manifest your individuality in the outside world. During this process, you will also learn to give words to many feelings which were previously an enigma.[52] The process is slow and requires significant dedication on your part. I would ask that you remain honest with yourself throughout; otherwise, your results will be colored and biased. You may come across some fears as you make your journey to the authentic self. You have to face these fears and move ahead. It is a long journey, so don't rush. Take your time.

---

[50] Heads, G. (2017). *Living Mindfully: Discovering Authenticity Through Mindfulness Coaching*. John Wiley & Sons.
[51] Carson, S. H., & Langer, E. J. (2006). Mindfulness and self-acceptance. *Journal of rational-emotive and cognitive-behavior therapy*, 24(1), 29-43.
[52] Fahkry, T. (2017). *Awaken Your Authentic Self*. Tony Fahkry.

"Being born gay, Black, and female is not a revolutionary act. Being proud to be a gay, Black female is."

~ LENA WAITHE

Chapter 9: Coming Out, Again

Unleashing The Buried Parts of My Queer Experience

Faggot, fruity, flame… words that would scar me so deep that their weight still held space in my mind six years after coming out of the closet. As you know, when I first came out, I was deathly afraid of how I would be received in the world. So much so that when my story hit the internet, I had a panic attack and could hardly breathe. Sitting in my room alone, reading the comments on social media, was even worse. "Burn in Hell, faggot," "Go kill yourself," "God doesn't love you," posted thousands of times written in different ways, all over Beyoncé's internet for the world to see.

Though I was mortified, none of those comments really mattered because I had no clue who those people were. It was the words of those closest to me that impacted me the most. "You're going to get AIDS," "I don't mind you being gay, so long as you don't act like a girl," "You're not gay you just have daddy issues."

Because of my love for those individuals, I still found myself trying to live up to their acceptable version of gay. There was still a little voice in my head saying, "don't be too gay," "watch your mannerisms," "that shirt is too flamboyant." It wasn't until a trip to Hawaii in June 2021 that I realized I wasn't truly free as I supposed. Even though I had come out to the world in 2015, I was still running from the words that taunted me my entire childhood. I was so worried about being accepted when I came out that I adopted another false persona just so that the people I love would still love me. It was through a great deal of self-reflection that I realized my entire life, I was taught to hide certain parts of me. Hide the gay Ben, the feminine Ben. Put the queer Ben away. Not loving and accepting all parts of my queerness has impacted all parts of my life. I've been trying to get people and lovers to choose me, but I still hadn't chosen me, still embarrassed to tell a random girl hitting on me that I'm gay.

Still nervous about revealing to a room full of straight identifying men that I'm gay. Still trying to find a masculine partner that would be acceptable by mainstream society. Still afraid to be my full self in front of my family. Still upholding an aura of masculinity, afraid that I won't attract a masculine man if I embrace the feminine side of me. Still embarrassed to embrace the fullness of my queerness. Whatever that still maybe....

Thanks to great self-reflection and the work of therapy, I was able to free myself from the shame, embarrassment, and even rage that had me bound. Today and forever, I choose me, ALL OF ME - the masculine, the feminine, the in-between. I reject heteronormative posturing and pick up the Ben that was dropped so many times. I pick up the Ben that was told to die. The words that were used to taunt me I actually embrace. Yes, I'm fruity, yes, I'm queer, yes, I'm a flame, and I love it.

They say sticks and stones may break your bones, but words can never hurt you. That's only a partial truth. Words can't hurt you if they don't have a place to land. But if you haven't fully embraced who you are, or you are ashamed of who you are, the words people use to taunt you will hurt you or anger you. If you called me dumb, that would not hurt my feelings at all because I know I'm smart and have the grades to prove it. If you said you throw like a girl, I would not be offended because I know plenty of girls who can throw really well, and I also know my strengths and weaknesses, and sports ain't a strength. If you called me a faggot, I'd say thank you because I love everything a faggot represents, queerness, realness, big bright, bold energy. When your words and opinions have no place to land, they can't hurt me. It is only in our insecurities that words can find space to harm us.

The Blessing and Curse of Coming Out

As we grow and change and reach a newfound understanding of who we are, we come out all over again. And this process is lifelong. In Chapter 8, we learned that Therapist *Alan Downs* calls this phenomenon the Birth of Authenticity. *The Velvet Rage* outlines the underlining and inherent shame that comes from parental rejection and/or growing up gay in homophobic spaces. The anger that comes from constantly trying to present an acceptable you that gets rejected is what Downs has coined "velvet rage." Our anger and our shame cause us to overcompensate and try to earn love and acceptance by being the best, better than others, and exemplary – trying to become someone we believe will make us more acceptable and loved. Though the book is mostly focused on the privileged white gay male experience, it rings true for most of the LGBTQIA+ community. According to Mental Health America, LGBTQ people experience mental illness at three times the rate of the non-LGBTQ population. LGBTQ youth are four times as likely to attempt suicide. Rates are even higher for trans and gender-non-conforming folks. These higher risks are linked to stigma and misunderstanding of LGBTQ people, even in a post-marriage equality U.S.A.

Once we face this shame and rage and overcome the stigma attached to being queer, we step into the birth of authenticity. We are free to discover the parts of ourselves that were hidden away, shamed away, beaten away, or prayed away. Most of us don't even realize we are responding to hidden shame. We numb the pain of parental or societal rejection, so deeply we do not even realize it is running the show.

Downs points out that the lack of any authentic validation, especially from a parent, results in destructive "velvet" rage. It lives in the silos of our psyche, nurturing seeds of unconscious self-hatred that manifest in so many ways: careless sexual choices, substance abuse, financial abandon, undisciplined career, self-sabotage, numerous short-term relationships, ignored opportunities, etc. Depression often rears its ugly head when life is good because deep down, we don't believe we deserve it.

Even as I write this book, I am in a season of unlearning. I'm undoing 30 years of hiding, shame, anger, and self-hatred. I'm doing away with the words, habits, behaviors, and even people that cause me not to choose myself. A friend asked me what choosing me looks like. At first, I had no idea, but then I realized I started choosing myself when I decided to pursue everything I didn't simply because I was gay. For instance, in 2021, I became a member of the world's first Black collegiate fraternity, Alpha Phi Alpha Fraternity, Inc.

Choosing me includes doing me and being me for me and no one else. Choosing me may result in losing some people who expect me to fit their idea of me. And that's ok. The connection must only be for a season.

In 2015, coming out exposed my truth, but I had no time to process the internal rejection and remove the internal voices that were telling me I was unworthy. I was out and proud but still being governed by the shame of being gay.

It is important that we all do some collective unlearning and restore our confidence in who we were created to be from birth. Becoming who we really are and loving that person is a journey. I am yet on my way to being my real authentic self and invite everyone to join me on the journey of discovering and loving the real you.

As you will read in the next several chapters, what you learned growing up about religion, homosexuality, and even Blackness has all been influenced by factors that don't sit in truth or reality. It is our job to wrestle with the truth and uproot the false and negative things that don't point us in the direction of truth and authenticity.

What have you not pursued because of your hidden queerness?

Coming Out as An Ally

Imagine feeling confused, alone, and worse—rejected—just for being who you are. This is the story of thousands of youth who identify as a member of the LGBTQIA+ community. It is so important that we continue to stand up for the members of the LGBTQIA+ community, especially our youth. We must show them that they aren't alone in their struggle for equality, inclusion, and acceptance.

Now, more than ever, advocates, teachers, parents, caregivers, youth, and communities are uniting across race, gender, and economic status to demand safe and affirming environments where LGBTQIA+ identifying youth can learn, grow, and thrive. Our LGBTQIA+ youth need us to prioritize equity and ensure our schools, social settings, and youth-serving environments are places where all youth are protected and empowered, no matter what part of the country they reside.

According to Human Rights Campaign's 2018 LGBTQ Youth Report:

- 67% of LGBTQ students hear their families make negative comments about LGBTQ people.
- While some students are open about their LGBTQ identity at school, only 21% are out at home.
- Privacy and confidentiality are critically important for LGBTQ youth, especially for those who do not have supportive families.
- Extreme rejecting behaviors can have dire consequences: Approximately 40% of the homeless youth population in the United States identify as LGBTQ, most as a result of rejection by immediate family members.

- Additionally, LGBTQ youth of color often face additional stress and adverse impacts on their health and well-being as a result of bias around their intersecting identities.

If you are interested in being an ally or advocate for LGBTQIA+ youth, you must first get an understanding of each youth's story to understand their needs and aspirations. For starters, young people today are exploring their genders in ways that expand beyond the scope of just male and female: binary (either male or female), non-binary (neither male nor female), universal (people everywhere are the same), and multi-gender (both male and female).

As more youth and young adults are given agency to express themselves and explore gender and sexuality, they find themselves discovering more parts about themselves. Today, more youth are identifying as lesbian, gay, bisexual, transgender, or queer than ever before, according to GLAAD's Harris Poll survey of LGBTQ acceptance.

Even still, most environments are too dangerous for youth to express themselves, especially in isolated parts of the country and the world. LGBTQIA+ youth who have rejecting families are eight times more likely to attempt suicide than those who do not have rejecting families, according to a study published in 2009 in the Journal of Pediatrics. On The Contrary, a Trevor Project survey found that just having one supportive adult in a young person's life reduces their risk of suicide by 40%.

It is so important that you read these next several chapters for clarity and understanding. They will help you challenge the awful religious rhetoric that is used to harm so many in the queer community. We need more people who identify as straight to stand in solidarity with the LGBTQIA+ community and have conversations in heteronormative spaces. Being a true ally means you are willing to get uncomfortable and make personal sacrifices.

What are you willing to sacrifice to stand up for the LGBTQAI+ community, especially our youth?

"My point, once again, is not that those ancient people told literal stories and we are now smart enough to take them symbolically, but that they told them symbolically and we are dumb enough to take them literally."

~ JOHN DOMINIC CROSSAN

Chapter 10: For the Bible Tells Me So

Picture it, Philly 1992, a bright-eyed young Black boy and all his friends in the hood were playing what looked like Church. In his friend's back yard, they set-up two rows of bronze metal folding chairs in front of a fixed stack of old plastic milk crates to form a makeshift podium.

"In the beginning...", the young boy yelled as he pointed his little finger toward the sky, "...God created the heavens and the...". Before he could even finish his sentence, all his friends stood up screaming "yes," "preach," and "amen."

Grinning from ear to ear, the young boy continued, lifting the Bible to the sky, "God made the animals, God made the trees, God made you and me." The commotion had gotten so loud that his friend's dad came to the back door and asked, "What is going on?" The boy turned around, annoyed because he had been interrupted, and said, "Having church!"

That little boy was me, and that friend's dad was Bishop TD Jakes, and he had just returned home from preaching *Woman, Thou Art Loosed.*

Just kidding! That wasn't Bishop TD Jakes, but he did first preach that sermon in 1992. If you know anything about a Sophia Petrillo "Picture It" story from the hit TV show Golden Girls, then you know it always closed with an extremely outlandish ending. The Bible has been my source of inspiration ever since I was in the first grade. While children would want to playhouse and doctor and cops and robbers, I would gather my friends and play Church. I would bribe them into the backyard with candy and snacks and begin preaching as I'd seen in movies. Not really knowing what I was talking about, I would just open the book and read from Genesis. I'm imagining now they were so quick to respond to my preaching because they wanted to get to the candy and snacks.

My immediate family was not religious at all. We didn't go to Church. Our Sundays were spent at home with friends playing in the streets. A definitive answer as to why I was drawn to the Bible and religion at such a young age has yet to be answered.

The only moment I vaguely can remember is being captivated by the story of Jesus and him being raised from the dead. Occasionally, while watching TV, they would break for a marathon and sell VHS copies of the *Animated Stories from the New Testament.* I would always beg my mom to buy them for us. One Christmas morning, I got my wish. Story after story, miracle after miracle, drew me into this world of possibilities. If this God could make their lives better, I wonder what he could do with mine.

As I grew older and could interpret scripture with greater comprehension, the book that brought me so much inspiration also began to bring me so much pain. Not only did my family not like me being gay or feminine, neither did the Bible.

This hurt and wildly confused me. How could I be what God does not like? And furthermore, how did I get this way? Throughout my life, I've heard and repeated that God doesn't like homosexuals, gay people shall not inherit the Kingdom of God, and being a sissy meant you were going to burn in Hell. The only proof that I had of the validity of this hate speech was the few scriptures in the Bible.

Before I decided to come out and live in my truth, I told my mentor and pastor that I was taking a break from ministry and taking time to really understand the Bible and why if being gay was an abomination, God hadn't cured me yet. That was in 2012. I didn't come out until three years later.

What I found shocked me to my core. I immediately grew angry at all the preachers that came before me for never addressing any of these issues. After a while, I figured these issues were never addressed because not too many people have a definitive understanding. And to explore the topic would be to shake one's faith.

I remember as a teen on a car ride back from burying a church member, I rode with my pastor and asked him about dinosaurs. Surely if the authors wrote about David conquering a lion and a bear mauling disobedient children that someone saw a dinosaur. He chuckled and did not answer. The assistant to the pastor came up with a story that didn't make any sense. So, I followed up by asking how dinosaurs were millions of years old, and the Bible was only thousands of years old. No one responded.

Their response is representative of how the Church responds to these deep questions concerning logic, time, and science. They do not lean in and explore. There is no response at all, or people become very defensive. I took the time to explore some issues, namely how the Bible was formed. Many judge and damn people from a book they barely understand themselves. It is important to note that my point is not to deter you from your faith but give us all insight into the Bible and disarm the hate speech that is used in judging one another.

If what we believe about Hell is true and "sinners" will spend an eternity burning, weeping, and in torturous pain, how can one so easily sentence their fellow brethren there. Furthermore, how could one stand so firmly on sending someone to Hell based on information they don't fully understand.

Do you know who wrote the Bible? Who authorized the editions? Who pulled together the books? What was excluded from the Bible? What was the process for determining what was approved for entry? Was it the Holy Spirit that approved the final version like Moses' revelation of the commandments? What book and verse tell this story?

I'm going to take a strong guess and say you don't have most of those answers. No worries, most people do not. Generally, we leave that up for scholars and theologians to understand. But isn't it our duty to understand? And wouldn't you want to understand, especially if you're going to use this book to sentence someone to Hell?

Join me on this quick journey. Take notes, develop your own questions, discuss with a friend. There's too much information to put in one book, let alone one chapter. I'm challenging you now to explore and go beyond what you learn and discover in this chapter.

Recording History

The cataloging of history is often controlled by a few influential people with political power and agendas. Those with the power to control the distribution of the story are the gatekeepers. In addition, humans have a habit of forgetting their own history and how they came to be. Our history can easily be misconstrued with the stroke of a pen or flick of a match. The more educated we become as a people, the more we are aware of these occurrences.

In 2015, a Black 15-year-old and his mother discovered that his textbook was telling a different story about slavery in America. McGraw-Hill's CEO David Levin had to issue an apology because the textbook published by his company omitted the brutality of the Atlantic Slave Trade and replaced the word "slave" with "worker" and "immigrant."

In McGraw-Hill's "World Geography" textbook, on a page titled: "Patterns of Immigration," a caption, overlapping a map of the United States, reads: "The Atlantic Slave Trade between the 1500s and 1800s brought millions of workers from Africa to the southern United States to work on agricultural plantations." This caption downplays the brutal removal of Africans from their homes and families.

In addition to replacing the word "slave" with "worker, the caption uses the verb "brought," an understatement that misrepresents the inhumane and deadly transportation of Africans across the Atlantic. The simple change of one word can alter an entire story. This is key to remember, as will later work through biblical translations.

History is rife with examples of political or ideological censorship and whitewashing (to alter in a way that favors, features, or caters to white people). Dictatorial regimes are famous for altering what contradicts their power and belief systems. This activity predates the formation of the Bible and continues today.

Here are some key examples of stories being altered or destroyed.

According to the Tanakh (Hebrew Bible), in the 7th century BC, King Jehoiakim of Judah burned part of a scroll that Baruch ben Neriah had written at prophet Jeremiah's dictation.

From 213-210 BC, the Chinese Emperor Shih Huang Ti thought that if he burned all the documents in his kingdom and killed hundreds of scholars, history would begin with him.

In 367 AD, Athanasius, the zealous bishop of Alexandria, issued an Easter letter in which he demanded that Egyptian monks destroy all such unacceptable writings, except for those he specifically listed as 'acceptable' even 'canonical' (a list that constitutes the present New Testament).

According to the Chronicle of Fredegar, Recared, King of the Visigoths (reigned 586–601 AD) and first Catholic king of Spain, following his conversion to Catholicism in 587 AD, ordered that all Arian books should be collected and burned; and all the books of Arian theology were reduced to ashes, along with the house in which they had been purposely collected.

In 1244, as an outcome of the Disputation of Paris, twenty-four carriage loads of Talmuds and other Jewish religious manuscripts were set on fire by French law officers in the streets of Paris.

In 1817, for the 300th anniversary of Martin Luther's launching of Protestantism, students held a major burning of "Un-German" books.

In 1933, in Nazi Germany, under the guidance of Joseph Goebbels, Reich Minister of Public Enlightenment and Propaganda, one-third of Germany's library holdings were destroyed.

In 2013, al-Qaeda-affiliated militants in Mali burned the library in Timbuktu, and in 2015 ISIS burned books from Mosul's library as a show of both ideological and territorial conquest.

While book burnings in our time have been acts of sensationalism and symbolism, in the past, torching texts was a tactic used by dictators, conquerors, and religious leaders to wipe the slate of history clean. We don't even have any idea of how much history was wiped away as millions of Africans were stolen from their homeland and shipped around the world.

It is impossible for us to know everything about everything when catalogs of stories and facts have been burned for good. It is through multiple events and centuries of decisions made by a few influential people with power that the path to understanding our world is shaped.

It is important to understand before we dive into how the Bible was formed and written, we understand how ancient humans began writing in the first place.

Scholars acknowledge two types of writing, proto-writing and true writing. Proto writing consists of visible marks and symbols that communicate limited information. True writing is the content of a linguistic utterance that is encoded so that another reader can reconstruct, with a fair degree of accuracy, the exact utterance written down.

The origins of proto writing appear nearly 12,000 years ago in the stone age during the start of the pottery phase of the Neolithic when clay tokens were used to record specific amounts of livestock or commodities.[53]

The best-known picture writing system of ideographic or early mnemonic symbols are Jiahu symbols, carved on tortoise shells in Jiahu in 6600 BC.[54], Vinča signs (Tărtăria tablets), in 5300 BC[55], and Early Indus script, in 3100 BC.

Recent developments have also found early humans as far back as 40,000 years ago developed a system of signs that is consistent across continents. Genevieve Von Petzinger spent years cataloging these symbols in Europe, visiting 52 caves in France, Spain, Italy, and Portugal. The symbols range from dots, lines, triangles, squares, and zigzags to more complex forms like ladder shapes, known as tectiforms.[56]

Scholars believe true writing was independently developed in at least four ancient civilizations: Mesopotamia (between 3400 and 3100 BC), Egypt (around 3250 BC)[57] China (1200 BC),[58] and lowland areas of Southern Mexico and Guatemala (by 500 BC).[59]

Writing today, in its most general terms, is a method of recording information and is composed of graphemes (a letter or a number of letters that represent a sound in a word) which may, in turn, be

---

[53] W. Hallo; W. Simpson (1971). *The Ancient Near East*. New York: Harcourt, Brace, Jovanovich. p. 25.
[54] *Archaeologists Rewrite History*. (n.d.). China Through a Lens. Retrieved September 10, 2021, from http://www.china.org.cn/english/2003/Jun/66806.htm
[55] Haarmann, H. (2002). *Geschichte der Schrift* (Vol. 2198). CH Beck.
[56] Von Petzinger, G. (2017). *The first signs: Unlocking the mysteries of the world's oldest symbols*. Simon and Schuster.
[57] Wengrow, D. (2011). The invention of writing in Egypt. Oriental Institute, University of Chicago.
[58] Boltz, W., & Boltz, W. G. (1994). *The origin and early development of the Chinese writing system* (Vol. 78). Eisenbrauns.
[59] Brian M. Fagan, Charlotte Beck, ed. (1996). *The Oxford Companion to Archaeology*. Oxford University Press. p. 762. ISBN 978-0-19-507618-9.

composed of glyphs[60] (an elemental symbol within an agreed set of symbols, intended to represent a readable character for the purposes of writing).

How Was the Bible Formed?

The Bible has been at the center of most conflicts, revolutions, wars, and peaceful eras throughout history. It always made me wonder how a book with so many messages of kindness, love, and generosity ignite such intense feelings of hostility.

Contrary to popular belief, the Bible was not carried to us by angels, flapping their wings, descending from the heavens. This truth may disappoint you even further. Jesus didn't write the Bible either. As a matter of fact, Jesus quite often quoted what was already written. Spirituality and inspiration aside, the Bible is a book that was written, compiled, and continues to be revised by humans just like you and me.

The word Bible comes from the Greek word Biblia, which means "books." The Bible is a collection of many books, like a library. Each biblical book has a unique history and takes a distinctive route on its way to inclusion in the Bible. Scholars dated the earliest biblical writings to the time of Moses, which may have been around 1500–1200 BC.[61] Some scholars claim that the earliest biblical texts were written down in the eighth or seventh century BC.[62] The exact dates of composition are truly unknown, and we have no concrete idea of who originally authored much of the Old Testament. Many theories but no exacts. When we read the Bible, most have the understanding that the words were written by man but inspired by God. Now that we know how ancient writing was formed, we have to ask ourselves how were

---

[60] Bricker, V. R., & Andrews, P. A. (1992). *Epigraphy* (Vol. 5). University of Texas Press.

[61] *How Was the Bible Written and Transmitted?* (n.d.). Bibleodyssey. Retrieved September 10, 2021, from https://www.bibleodyssey.org/en/tools/bible-basics/how-was-the-bible-written-and-transmitted

[62] *How Was the Bible Written and Transmitted?* (n.d.). Bibleodyssey. Retrieved September 10, 2021, from https://www.bibleodyssey.org/en/tools/bible-basics/how-was-the-bible-written-and-transmitted

the text that make up the Bible originally captured? One can hypothesize that before writing, humans shared stories, from those stories symbols, from those symbols text. Now it begs the question of how accurate the information was with each passing of the story.

The earliest biblical texts were written on scrolls made from papyrus (plant-based paper) or parchment (animal skins). It is also believed that prior to scrolls, the Bible was passed down via storytelling from generation to generation, but there is no strong evidence of that occurrence. But one would have to believe that the story of creation was told and retold.

None of the books of the Bible, to our knowledge, were written by Adam or Eve or any of the early biblical characters. And if everything was truly destroyed in the flood, the stories of anything prior had to live with Noah. What we do know for sure is that only in the second or third century AD did scribes begin to write on papyrus or parchment that was folded and stitched into a codex or book. This formal process was thousands of years after the original occurrence of events. So much could have happened in between that time.

Scribes were very key in the development of the Bible. Scribes did all the work of composing, preserving, and transcribing scrolls. Reading and writing wasn't a common skill in ancient times, so Scribes were essentially the true gatekeepers. Scribes often edited and condensed several different scrolls that told the same story. No original manuscripts of any of the books in the Bible exist.

Over the years, these stories were rewritten hundreds of times with many changes, additions, errors, and omissions along the way. As a matter of fact, the word homosexual wasn't even added to the Bible until 1946. But we'll discuss that later in the next chapter. What we do know for sure is there aren't too many firsthand accounts in the Bible. It's a collection of stories told by "witnesses."

If history has taught us one lesson, it is that whoever controls the pen controls the story and everything in it. There are many stories and versions of those stories told throughout the decades, with each one slightly different than the last.

To understand the entire concept of what the Bible could mean, we would have to go back to the origins of the book itself. Was the Bible already in the process of being formed right after the first revelation in Genesis? If not, then when and how did the process even begin? To answer those questions, we need to take a deep dive into the information available to us. For instance, as Jewish traditions suggest,[63] during 500 BC, most of the writings that are now recognized as the Old Testament were hailed as the final word of God after many processes of acceptance.

Many of the Old Testament stories are also like stories in other histories. The great flood story[64] can be traced as far back as 3500 BC to the Sumerians, the Old Babylonians, and the Jewish people.

While the Jewish people believed every word to be a divine revelation, more religious writings were being revealed during the intertestamental period, the 400 years that took place between the Old and New Testaments. They had to get a handle on these other texts.

The Church doesn't speak much about all that took place over this 400-year period because there's very little account of it in the Bible. But it's very important to understand what happened to Jewish people during this time and who had control over the many scrolls kept by the Scribes. The Apocrypha, a group of books consisting of historical accounts of God's people, including 1 & 2 Maccabees, were developed during this time. Although accurate portrayals of history, this work is

---

[63] History.com Editors. (2019, April 23). The Bible. HISTORY. https://www.history.com/topics/religion/bible
[64] History.com Editors. (2019, October 8). Sumer. HISTORY. https://www.history.com/topics/ancient-middle-east/sumer

not regarded as Scripture because there is no prophetic inspiration.

At the beginning of the intertestamental period, the Jewish people were under the rule of Persia, who allowed them to return to the land of Judah, ending the time of exile. They also began to rebuild the temple. In 331 BC, Persia was conquered by Greece under the reign of Alexander the Great, who ruled Judea until 164 BC. The New Testament is written in the Greek language for this reason. The Greeks had a major influence over the Jewish people. One hundred years later, Rome conquered the land, removing any independence from Judea. Rome brought law, persecution, and control to the people of Judea.

During Jesus Christ's age, the Old Testament was regarded as the Holy Scripture, and the writers of the New Testament even quoted it. When Jerusalem was in ruins after 70 AD, the Jewish people and Scriptures were all over the place.[65] They panicked and thought about how to conserve those sacred texts. Then in 90 AD, the Council of Jamnia was established to helped figure out the canonicity of the 39 books of the Old Testament.[66]

Flavius Josephus recognized the books in 95 AD[67]; some books were readily accepted into the canon scripture, while some caused doubt before getting accepted, and others didn't get accepted at all. Flavius Josephus, original name Joseph Ben Matthias, was a Jewish priest, scholar, and historian who wrote valuable works on the Jewish revolt of 66–70 AD and on earlier Jewish history. His major books are History of the Jewish War (75–79 AD), The Antiquities of the Jews (93 AD), and Against Apion.

The books that were ultimately rejected by Jews[68] based on doubt

---

[65] Siege of Jerusalem | Facts & Summary. (n.d.). Encyclopedia Britannica. Retrieved September 10, 2021, from https://www.britannica.com/event/Siege-of-Jerusalem-70
[66] Newman, R. C. (1976). The council of Jamnia and the Old Testament canon. Westminster Theological Journal, 38(4), 319-348.
[67] Weiss, J. (2016). Flavius Josephus, 1492. International Journal of the Classical Tradition, 23(3), 180-195.
[68] How Was the Bible Written and Transmitted? (n.d.). Bibleodyssey. Retrieved September 10, 2021, from https://www.bibleodyssey.org/en/tools/bible-basics/how-was-the-bible-written-and-transmitted

and conflict were later added to a codex of Christian scriptures that the Greek Christians adopted because they couldn't follow Hebrew. The books were rejected by Martin Luther as well during the Protestant Reformation. The Protestant Reformation was the 16th-century religious, political, intellectual, and cultural cataclysm where reformers like Henry VIII and Martin Luther challenged papal authority and questioned the Catholic Church's ability to define Christian practice.[69] They argued for a religious and political redistribution of power. The disruption triggered wars, persecutions, and a rush to get a handle on the Holy text.

In the end, the Roman Catholic church chose to formalize scripture in 1546.[70] They wanted to support the doctrines that mentioned the prayers for the dead and Purgatory, which originally have no basis in the Bible.

The Protestant Church rejected some of the formalized scripture due to theological and historical errors, as well as the fact that Jews rejected those books because they believed that the scripture had ended in the 4th century BC.[71] There was doubt because the Apocryphal was never quoted by Christ or any of the writers of the New Testament. When it comes to the New Testament, Christians of earlier times chose to compile and collect the words and quotes of the rising Church's apostles.

During the first couple of centuries, religious scripture was passed around with people either accepting them completely, somewhat or not at all. Some of those texts were even considered scripture in the apostolic period, like Peter considering Paul's letters as scripture in

---

[69] History.com Editors. (2021, September 9). *The Reformation*. HISTORY. https://www.history.com/topics/reformation/reformation
[70] *Council of Trent | Definition, Summary, Significance, Results, & Facts*. (2021, August 19). Encyclopedia Britannica. https://www.britannica.com/event/Council-of-Trent
[71]*Biblical literature - Determination of the canon in the 4th century*. (n.d.). Encyclopedia Britannica. Retrieved September 10, 2021, from https://www.britannica.com/topic/biblical-literature/Determination-of-the-canon-in-the-4th-century

Peter 3:16.

Matthew, Mark, Luke, and John were the four gospels that laid the foundation for those texts to be considered scripture because of their apostolic roots. In 397 AD, the Council of Carthage recognized the 27 books of the New Testament,[72] being the first to do so.

Even though the council recognized them easily enough, some of the Apocrypha was still accepted as canon by a few people. A few of the books did shed some historically accurate facts regarding the practices of the early Church.

There were even some books that were given the names of Mary, Judas, and Peter. Some were written as political or religious propaganda. Today, some authors use the Nag Hammadi documents that were discovered in 1945 in Egypt to portray them as lost books of the Bible.[73] Included in those documents were the Gospels of Truth, Thomas, Philip, Egyptians, and Mary. There are those who argue that there were 80 gospels in total.

The process for checking the authenticity and accuracy of text used by Jewish and Catholic leadership is unknown. We are taught that the Bible was formed by people who understood God's sovereignty, His divine revelations, and inspirations to reveal Himself and His word to the world. However, the book was indeed compiled and edited according to the people of that time. Whether they had personal or political gain through their work, their process remains vague. Who voted, how they voted, the intentions behind their vote are simply unknown.

When we talk about the Bible, we cannot simply disregard that with

---

[72] *biblestudying.net*. (n.d.). Bible Study. Retrieved September 10, 2021, from https://www.biblestudying.net/NTcanon.html

[73] Staff, B. A. S. (2020, December 26). *The Nag Hammadi Codices and Gnostic Christianity*. Biblical Archaeology Society. https://www.biblicalarchaeology.org/daily/biblical-artifacts/the-nag-hammadi-codices/

every few decades, new revisions and editions have been released based on the people in power at the time. The Bible was done being compiled and added to a long time ago, but modifications are still being made. The book itself contains the same message; it's the details around it that keep changing throughout the years. The Holy Bible has been translated into so many languages – around 3,324 of them, to be more exact.

A question regarding the authenticity of every word of the Bible used to haunt me when I was younger and more confused about my existence in the world around me. Coming from a Black church background, it was almost blasphemous to question God or the Bible. However, I couldn't stop myself from wondering, just like I couldn't stop wondering about dinosaurs. Most people who belong to a religious community goes through a phase where they question the things they have been taught, whether they want to acknowledge that or not.

I was lost about my direction in life, and I turned to the Church. I had always heard how God helped people discover not only themselves but also the world with a deeper and much clearer perspective. The world still did not make sense to me, even after studying the Bible. In fact, it raised more questions than answers. I was so interested in discovering all I could about the Bible that I enrolled in the True Light Fellowship School of Biblical Studies. I was the only teenager in a school full of adults and ministry leadership. As I went deeper and deeper into my studies, I learned that there are many things that indeed do not make much sense.

For me, I was a bit surprised as I discovered that the Bible was not as infallible as everyone would lead you to believe. Just like any other book regarding history and accuracy, it is flawed in many aspects. It is not flawed in the sense of God's word and the divine revelation that Jesus received. The question about how much of it all was documented and reported accurately and completely remains nonetheless. It was especially the historical accuracy of the Bible that had me befuddled.

The errors and flaws of biblical history can no longer be overlooked as more and more details and factors surface, specifically regarding the first few centuries when the revelations, events, stories, and quotes were compiled.

Errors In the Bible

At its core, the Bible is a historical text, and those are famously known for their errors regarding historical accuracy. When it comes to books, people try their best to portray the most accurate version of events in the past when writing, but it is still acceptable, albeit with some accountability. However, the Bible is supposed to be perfect because people follow the book's words so literally and seriously. With such a serious and severe importance in society, one can understand why the Bible's details are expected to be perfect.

Making a mistake or an error when writing a book like the Bible can have serious consequences. Take interchanging the words kill and murder for instance. When the Bible condemned an act, some versions note it as 'thou shalt not,' which is a perfect translation from Hebrew to English. However, over the years and the number of modifications and translations that the Bible has gone through, it is only expected that the translation could lose its original meaning. It could portray the command of God as something else entirely due to simply being mistranslated.

There's a huge difference between 'thou shalt not kill' and 'thou shalt not murder. To kill is to take life. To murder is to take life with no moral justification. We kill animals to eat. We even kill plants to eat. Does that mean we are breaking one of God's commandments?

In Biblical Hebrew, harag, which translates as killing, and ratzah, which translates as murder, are two different words as well with two very different moral connotations. The Hebrew version of the commandment uses the word ratzah, which means that the proper translation of the commandment from Hebrew into English is, "thou shalt not murder."

That is one reason why experts and historians have found multiple errors and historical inaccuracies in the Bible. As I dived deeper into the theology of Christianity and then studied history on its own, without the added perspective of Christianity, I realized that there were many events and stories added in the New Testament that either did not happen or represent a fictitious view of our world. They pertain more to mythology than anything real and accurate based on events that happened or people that existed.

Historical Errors in The Bible

To get started, let's point out how historians of that period, people who lived and recorded the major events of their lifetime, have no records of biblical events like the crucifixion, resurrection, the risings saints of Matthew, earthquake, etc. For example, Philo Judaeus was alive around 50 AD[74], and throughout all his records and texts, there are no such events mentioned as the ones included in the gospels.

Even the records of the Roman Pilate do not include anything about a person named Jesus Christ. If Jesus was alive at the time and doing the things the gospels mention him doing, then why didn't these people record such important and world-changing events in their records?

The famous punishment of being crucified at the cross, as the gospels mention, for his crimes against the Roman Pilate does not

---

[74] *Philo Judaeus | Encyclopedia.com*. (n.d.). Encyclopedia. Retrieved September 10, 2021, from https://www.encyclopedia.com/people/philosophy-and-religion/philosophy-biographies/philo-judaeus

exist in factual form. There are simply no records of a man named Jesus Christ being crucified.[75] However, according to Al-Quran 4:157, Hebrews 5:7, and Psalms 20:6, Christ was saved by God and never actually died at the cross. Even the much talked about earthquake or darkness in Matthew after the crucifixion events were not recorded in historical accounts.

So, does that mean Christ wasn't crucified just because other history books can't account for it? Or did the devil erase Jesus from historic accounts through the actions of man?

Another famous event recorded in the gospel of Matthew in the New Testament is Herod's Slaughter of the Innocents. Scholars and historians have expressed their expert opinions that the event is nothing but stories of pagan mythology.[76] For instance, sung-gods of Egypt, Rome, and Greece had their lives in danger ever since they were born. Therefore, a command was passed that called for the executions of all newborns. Moreover, secular scholars consider Jesus Christ a sun-God himself because a similar event occurred during his lifetime.

Another intriguing discovery was when I found out that Jesus title was not 'Son of God;'[77] instead, he was the 'Sun of God.' His titles like 'God the Son' refer to paganism because 'God the Son' means the trinity in paganism. Even the title 'Lamb of God' was not exclusive to Christ because the Hindu savior god, Krishna, held the title when he existed centuries before Jesus Christ.[78]

Like that, there is glaring evidence of historical errors when it

---

[75] Jarus, O. (2019, August 2). *Who Was Jesus?* Livescience.Com. https://www.livescience.com/3482-jesus-man.html

[76] *The Slaughter of the Innocents - Associates for Biblical Research.* (n.d.). Biblearchaeology. Retrieved September 10, 2021, from https://biblearchaeology.org/research/new-testament-era/2411-the-slaughter-of-the-innocents-historical-fact-or-legendary-fiction

[77] *Why Was Jesus Called the Son of God?* (n.d.). Learn Religions. Retrieved September 10, 2021, from https://www.learnreligions.com/origin-of-the-son-of-god-700710

[78] *KRISHNA AND CHRIST.* (n.d.). University of Idaho. Retrieved September 10, 2021, from https://www.webpages.uidaho.edu/ngier/KrishnaChrist.htm

comes to biblical history. One such category of errors that many experts and scholars have commented on is the number of geographical errors in the Bible.

There is a story talked about in the gospel about the Gadarene swine. It mentions how the Gadarene rushed down a cliff and then drowned in the Sea of Galilee. A Jewish scholar has debunked that as geographically and historically incorrect because Gadera is located miles away from the sea, which means that it is unlikely to have happened simply due to geography.[79] Similarly, according to scholars and experts in the field, there are other geographical errors in the gospels that prove how the accuracy of biblical events and history is up for question.

These errors are not meant to disprove the legitimacy of the Bible, God's existence, or go against the Christian faith. They are only meant to shed light on the inaccuracies documented by humans, voted on by a council of humans, and considered the infallible word of God by humans.

Are you following along yet?

How many times did your brain reject the facts I've just laid out before you? It's ok I went through the same process. The quicker you get rid of the notion that the Bible is perfect and God would not allow any mistakes in it, the quicker you can get through this process.

Contradictions In the Bible

There are so many statements in the Bible that if considered true, without further exploration and investigation, we'd always be at odds with one another. If any preacher preached these scriptures together in one sermon, they'd have a hard time making the sell. I'm just going

---

[79] American Atheists. (2017, March 29). *Did Jesus Exist?* https://www.atheists.org/activism/resources/did-jesus-exist/

to simply lay the pairs out together and let you be the judge. Hold on because it's about to be a little bit of a roller coaster.

"For **whosoever shall call upon the name of the Lord** shall be saved." - Romans 10:13.
Vs
"**Not everyone who says to me, 'Lord, Lord,'** will enter the kingdom of heaven..." - *Matthew 7:21.*

"Thou shalt **not kill**." - Exodus 20:1.
Vs
"Thus sayeth the Lord God of Israel... **slay every man** his brother, companion, neighbor." - Exodus 32:27.

"For by grace are ye **saved through faith...not of works**." - Ephesians 2:8-9.
Vs
"Ye see then how that **by works** a man is justified, and **not by faith only**." - *James 2:24.*

Rejoice not when thine enemy falleth... - Proverbs 24:17.
Vs
The righteous shall rejoice when he seeth the vengeance... - *Psalms 58:1.*

"And [Judas] cast down the pieces of silver in the temple, and departed, and went and **hanged himself**." - *Matthew 27:5.*
Vs
"Now [Judas] purchased a field with the reward of iniquity; and **falling headlong**, he burst asunder in the midst, and all his bowels gushed out." - *Acts 1:18*

"**Answer not a fool** according to his folly, lest thou also be like unto him." - Proverbs 26:4.
Vs
"**Answer a fool** according to his folly, lest he be wise in his own conceit." - *Proverbs 26:5*

"Submit yourself to every ordinance of man...to the king, as supreme; Or unto governors." - *I Peter 2:13*.
Vs
"We ought to **obey God rather than men**." - *Acts 5:29*

"**Two and twenty years old** was Ahaziah when he began to reign." - *II Kings 8:26*.
Vs
"**Forty and two years old** was Ahaziah when he began to reign." - *II Chronicles 22:2*

"For every man shall **bear his own burden**." - *Galatians 6:5*.
Vs
"**Bear ye one another's burdens**, and so fulfill the law of Christ." - *Galatians 6:2*.

"**No man hath seen God** at any time." - *John 1:18*.
Vs
"For **I have seen God** face to face." - *Genesis 32:30*.

"God is not a man, that he should lie; **neither the son of man, that he should repent**..." -*Numbers 23:19*.
Vs
"**And the Lord repented** of the evil which he thought to do unto his people." - *Exodus 32:14*.

"Moreover of the children of the strangers that do sojourn among you, of them shall ye buy...and they shall be your possession...**they shall be your bondmen forever**." - *Leviticus 25:45-46*.
Vs
"Undo the heavy burdens...**let the oppressed go free**,...break every yoke." - *Isaiah 58:6*

"And of every living thing of all flesh, **two of every sort** shalt thou bring into the ark." - *Genesis 6:19*.
Vs
"Of every clean beast thou shalt take to thee **by sevens**, the male and his female: and of beasts that are not clean by two, the male and

his female." - *Genesis 7:2*.

"Therefore **Michal the daughter of Saul had no child** unto the day of her death." - *II Samuel 6:23*.

Vs

"But the king took the two sons of Rizpah...and the **five sons of Michal the daughter of Saul**." —*II Samuel 21:8*.

Let those sit for a minute. Actually, you should go back and read them again. Wild, right? Some contradictions are right in the same book, in the same chapter, just verses apart! Again, the purpose of placing these scriptures before you is not to refute God's existence but demonstrate man's ability to err on behalf of God. Some contradictions were as small as how old someone was or what day something happened. My point is if we took all of them as infallible truth, the Bible would always be at odds with itself.

The Fallacy of The Literalist

Whether online or physical, we go to the store, pick out a good book, and sit down to read. Whenever we read a book, no matter the genre or subject matter, we always keep an open mind. We know that whatever we read on the pages more than often has double meanings or a subtle message that readers are meant to grasp through their comprehension skills alone. However, when it comes to the Bible, people tend to leave that skillful comprehension aside. They look at every word, phrase, verse, and quote with a literal meaning.

Of course, there are no prescribed ways of reading or understanding the Bible as it was. Many aspects of the Bible are merely symbolic and not meant to be taken literally and at face value. Some experts believe that this is because of the Protestant reformation.

Before then, people turned to the Church for the final word or information regarding religion or scripture. Mostly because most people could not read or write, there weren't millions of copies of the Bible laying around, and the Pharisees thought laymen weren't capable of understanding scripture. The Church was a living, breathing people with sound minds that were capable of discerning a situation and coming up with a reasonable solution.

As Luther and his allies opposed the Church and their teachings, people looked towards a new source of authority; the Bible. While defending it from liberals or the papists, Evangelical Protestants turned the Bible into being the center of the faith when it is actually not.[80] A religion, for all intents and purposes, is firstly about the figure or entity that is worshipped or believed to be the ultimate authority. Then there are the doctrines, prophets, and so on and so forth. So, how come the Bible has become the focal point of Christianity when it is merely a guidebook for those that want to learn or discover new things about the religion?

One of the biggest drawbacks of this literalist movement is that there is no presence of someone or something that can adhere to a situation. For example, if there are disagreements regarding something about the religion, questions, and queries, or even confusion regarding old and new discoveries, how will the Bible be able to come up with sound resolutions? How can a book, at its core written and compiled by humans thousands of years ago, fully answer to the troubles of humans today?

That is why when it comes to complex topics like gender, identity, and orientation, that are so deeply layered, it's impossible to look to the Bible for answers. Questions regarding different aspects of our world that are only just developing require complex answers that the Bible, in all honesty, cannot give.

---

[80] McLean, J. (n.d.). *Luther and Protestantism | Western Civilization.* Lumenlearning. Retrieved September 10, 2021, from https://courses.lumenlearning.com/suny-hccc-worldhistory/chapter/luther-and-protestantism/

Questions about homosexuality require a broader and more elaborate explanation than just referring to it as an 'abomination' as some biblical translations do. There are many other situations and questions like that that require more explanations than just what the verses in the Bible provide. We need someone with the capability of studying those verses and coming up with answers regarding the theology of Christianity. A book is not capable of doing that.

As a young person who had heard that the Bible could answer all your questions in life, I turned towards it myself during my phase of being lost about my sexuality. I spent nights upon nights turning pages of the Holy book, trying to find the right verse or the right event that would help me figure out how I was feeling or thinking. Then when I only found things that confused me further, I had to realize that the Bible, at the end of the day, was not the final authority.

I had to study it over and over again, then realized that the words are not meant to be taken with absolute and ultimate finality. The words, stories, and verses that portray the message of God should not be read with a literal perspective. You are meant to understand every nuance of the story and historical events that occurred.

If you read between the lines, you will realize that the message of the Bible is not to remember every verse by heart. You are supposed to draw your own conclusions as well. Sometimes those conclusions will not be noted down in the Bible. So long as they align with God's principles of love, you will be alright.

Many people have drawn their own conclusions, but they have been led astray, thinking they were doing the work of God simply because the Bible said it. What they failed to do is measure it against God's love and morality. Do you think God really wanted children to be stoned to death for disobeying their parents?[81] Or women to feel safe after

---

[81] Deuteronomy 21:18-21

marrying her rapist?[82]

A religion of any nature is not about simply following the doctrines or commands in it. Religion is about understanding what God wants you to see and understand through His actions, words, and decisions. Past events would help you draw comparisons and parallels with your own life. If you study the Bible enough, you will be able to tell what is written between the lines. At the end of the day, religion is about what God speaks in your heart, not in a book.

A book such as the Bible was the creation of humans that, no matter what, had their own personal agendas, believed in specific things and were very much capable of making mistakes. If we were to take their words literally and to heart, we would be stuck with questions our entire lives. For example, the events and things discussed in the Bible were regarding a time that was much different and simpler than ours. A time with different sets of traditions, myths, societal norms, and people. The present time and world are not at all like those.

We have many more things to answer for, and that is why we turn towards the Bible, but when the Bible is taken much too literally, it poses a barrier because of those factors. It creates a gap in understanding and comprehension because the problems of those times do not translate to that of ours. We have to keep guessing and assuming about what could be the right and divine answer to our questions. With the help of learned people who have studied the Bible, such as myself, Christians are able to get their problems or issues discussed with the hope of figuring out what could be done.

The Bible tells us about the basic facts of Christianity, but it cannot be trusted with accurate information or the best solutions to our much too modern troubles and struggles. The Bible tells us to kill our disobedient children and pluck out our eyes for lusting. How's that for

---

[82] Deuteronomy 22:28-29

modern-day problems?

The Bible has been used by people and movements that don't represent the love of God. In modern times it was used to keep Africans mentally enslaved in America, it was used to keep interracial couples from getting married, it was used by the Klu Klux Klan to justify their brutality, and now it is being used to condemn the LGBTQIA+ community.

What has been consistent is eventually, humans saw the errors of their ways and stopped using the Bible as a weapon. How long will it take us to stop using the Bible as a weapon against God's beloved people? What will the future say about our current actions? Can you imagine the Bible being used as a tool to keep Blacks and whites from getting married? Well, it was. Things like homosexuality, diversity of religion, discrimination, and other such complex topics could not be argued or debated about if you were to take the Bible at face value. What we have to do is make sure that we understand the subtle hints and clues hidden inside the commandments, gospels, and books of the Bible so that we can better understand what God wishes to convey to His creations.

Know God and The Bible for Yourself

So much is to be said about a person whose relationship with God is contrary to the love of God. How can you hate your brother whom you see every day and love a God whom you've never met? The Bible is written with scriptures telling us to love. Love is the principal instruction. Love is the principal example. Yet most somehow miss that and head straight to the 'thou shalt not.'

What is it about us that causes us to want to be superior to another? To have a one-up on our brother? To be seen as better? We're drawn into the doctrine and the mouthpieces that spew hate and division. We take the worst parts of the Bible and choose that to live by, overlooking mountains of text that tell us to love and judge not.

Humanity is one of God's greatest inventions but also one of God's most complex. Humans lie, humans steal, humans kill, humans hate, humans envy, humans enslave, humans manipulate text to support their agenda: all in the name of God. If humans can do this now and have done so throughout history, what makes you believe none of this happened in the formation and translation of the Bible? Is it because they said it was God? Who are they, and how did they get in charge? God is not the author of confusion, or is He? Because I know I sure am confused. How could a God of love be so cruel and hateful at the same time? How do you make me in your image and then tell me I am an abomination or did He?

We have to be very careful when the "instructions" and "commandments" of God are counter to the love of God. Humanity has painted God as this big bad deity who is waiting for the chance to pounce on us for being imperfect. Man did that and supported it with stories that are counter to God. If there can be false prophets, who lie in the name of God and lead people to destruction today, how come that couldn't have happened in the days of old?

In the year of our Lord 2020, thousands of pastors and prophets decreed and declared that President Donald Trump would be re-elected President of the United States. But he lost the election by millions of votes. They, "representing God," cursed anyone who didn't vote for him. His chief intercessor and pastor Paula White said disobeying President Trump was like disobeying God. They, being the "representatives of God," chose to overlook Donald Trump's - bigotry, racism, hatred, division, lack of biblical knowledge, lack of church attendance, criminal investigations, sexual assault charges, hush money for a porn star, lack of respect for the law, foul mouth and Twitter fingers, bullying minorities, women, and children, stealing from the less fortunate, thousands upon thousands of lies, scandals, crooked connections, mob ties, cult ties, white supremacist ties, domestic terrorist ties, tyranny ties, espionage, constitutional treason, fraud, tax evasion, - and boosted him up as God's chosen and upright.

If these nut jobs can do this right before our eyes on national television, what more do you think could have been done when information and agency weren't so available in ancient civilizations?

You must know God for yourself. You must know love for yourself. You must know Bible for yourself. And you must go beyond the text and tap into God. The Bible, though imperfect, is a guide. It is our source of inspiration. It is the tool that we use to find the message of Love God wants to be shared on earth. It is a guide that should lead you to a better you and lead you to building a better world. Not tearing it and others down.

We will never agree on Bible. The variables in its founding are to spread for common consensus. We have no idea who authored the original text of most of the Bible nor the methods used to bring thousands of years' worth of text together to formulate the Bible. We can speculate, theorize, and guess, but we'll never know. What we do know is we have a choice. A choice on what we decide to believe and live by. After all, isn't that the main part of our religion, faith?

What do you believe and why? Does your belief do more harm than good? Does your belief devalue another human or lift them up? Does your belief impede on their business and their choices, or does it allow free will just like God gave us free will? Is your belief wrapped up in love or entangled in judgment?

"One of the most painful scenarios of Black church life is repeated Sunday after Sunday with little notice or collective outrage. A Black minister will preach a sermon railing against sexual ills, especially homosexuality. At the close of the sermon, a soloist, who everybody knows is gay, will rise to perform a moving number, as the preacher extends an invitation to visitors to join the church. The soloist is, in effect, being asked to sign his theological death sentence. His presence at the end of such a sermon symbolizes a silent endorsement of the preacher's message. Ironically, the presence of his gay Christian body at the highest moment of worship also negates the preacher's attempt to censure his presence, to erase his body, to deny his legitimacy as a child of God."

~ *MICHAEL ERIC DYSON*

Chapter 11: Sexuality, Religion, and the Black Church

What Is the Black Church?

Black religious institutions have been the most important institutions in the Black community; that's not opinion but fact. If you are Black in America, religious or not, you have benefited from the actions of the Black religious community. Black Religious Institutions, namely the Black Church and the Nation of Islam, have been the center of Black liberation and empowerment. Two of our most beloved civil rights leaders were ministers who represented the Black Church and the Nation of Islam – Dr. Martin Luther King Jr. and Malcolm X. Many of our Black empowerment leaders today still emerge from Black religious institutions. Black Americans are among the most religious in the country, reflected in church attendance, daily prayer, and the personal importance of religion in our lives.[83]. Today, roughly eight-in-ten (79%) of Black Americans self-identify as Christian, (5%) Catholicism, and (2%) Islam.[84]

For centuries, Black Religious Institutions have served as a crucial hub for the Black community, providing social, economic, moral, and wellness support, as well as a place to build community and have a sense of belonging. In our earliest years in America, Christianity was forced on Black slaves. The Bible, used as a form of control and mental oppression, was the tool used to enforce slavery. Slaves in the Caribbean were even given a different version of the Bible that removed stories about the liberation of the Children of Israel for fears that it would cause a rebellion. The Slave Bible told of Joseph's enslavement but left out the parts where Moses led the Israelites to freedom. As soon as slaves learned to read and write English, they

---

[83] Sahgal, N., & Smith, G. (2009). A religious portrait of African Americans, US Religious Landscape Survey.
[84] Sahgal, N., & Smith, G. (2009). A religious portrait of African Americans, US Religious Landscape Survey.

began to interpret the Bible differently and began to protest the idea of the biblical justification for slavery.

Religion became a powerful and profound sense of hope for Black slaves. Slaves clung to Christianity in hopes that God would care for them during their most difficult times. The hope was Christ would return and save them from their suffering. And if Christ didn't come before they died, the good submissive life they lived would grant them a better one in the afterlife. The idea that there was a land flowing with milk and honey and a place with many mansions was their hope. Many believed and still believe today that at the end of this terrible life is a reward. Still hanging on to that hope and faith, Jesus remains a staple in the Black community.

Many Muslims were also forced into Christianity. An estimated 30% of slaves brought to the Americas from West/Central Africa were Muslims.[85] Only a few were permitted to maintain their religion. There are records of individuals such as Omar ibn Said who lived his life as a Muslim Black slave.[86] At the turn of the 19th century, many Black people converted to Islam, mainly through the influence of Black Nationalist groups that preached with distinctive Islamic practices, including the Moorish Science Temple of America, founded in 1913, and the Nation of Islam, founded in the 1930s.

The Nation of Islam was created by Wallace Fard Muhammad. Fard, who was bi-racial, provided three main principles that served as the foundation of the nation: "Allah is God, the white man is the devil, and the so-called Negroes are the Asiatic Black people, the cream of the planet earth."[87] In 1934, The Prophet Elijah Muhammad became the

---

[85] Potts, D., & Stock, R. (1997). Africa South of the Sahara: A Geographical Interpretation. *The Geographical Journal*, 163(1), 94. https://doi.org/10.2307/3059691
[86] *How this slave manuscript challenges an American narrative.* (2019, April 24). PBS NewsHour. https://www.pbs.org/newshour/show/how-the-autobiography-of-a-muslim-slave-is-challenging-an-american-narrative

[87] Brooks, R. L. (1996). *Integration or Separation?*. Harvard University Press.

leader of the nation. Prophet Muhammad influenced the civil rights era and shepherded Malcolm X and Heavyweight Champion Muhammad Ali.

Most of my lived experience is from a Christian perspective. But I wanted to include both stories of the founding of the Black Church and Nation of Islam, considering how influential both religious institutions are on the Black family.

Most of my family identifies as Christian, though I grew up with some very militant Muslim uncles who did not play about their religion. I spent many thanksgivings listening to my Christian uncles, arguing with my Muslim uncles. We'll talk about how white supremacy caused division in Black religion in Chapter 14.

The Black Church was born out of slavery and shaped in the slaves' attempts at liberation and building a sense of community. Traditionally, the Black Church was comprised of seven Black American protestant denominations with their roots in emancipation including, the African Methodist Episcopal Church, the Church of God in Christ, and Progressive and National Baptist Conventions. Since then, there have been hundreds of Black-led denominations, but they all have been modeled on the traditions of the original Black churches.

The Black Church represents a movement that took what once was used to oppress our people to free our people. To Black people, the Black Church is more than just a religious institution. It extends into our social, familial, and cultural lives, making it difficult to separate the church from other aspects of our lives. This has been both a blessing and a curse for the Black community. Much of the religious dogma that extends from the church also spills into Black family life, whether the family is religious or not. There are so many issues impacting the Black family that the Black Church is silent or complicit about. Most are either perpetuating stereotypes or spreading misinformation. One of the tabooest topics in the Black Church is sex and sexuality. You can talk about anything and everyone, but you better not talk about sex. The only thing we learned about sex was don't have it until you are married and don't be gay. Even if most people suspected someone was gay or even knew they were gay, it was forbidden to address it other than to keep announcing that being gay is a sin. Many would murmur about the feminine choir director but never dive into the topic from an enlightened perspective.

As a teen, there were so many times I wanted to share with my youth leaders about my struggle with sexual identity, but I didn't know how I would be received. One time after impassioned spirit-filled youth service, many of the youth began to open up about a lot of struggles they were facing. We spoke about depression, suicide, sex, marijuana, peer pressure, and so many other things teens struggle with. A youth leader, whom I highly respected, said to a group of us junior youth leaders who were hanging out in the back of the church, 'if you're having sex, you're nasty, and if you're gay stay in the closet, I don't want nobody coming out around me.' I immediately wondered, is she talking about me? Does she know something about the gay youth messing around with each other? Her announcement frightened me but equally surprised me. Why wouldn't you want a young person who is in your charge to confide in you? So, in the closet, I remained.

Her response to sex and sexuality is no different from many leaders in the Black Church. And the Black Church's response is no different from society's response to sex and sexuality.

Is Sex the Missing Link?

Sex is God's greatest gift given to mankind, for within it, you have the power to create life and the power to connect with a human being in the most intimate way. Sex is the ultimate form of human vulnerability. Our relationship to sex and how we are introduced to sex is tied to so many other areas in our lives. Without sex, none of us would be here. Without sex, life would cease to exist. So, if sex is the key to life, how come it is shunned upon by so many, especially in the church? Why are we so embarrassed to talk about sex and sexuality?

There are many reasons why sex is a sensitive topic that many don't like to discuss. Whether through sex education at school, Sunday School at church, or at home with family, most of us learned early on that sex is wrong, and you should only have it when you become an adult. Now, while I do promote no sex until adulthood, most people fail to give instructions or a proper introduction to sex once teens do become young adults.

Many of us have been punished, and some severely, for mutually exploring our sexuality as a child with a friend, cousin, or neighbor. As much as people do not like to talk about it, our first act of sexual interaction is usually with the people who are around us. We get curious, we explore, we look, we question, we act, but at the end of it all, we do it in secrecy because we are taught that sex exploration is bad. We, until a new relationship with sex is formed, connect sex, sexual thoughts, and sexual activity with shame. That's why most people, even as adults, after they are "fulfilled," whether with someone else or individually, feel shame as if what they just did was wrong.

Shame is a social construct created by socialization and cultural or familial norms. Shame is a social emotion because it is different from normal emotions like feeling happy, sad, or angry. We learn shame based on what is socially acceptable. In some cultures, men holding hands as they walk or men kissing as they greet is socially acceptable. In 2005, President George W. Bush and Saudi Crown Prince Abdullah were photographed holding hands, walking through a garden in Texas. Americans lost their minds, and the American news media went crazy over something that is completely normal in Saudi Arabian culture. Forget the political ramifications of a US president walking with a Saudi Prince, many shamed President Bush on the hand holding act alone.

There was one time when I was so excited to see my best guy cousin visit me at my home in Philadelphia. We were young teens, maybe around 13 / 14 years old. As soon as he arrived, we grabbed hands and started skipping up the street to the corner store to buy our favorite snacks. A couple of older boys on the block called us back down the street. Surprised that they even acknowledged us, we went running back down the street holding hands. As soon as we got there, they made fun of us and mimicked our handholding and skipping, and even over feminized the act.

Immediately we both felt shame and were equally embarrassed as all my friends were there to witness. That quick moment of innocent banter and shaming destroyed years of friendship. My favorite cousin and I were never the same. Our friendship did not feel the same. We looked at each other differently. We even started treating each other differently. We'd make sure we weren't too close to one another, making sure we didn't hold hands, hug too tight; as a matter of fact, I think we stop hugging altogether. Shame can take what is innocent and turn it into something traumatic. Shame can take what is natural and make it taboo. There was nothing perverted or sexual about me and my cousin holding hands and expressing our excitement and love for one another. He was my very best friend who I loved very much. But men expressing any type of affection for another man is seen as gay. Now yes, I am gay, but my cousin is not, but we were shamed into believing our affection for one another was sexual, and that is not right. So many men grow up with so many underlying issues because their natural desire to show affection, emotion, and love is erroneously connected to sexuality.

These natural desires fall outside of the "Man Box," a rigid construct of cultural ideas about male identity, including all the things society says it takes to be a man. In a 2017 study conducted by Promundo and Axe, young men aged 18 to 30 in the US, UK, and Mexico felt pushed to live in the "Man Box." This includes being self-sufficient, acting tough, looking physically attractive, sticking to rigid gender roles, being heterosexual, being homophobic, having sexual prowess, and using aggression to resolve conflicts.[88]

The behaviors outlined in the "Man Box" strongly align with the traits of toxic masculinity, which is a term often used to describe the negative aspects of exaggerated masculine traits. Toxic masculinity is defined by adherence to traditional male gender roles that consequently stigmatize and limit the emotions boys and men may comfortably express while elevating other emotions.[89] Though the impacts of toxic masculinity aren't new, the term didn't originate until the mythopoetic men's movement of the 1980s and 1990s. Masculinity becomes toxic when people equate manliness to strength, lack of emotion, self-sufficiency, dominance, or sexual virility. The outcomes are generally harmful to environments and can turn violent.

In 2018, The American Psychological Association warned that "traditional masculinity ideology" is associated with negative effects on mental and physical health.[90] The new "Guidelines for the Psychological Practice with Boys and Men" marks the first-ever report published by the association aimed at helping practitioners care for their male patients. The association also introduced new guidelines for therapists working with boys and men, warning that extreme forms of certain "traditional" masculine traits are linked to

---

[88] Heilman, B., Barker, G., & Harrison, A. (2017). *The man box: A study on being a young man in the US, UK, and Mexico*. Promundo.
[89] Wikipedia contributors. (2020, December 28). *Toxic masculinity*. Wikipedia. https://en.wikipedia.org/w/index.php?title=Toxic_masculinity&oldid=996812557

[90] American Psychological Association. (2019). APA guidelines for psychological practice with boys and men. 2018.

aggression, misogyny, and negative health outcomes. According to social learning theory, teaching boys to suppress vulnerable emotions, as in the saying "big boys don't cry," is a significant part of gender socialization in Western society.[91]

While the evidence is becoming clear about the harmful impacts of this toxicity, many still refuse to acknowledge the truth. Many conservatives and representatives of major ministries believe that accusations of toxic masculinity are an attack on manhood itself, while many progressives argue that addressing toxic masculinity is an essential pathway to gender equality. We must begin to have more conversations about sex, sexuality, gender, gender roles, orientation, nonconformity, and so much else. The more we remain quiet or approach these issues from an age-old judgmental perspective, the more issues we will have in our society.

Dethroning Toxic Masculinity

The year 2019 was a big year for addressing toxic masculinity. We were on the heels of the #MeToo movement, which exposed the many ways women are sexualized and taken advantage of sexually. The movement gave women agency and language to express long-felt feelings and a megaphone to call out men for their egregious behavior. There were also allegations of women sexually harassing men. Most men would never come forward complaining about sexual advances or inappropriate behavior from a woman because it is outside of the "Man Box." Our inability to properly deal with sex and sexuality leads to so many underlining issues.

American Activist Tarana Burke began using the phrase "Me Too" in 2006 to raise awareness of women who had been abused. A little over a century later, it found global recognition after a viral tweet by

---

[91] Wikipedia contributors. (2020b, December 28). *Toxic masculinity*. Wikipedia. https://en.wikipedia.org/w/index.php?title=Toxic_masculinity&oldid=996812557

actress Alyssa Milano. Milano was one of the women who accused Hollywood producer Harvey Weinstein of sexual assault. Corporate executives and celebrities who were, prior to the movement, protected by their money, fame, and power were being taken down, and some were carted off to jail. Big names included Harvey Weinstein, FOX host Bill O'Reilly, comedian Bill Cosby, NBC Today host Matt Lauer, and FOX News Chairman and CEO Roger Ailes, just to name a few. A New York Times report showed that at least 200 prominent, powerful men lost their jobs after public allegations of sexual harassment since the movement started. Prior to the movement, these men were untouchable.

The year 2019 was also a big year for me; I had the honor of speaking at President Barack Obama's My Brother's Keeper Rising Conference in Oakland, California, a gathering of young boys and men of color and the professionals that work with them. I led a conversation on the main stage about the responsibility of men of color in the lives of women and the LGBTQIA+ community. I took the stage a day after President Obama and NBA Superstar Steph Curry rocked the house. The president boldly spoke about how to be a man and the need to combat stereotypes of masculinity that trap young men, specifically young men of color.

At the start of the panel, President Obama had introduced himself as "Michelle's husband" and the Golden State Warriors player as "Ayesha's husband." They addressed the need to get rid of old views on masculinity and define ourselves by our ability to help one another out instead of tearing one another down. President Obama also spoke about how racism plays a role in perpetuating toxic masculinity in communities of color. "Racism, historically in this society, sends a message that you are 'less than'... we feel we have to compensate by exaggerating stereotypical ways men are supposed to act. And that's a trap."

I was relieved to see that the president's message was well-received, considering I would be speaking about similar issues the next day. It also gave me personal cool points and free reign to say, 'like President Obama said yesterday.'

I shared the stage with some really powerful women who had some gems to share with the auditorium full of young leaders from across the country. Alicia Garza, co-founder of Black Lives Matter; Ericka Huggins, Activist and former Black Panther Party Leader; Aja Brown, Mayor of Compton, and MJ Rodriguez, actress and activist, all took the stage and joined me and shedding light on how young men can be better sisters' keepers.

We spoke about love, sexuality, gender, standing up for one another, and being proud of who we are and who we love. Garza floored the crowd when she said as a Black queer woman, she is tired of being accepted and included. She doesn't want to be included in spaces as an afterthought; she wants everyone to be a part because we're human. She challenged the young leaders to activate the artist inside of them and step outside of "weird boxes that we didn't build" and "design our own way of being together in connection in the relationship because our survival depends on that." Trans actress and star of the hit show Pose, MJ Rodriquez, spoke about how she felt so proud when NBA Superstar Lebron James honored her and a few other trailblazing women in a post on his social media. On Instagram, James thanked some notable women for their important and inspiring work with a slideshow of their magazine covers. Along with Beyoncé, Issa Rae, and Zendaya was Out Magazine's cover featuring the transgender cast of FX's Pose. He posted, "Nothing in this world is more POWERFUL than Colored Women!! Thank you all for continuing to not settle and setting great examples in life for so many looking up to you for inspiration/guidance and love!! My daughter is watching!"

Though the post included a diverse set of Black women in the industry, James received backlash because of how people still view transgender members of our society.

"When LeBron James did that, I thought that was quite amazing because not a lot of African American men address these things out in public, and he is someone who is so sure in who he is he had no problem doing [that]," shared Rodriquez. She challenged everyone to be courageous and have these conversations and stand up for and protect women of her experience.

Mayor Brown urged everyone to find a space in their community, whether large or small, to have real conversations. "I can tell you that in our city Compton we started an open mic... any place that you can gather a few people and have a real conversation you will be amazed at what can happen with just talking to one another." Mayor Brown explained that in order for us to have a real impact on each other's lives we need to be "transparent and vulnerable" because we are all connected.

I asked Ericka Huggins how we can start to have these conversations earlier to impact future generations because it seems as if older generations are stuck in their ways and attack anything that's outside of the "Man Box."

Earlier that year, giant razor maker Gillette jumped into the toxicity conversation with a nearly 2-minute-long ad promoting the ideals of the #MeToo movement. While the ad opened the door for transformative conversations, it did not come without its huge share of backlash and criticism.

The first half of the ad portrays males as impolite, sexually harassing women, mansplaining, and bullying. Halfway through, the narrator states that something has changed and that "there will be no going back."

"You can't hide from it. You can't laugh it off, making the same old excuses," the narrator explains. Then the ad showcases caring and empathetic men who intervene to stop men from catcalling or bullying. The ad concluded with, "It's only by challenging ourselves to do more that we can get closer to our best."

Many saw this as an attack on manhood and even threatened to boycott the razor maker unless the ad was pulled. Gillette stood its ground, and the ad continued to play.

"I'm not your typical set of identities," Huggins shared. "I've been married, my partner now is a woman, I have three children, they do not each have the same father, not because of promiscuity as is the stereotype." The crowd, along with myself, was intrigued.

"But because of these embedded assumptions that we're walking around with, we don't know necessarily how to support boys and young men being exactly who they are." She pretty much summed up the issue in that one sentence. "I told both of my sons if you ever feel that you are attracted to the same sex, its fine; if you ever feel like you don't understand what it means to be with a woman, talk to me..."

She encouraged everyone, youth, and their mentors alike, to take a look inside and deal with self-first.

"I always say that freedom is an inside job... in order for me to have those conversations; I had to be secure in who I am and all my coinciding identities."

She explained that one of the most horrific aspects of toxicity is what we force our children to live by.

"Based on our socialization we expect boys to be a particular way and we expect boys not to cry, that is inhumane, that is toxic, that's violence because what that means is that we're asking a human being to sublimate and suppress human emotion and we ask little girls to be ladies, I don't even know what that is."

She closed out by saying if we're going to be effective mentors and examples for the next generation, we need to be able to have these conversations from a place of enlightenment. As President Obama closed with, trying to live up to society's outdated version of manhood, "...is a self-defeating model for being a man."

Thankfully, there is light at the end of the tunnel. Today's generation is a bit more fluid and freer. They are combating toxicity, embracing emotions, and overcoming gender norms. They have even coined the desired nonsexual male connection, bromance. A bromance is a close but nonsexual relationship between two or more men. It is an exceptionally tight, affectionate male bonding relationship exceeding that of usual friendship and is distinguished by a particularly high level of emotional intimacy. Some famous bromances include President Barack Obama and President Joe Biden, The Rock and Kevin Hart, Matt Damon and Ben Affleck, Kanye West and Jay-Z, Will Smith and Duane Martin, Justin Bieber and Chris Brown, and the list goes on.

Though the concept of a bromance isn't new, its emergence is seen as reflective of a broader acceptance of non-heteronormative cultural expressions as well as the prospect of a same-sex intimacy that transcends matters of sexual orientation".[92] Even in our movies, we see creatives explore Black bromances. In the iconic film The Last Black Man in San Francisco, straight best friends Jimmie and Montgomery are the perfect example of what a bromance looks like that is free from the traditional context of gender and gender norms. Jimmie and Montgomery are physically affectionate and emotionally connected as they navigate the gentrification happening in their

---

[92] DeAngelis, M. (2014). *Reading the bromance: Homosocial relationships in film and television*. Wayne State University Press.

community. To see two strong Black male leads play out their love for one another in a nontoxic and non-hypersexualized setting was empowering. It was an example of what life could be like for young Black men if we'd only remove the toxicity attached to masculinity and the misconceptions attached to sexuality.

More and more people are caring less about whether their actions or connections are perceived as sexual. Unfortunately, there are many spaces that are still being led by people who are less fluid and freer. They continue to shame people for who they are. Men are condemned for being too aggressive and shamed for being too feminine. Anyone trying to live up to these standards is sure to suffer from mental dysfunction. Societies standards are all jacked up. Shaming and condemnation for being who you are is truly an act of violence.

Sex Shaming and The Black Church

Sex shaming is not a new phenomenon; it has been going on for centuries, and it's especially hard for women and members of the LGBTQIA+ community. I always wondered why in the Bible, mostly women were punished for sexual acts and seen as promiscuous, and the men were mostly left alone. Last I checked, it takes two to tango.

The Bible has many instances and events of women being discriminated against. For instance, the word for woman in Hebrew, 'naqeba,' literally means 'orifice bearer.' There are many incidences that prove how women have been portrayed as simple objects or property of their fathers or husbands in the Bible. They were viewed as just an asset to be owned by men and used to procreate. The burial of girl babies was a common practice in old times. The Bible has many stories where women are only used as objects or shown to be inferior to men naturally. The fundamentalist sexism that is prevalent in Christianity is when anything feminine is portrayed as weaker or less than anything masculine. Whatever a person's gender identity or sexual orientation, their behavior would be seen as either feminine or masculine and hence, narrate their standing in society. The mere fact that women were not allowed to have leadership roles - a practice still being followed by Christian churches - is proof of how the church objectifies women.

The story that bewildered me the most was the woman who was caught in the act of adultery in the seventh chapter of the book of John. The Pharisees brought this unnamed woman before Jesus in a public spectacle and suggested she be stoned to death based on scriptural instruction. Jesus, in all his wisdom, love, and grace, said, 'He who is without sin cast the first stone.' The crowd dispersed because only Christ was sinless, and the woman was sent on her way. What I often wondered was, where was the man with whom she was caught sleeping, and why wasn't he about to be stoned as well?

Now, the Bible does condemn both men and women for adulterous acts. The Ten Commandments forbid it, Leviticus and Deuteronomy say people who commit adultery must die, the prophets condemn it and the New Testament writers, borrowing from Old Testament scripture, view adultery as a sin. But upon further study, I learned men were freer to explore their sexual appetites than women.

Does that sound like a just God to you? Can you imagine God saying, "Let us make man in our image; men can have all the sex they want, and women can't"?

A man did not have to be faithful to one woman. If he was married, he could sleep with another unmarried woman[93] and he could get married as many times as he liked.[94] The only time punishment to a man was applied was if he slept with someone else's wife or fiancé.[95] The unjust part about all of this is that women were objectified and not

---
[93] Exodus 22:16-17
[94] Deuteronomy 21:15
[95] Deuteronomy 22:22-26

permitted to explore their sexuality. A woman had to be faithful to her husband alone, was expected to be a virgin until she married, and if she got raped and didn't tell anybody, she was put to death or had to marry her rapist.[96]

This could partly explain why today, men are encouraged to explore their sexuality and sleep with multiple women before marriage, while women are encouraged to stay virtuous and holy until marriage. Women always seem to get the bad end of the stick in these regards. Growing up, I have witnessed young women get torn apart for getting pregnant while the man is praised for stepping up and being a father. And don't let the young woman have a position in the church. She is generally sat down, never to be seen or heard from again until after she has had the baby. How do you praise one and shame the other for the same baby?

There are so many stories of male chauvinism in Black Church culture that go unaddressed. Just in the last few years alone, mainstream pastors have been caught cheating on their wives with no consequence. One pastor was caught in the act with his parishioner's wife in her daughter's bed. He was forced to jump out of the window naked because the husband went to get his gun. He was never disciplined and defiantly remained in position. There was another pastor who was caught cheating on his wife multiple times between 2018 and 2020. He was never disciplined and remained in position. There was a pastor who was accused of sleeping with multiple women. He denied it even though she had pictorial evidence.

His congregation eviscerated her, even threatened to harm her and her family. Lastly, there was a bishop exposed for sleeping with multiple young adult Black men, seducing them with trips and gifts purchased with church funds. His congregation eviscerated the young

---

[96] Deuteronomy 22:23-29

men accusing him. He was never disciplined and remained in position. This pattern of protecting men and their sexual exploitations is hypocritical to how women and members of the LGBTQIA+ community are treated in the church. It is harmful to the Black community.

This protection goes beyond promiscuity. The amount of molestation, child abuse, and inappropriate sexual behavior with teens continues to go unaddressed. In 2014, Bronx pastor Michael Clare admitted to raping two teen girls. In 2018, North Carolina pastor Glenn Collins was charged with at least 128 counts of child sex abuse after raping four children and abusing others over a span of 13 years (1996-2009). In 2019, Ohio church leader Arthur Dade Jr. (known as "Apostle Dade") was convicted of raping a 10-year-old boy in the backseat of his car. Where is the outcry from the church? Where is the march to protect our babies? Where is the official church declaration against child abuse? Nope, some ministries are investing in anti-gay rallies and signing anti-gay declarations. One Bishop led a 25,000-person anti-gay march through the streets of Atlanta and ended up being found in a relationship with several men. The madness runs too deep.

And just when you think you have heard it all, in Jacksonville, former megachurch pastor Darrell Gilyard was back in the pulpit less than two months after his release from prison for committing sex crimes against minors. Gilyard pleaded guilty in 2009 to lewd or lascivious conduct and molestation involving two girls younger than 16. His 2007 resignation after 15 years as pastor of Jacksonville's Shiloh Metropolitan Baptist Church, a 7,000-member predominantly Black congregation, marked the fifth pastorate he lost due to allegations of sexual misconduct.[97] In 2004, Gilyard admitted to

---

[97] Allen, B. (2014, April 25). *Probation terms altered to permit sex offender pastor to minister to children* –. Baptist News Global. https://baptistnews.com/article/sex-offender-pastor-can-minister-to-children/#.X_D07NhKjZs

fathering the child of a woman who had accused him of raping her during a 2004 counseling session, according to court records. His accusations go all the way back to the early '90s from hundreds of women in Texas and Oklahoma.[98]

Gilyard said he initially intended to decline the offer to preach because he did not want to subject the church to negative press or go through it again himself. He also did not want to violate the terms of his three-year probation, which included avoiding contact with minors.[99]

Here is how the church and the state responded. Instead of the church opting not to have a convicted sex offender in the pulpit who was not allowed around minors, they chose to keep minors out of the service. A representative from the church claimed Gilyard was brought on because the church was going under. On Gilyard's first-day preaching service, attendance jumped from the normal five-ten attendees to 150.[100]

Though 150 people showed up to hear him preach, the local community was outraged. His presence prompted protests and a visit from Jacksonville Baptist Association, which resulted in an agreement that the church would "leave the fellowship" of the Southern Baptist Convention regional affiliate.[101]

In 2014, Gilyard's lawyer convinced a judge to modify the probation so he can "minister to children under the age of 18 as long as the children are supervised by an adult other than the defendant." The

---

[98] Allen, B. (2014, April 25). *Probation terms altered to permit sex offender pastor to minister to children –*. Baptist News Global. https://baptistnews.com/article/sex-offender-pastor-can-minister-to-children/#.X_D07NhKjZs

[99] Harris, J. (2020, March 11). *Pastor convicted of sex crimes is preaching at Jacksonville church, again*. WJXT. https://www.news4jax.com/news/local/2020/03/10/pastor-convicted-of-sex-crimes-is-preaching-at-jacksonville-church-again/

[100] Harris, J. (2020, March 11). *Pastor convicted of sex crimes is preaching at Jacksonville church, again*. WJXT. https://www.news4jax.com/news/local/2020/03/10/pastor-convicted-of-sex-crimes-is-preaching-at-jacksonville-church-again/

[101] Allen, B. (2014b, April 25). *Probation terms altered to permit sex offender pastor to minister to children –*. Baptist News Global. https://baptistnews.com/article/sex-offender-pastor-can-minister-to-children/#.X_D07NhKjZs

State Attorney's Office did not object to the change.[102] Gilyard is now the pastor of Mount Ararat Baptist Church in Jacksonville. The Florida Department of Law Enforcement says that Gilyard is not on probation and can work wherever he wants to. The church is across from Stanton College Preparatory School, but Gilyard, a registered sex offender, is not in violation of any laws by having a job near a school.[103]

insert very deep sigh and long dramatic pause

I am outraged. I am saddened. I am disappointed.

I can't be gay and preach in your pulpit, but Gilyard can be a convicted sex offender of minors with two centuries worth of paper trails of allegations and convictions. I can't be gay and protected by state law, but Gilyard can be a convicted sex offender of minors and permitted by the state to work with minors right next to a grade school.

insert another very deep sigh and long dramatic pause

Make. It. Make. Sense.

We can no longer take our cues from the traditional Black Church regarding queerness, gender, and sexuality. The institution does not have the capacity to engage in meaningful conversations at this point. There must be an undoing before the doing, a rework before the work. Before we get to queerness, we need to peel back the centuries of European terror and control that destroyed African spirituality and uproot the influences of white supremacy on Black religion.

Top 5 Issues to Address in Black Church

The urgency of these conversations is now. We can no longer turn a

---

[102] Pulliam, T. & News4Jax.com Staff. (2014, April 19). *Judge modifies pastor's sex offender probation.* WJXT. https://www.news4jax.com/news/2014/04/19/judge-modifies-pastors-sex-offender-probation/

[103] Pulliam, T. & News4Jax.com Staff. (2014, April 19). *Judge modifies pastor's sex offender probation.* WJXT. https://www.news4jax.com/news/2014/04/19/judge-modifies-pastors-sex-offender-probation/

blind eye when it comes to stigmas perpetuated by the Black Church that harm our Black communities. There is a myriad of probable motivations on why the Black Church has lacked conviction and urgency in dealing with these historical influences. For one, maintaining the status quo has kept many religious leaders whom I've talked to from dealing with much of these unequivocal truths. Here are the top 5 issues the Black Church must come to terms with before we can have a conversation about sex, sexuality, queerness, and gender.

1. Jesus is not white (Artist da Vinci, Michelangelo, and Sallman famously painted the white Jesus).

2. Many parts of the Bible were written from an Androcentric point of view and perpetuated toxic masculinity (It catered to heterosexual men and their needs and favored men over women).

3. Throughout history, the Bible has been influenced, manipulated, and incorrectly translated by white men. (Of recent the Slave Bible and the addition of the word homosexual in 1946).

4. The Bible is rife with commandments, customs, and practices that are ungodly and anti-love. Throughout history and still today, the Bible is used to reign terror on marginalized communities.

5. Africans had strong relationships with God pre-Atlantic Slave Trade. At least 30% of captured slaves were literate Muslims, while others had strong spiritual customs. White terror stripped Africans of their religious practices and disconnected us from many of our spiritual virtues. The big reason why there is a huge difference between the Anglo-Christian experience and the Black Christian experience is that many of our spiritual customs and expressions were infused in church services from the founding of the Black church.

Coming to terms with these truths will allow our community to begin the process of destroying the influence of strongholds that have hindered our ability to spiritually live life fully free. Free to express who we are, free from condemnation, free from manipulation, free to love who we want, free to explore the depth of God, free to be who God designed us to be.

Until this moment of great reconciliation, we must continue to call out sexual abuse, gender bias, and homophobia in the church. The power structures that permit this ungodly part of church culture to flourish runs deep. All the things Jesus fought against are what's keeping this power structure in place – corruption, money, greed, perfection, and performative ministry. And this is not opinion; I've witnessed it firsthand and read about it in newspapers more times than I'd like to. And many of these patterns have spilled over into Black life. Families are hush-hush about instances of sexual abuse, will protect the abuser and shame the abused, what goes on in this house stays in this house, avoid therapy and put-up facades of perfection.

The Black Church is the staple of the Black community, the place where we find hope, feel welcome, have a sense of community. Nevertheless, if the Black Church is your example of how to deal with sex and sexuality, you are in danger. When your highest spiritual order is out of order in any regard, dismay is soon to follow.

The Black Church must destroy the white savior complex that was rooted in the founding of the American Black Church - Black people waiting for a white savior to come and rescue them from all evil. Black slaves begging for a white God to save them from white people. Think for a moment how much sense that makes.

God has now given us the power and wisdom to overcome any hurdle faced before us. Though there's much work to be done, we've come a long way from the slave house. Oppression is before us; discrimination is before us, hate is before us, abuse is before us, violence is before us, what will we do about it?

I'm so thankful for organizations like Children of Combahee who mobilizes against child sexual abuse in Black churches using womanist pastoral and theological methods. Named after Harriet Tubman's 1863 Combahee River Raid and the 1970s radical Black feminist organization of survivor--activists, the Combahee River Collective, this project builds on a longstanding legacy of resistance, healing, and communal reckoning around issues of racial, sexual, and gendered violence in Black communities.

I am also thankful for the hundreds of trailblazers that fight against oppression in the church and work to make communities safer and welcoming to everyone. We need more liberators.

There is no greater example of love than Jesus laying down His life for His friends. What are you willing to lay down, give up, and sacrifice for the liberation of your fellow brethren? How hard are you willing to challenge your own beliefs so that others can begin to be free, including yourself?

Activist Tarana Burke fought for over a century to bring awareness to the abuse women were facing all over the world. She fought, sacrificed, suffered immense criticism and backlash, but she never gave up. And now, her movement has freed millions of women across the globe. The ways of the world aren't perfect toward women, but power structures have been challenged, and predatorial protection has been chiseled away. The #MeToo movement transformed American culture and way of life. It shook and is still shaking power structures in the most visible way.

It seems as though the cover-ups and scandals of the world are no different than the cover-ups and scandals in the church. The only difference is the church blames the devil for the offense, 'the devil made me do it.'

What can we do to shake the power structures of the Black Church to rid us of discrimination, gender bias, and homophobia? I know conversations this deep scare people, but we must start somewhere.

One of Garza's closing comments at the Obama Foundation summit really struck me as an amazing first step in this fight for equality.

"...love in public. One of the reasons that we know that trans women, in particular, are being killed at astronomical rates is because people are afraid to love in public. One of the reasons that we know that violence is impacting our communities in such a deep, deep way is because we are afraid to love in public."

Many people are turning away from church in the traditional sense and looking for communities that promote love and acceptance. I've noticed Sunday Funday brunches are becoming more popular than a traditional church. The impact of new age religiosities such as the Black consciousness movement and Black liberation theology may define what the Black Church looks like in the next century. Where will you be?

Why Is Sexuality Important?

Sexuality has always been one of the most basic components of one's identity and personality. It helps you form a sense of self. Our mental health is closely related to our sexuality. Sexuality is different from gender. Gender is how you choose to identify. Sexuality depends on who you are attracted to, based upon mental, physical, or emotional connection.

Everyone has somewhat of the same starting point in life from a discovery point of view. We have experiences that teach us about our surroundings and everything in it. Then something happens to trigger the epiphany that helps us realize who we really are. It can take either minutes or years for a person to come to terms with their sexual identity because of the constant stigma and judgment in society.

Some people get to celebrate their sexuality and live a life of acceptance. However, there are still people in the world who do not even get to come out due to the backlash they know they would face. Sexuality is all about learning to understand what kind of people you can connect with and the kind of person you really are.

Our lives are shrouded in discrimination from every angle, and we cannot help but question every part of ourselves, especially our sexual orientation. The world is progressing but not altogether or fast enough. That is exactly why it is important for us to identify ourselves truthfully. We have to be true to our sexuality, no matter how much the world may not accept it or let us have basic rights. Our self-acceptance is key; it's the first step towards making the world a better place for us all to inhabit without anyone being discriminated against based on who they love.

Sexuality And the Catholic Church

The Catholic Church in the USA is comprised of around 70 million members, with a network that spreads throughout the nation. The Catholic Church is a bit different in its opinions and perspective of different sexual orientations. Even though the Catholic Church has never claimed homosexuality to be a sin, they do not have a positively accepting attitude towards it either. There is a document that contains letters called the Catechism of the Catholic Church. The document teaches how homosexuality is against the natural way of life.

The Catholic Church is different from other fundamental churches of Christianity. The Catechism may talk about homosexuality in a reparative way by mentioning how such people should choose a life of chastity and abstinence. However, it does talk about homosexual people in a respectful way and behooves people to treat them with acceptance as no judgment against them would be tolerated.

The biggest question that arises here is why does the Catholic

Church not talk about sexuality, gender, orientation, or sex in general? There are some denominations of the Christian Church that advocate for sexual education, women's rights, abortions, and homosexuality. These are topics that most Christians stay away from due to their conservative fundamentalist views. They refuse to even acknowledge the existence of these global issues. Why? It is quite simply rooted in the patriarchy that rules over the Catholic churches. Women are not appointed in any significant or leadership roles. They are not considered when major policies or changes are being discussed. Catholicism has been a victim of patriarchy and its sexist views for a very long time. What's more, these views align with the patriarchal politics of the country and many parts of the world. It serves a purpose that is not divine in any way. The sexism that is prevalent in Catholic churches gives way to a barrier that doesn't allow the church to talk about such matters.

The Catholic Church, above all churches, should be the main one advocating for conversations about sex and sexuality. The amount of sexual child abuse, scandal, and the cover-up that occurs makes me wonder why people still attend. Why isn't anyone concerned about the children? In 2020, Pope Francis asked Cardinal Vincent Nichols, the leader of the Catholic Church in England and Wales, to stay in his post, despite a damning report that criticized his leadership and concluded that the church repeatedly prioritized its reputation over the welfare of child sex abuse victims.

The independent inquiry into child sexual abuse (IICSA) said the Vatican's failure to cooperate with the investigation "passes understanding." The 162-page report mentioned, "The church's neglect of the physical, emotional and spiritual wellbeing of children and young people in favor of protecting its reputation was in conflict with its mission of love and care for the innocent and vulnerable."[104] Between 1970 and 2015, the church in England and Wales received more than 900 complaints involving more than 3,000 instances of child sexual abuse, made against more than 900 individuals, including priests, monks, and volunteers. In 2018, in my home state of Pennsylvania alone, a report uncovered 1,000 identifiable victims of child abuse with thousands of more instances that were never filed. In a scathing report filed by a grand jury, it was discovered that bishops and other leaders of the Roman Catholic Church in Pennsylvania covered up child sexual abuse by more than 300 priests over a period of 70 years, persuading victims not to report the abuse and law enforcement not to investigate it.[105]

How dare the issue of homosexuality be bigger than children being abused and taken advantage of by religious institutions? That's so crazy to me. You will march against me for no wrongdoing but be silent about the damning behavior of religious leaders.

Sexuality And the Church Overall

The church has many different schools of thought regarding sexuality. Some churches only accept a chaste way of living, whether a person is heterosexual or not, while others are vehemently against homosexuality, while others accept it without providing the opportunity of same-sex marriage.

Sexuality has always been a controversial topic when discussed in the church. Christianity has evolved over the decades, but there are still branches that refuse to progress along with the trends of the world. When it comes to homosexuality or the LGBTQIA+ community,

---

[104] *The Roman Catholic Church Investigation Report.* (2020, November 10). IICSA. https://www.iicsa.org.uk/reports-recommendations/publications/investigation/roman-catholic-church
[105] *Holdings: 40th statewide investigating grand jury : (n.d.).* Villanova. Retrieved September 10, 2021, from https://library.villanova.edu/Find/Record/1902651

the church can never give a straight answer. There are many Christians who think that anything other than heterosexuality is a mockery of Adam and Eve, the original ideal couple and the parents of humanity. However, the church is always in a grey area regarding it.

Some Christian churches preach that the concept of homosexuality is immoral, sinful, or even downright the tricks of Satan to manipulate humanity. They think that such immoral sexuality could only be the work of Satan because they cannot understand how two same-sex people can fall in love. For them, love is not the basis of such a relationship. They think that homosexuality is a disorder or mental illness, rather than just the ability of a person to love another without the question of their sex. Generally, the church frowns upon the idea of same-sex marriages, but there are some affirming ministries and denominations that have made a welcoming home for LGBTQIA+ members, such as myself.

The rights of the LGBTQIA+ community and the mere acceptance of them in churches are rooted in sexism. The minute a person shows the hint of nature, behavior, or way of living that is inherently 'feminine' by society, they are deemed as less than. Most homosexual people are discriminated against due to some of their 'feminine' behavior when, in fact, 'femininity' is subjective. The patriarchal society has defined femininity according to its own standards. Men have always found a way to make women feel weaker or inferior to them due to their femininity when it should be the opposite. [106] All members of the LGBTQIA+ are discriminated against because of the unique traits that make us different and cause us not to fit "the norm." We are all God's creations made in the image and likeness of God and the universe, complex yet complete. The quicker we can strip

---

[106] Herrin, H. (n.d). *Sexuality, Gender and the Religious Right: Youth Advocacy on LGBT Rights in the United States.* Awid. https://www.awid.org/sites/default/files/atoms/files/feminists_on_the_frontlines_-_sexuality_gender_and_the_religious_right_youth_advocacy_on_lgbt_rights_-_us.pdf.

ourselves of this patriarchal mindset and accept people for who they choose to be, the quicker we can get to a more harmonious society.

Biblical Cultures Views on Homosexuality

Jews

Being cited often and popular amongst the conservative religious community, orthodox Jews would debate that male homosexuality has been condemned in the book of Leviticus quite clearly. The book states that male homosexual acts are sins and shall be punished by death. It does not say anything about lesbian relationships, but some Rabbis have put it in the same category, following the same principle. Some people argue that the harsh words against homosexuality used in Leviticus are against the acts themselves, not the people.

Though, it goes to say that the logic behind such condemnation is that same-sex couples are childless and thus, do not follow the divine command to procreate. Liberal Jews consider it a hurdle in their progress to accepting homosexual people into their community. Modern Rabbis and Jews are more accepting of homosexuals because they believe since God created gay people too, then they deserve love and respect just like any other human. The Reform movement sought to decriminalize homosexual relations and curb discrimination against LGBTQIA+ people. Now, due to the Reform, many openly gay couples can have their marriages and ceremonies officiated by Rabbis or get into Reform rabbinical institutions. [107]

Persians

Iran is a country ruled by Islamic Law. That may already give an idea as to how the homosexual people in the country fare. Many

---

[107] M. (2002, September 5). *Jewish Views on Homosexuality*. My Jewish Learning. https://www.myjewishlearning.com/article/homosexuality-in-jewish-thought/

Persians think that homosexuality is a recent phenomenon provoked and encouraged by the Western world. However, studies and research prove the existence of homosexuality throughout the history of Iran. There are highlighted cases that can be studied to analyze the systemic oppression of gay people throughout the history of the country. Decades of suppression have given birth to a culture where the existence of gay people is not deniable but also something extremely risky.

In Iran, being gay or performing acts of homosexuality is punishable by death as per Islamic Law. Homosexuality is deathly prohibited in Islam, and thus the country has become a prison of sorts for the homosexual people living in it. The more liberal Persians, of which there are few, do not condemn homosexuality and would advocate for it. However, the recent cases of executions carried out over charges of homosexuality have caused silence to grow over the community. The gay people living in Iran have established their own society and culture where they cannot live in freedom but have learned to cope with their reality. Some choose to leave the country, while others stay and learn to exist in a risky and hidden manner.[108]

Greeks

Ancient Greece has become widely popular amongst people regarding its culture of same-sex relationships. Many people consider Ancient Greece culture as the pinnacle of homosexual freedom when it isn't so. The earlier 5th century BC was when Athens was in the throes of homosexual relationships.

The history of Greece is quite complex when it comes to homosexuality. There were a hundred years or so where the nation was openly advocating for and partaking in homosexuality. It was

---

[108] Yadegarfard, M. (2019). How are Iranian gay men coping with systematic suppression under Islamic law? A qualitative study. *Sexuality & Culture*, 23(4), 1250-1273.

even considered a basic rite of passage for the elites. Then some societies started condemning it, and it became an act of immorality. Homosexuality has always been a complicated part of Greek history, but no one can deny how the Greeks were open to it and vehemently supported it to the extreme at one point.[109]

Romans

The sexuality of the Romans later went on to become the backdrop of the perspective Christianity would take on in the future. The Romans were not particularly inclined to partake in homosexual acts, considering it as something that did not go along well with their concept of a warrior's way. They considered a warrior to be dominant and powerful, someone who could not be a passive partner in sexual relations. For them, sexual dominance was what mattered and not the sexuality of a person. Even so, the Romans had a different attitude towards homosexuality.

In Rome, the Greek model was revered, and people would follow the traditions regarding arts and literature. That was why homosexuality was still very much present in Roman society. The only thing that the Romans had changed was that no adult man could be sexually involved with a young boy. They would take up slaves and treat them with love and affection. Those slaves were even known to go on and inherit rewards.

The Roman culture, however, was quite complicated in its acceptance of homosexuality. They accepted the parts where they could have relationships with young slaves, but anything that suggested passivity in sexual relations was immediately condemned, and thus homosexuality was regaled as not a warrior's lifestyle. There are many documented incidences of Roman emperors and elites

---

[109] Hubbard, T. K. (2020). Historical Views of Homosexuality: Ancient Greece. In *Oxford Research Encyclopedia of Politics*.

engaging in homosexuality only because they could afford slaves. Though, it was quite unheard of for the lower class.[110]

As for the global perspective on homosexuality in ancient times, it was all over the spectrum. Some parts of the world celebrated healthy expressions of sexuality, such as in Greece, Egypt, or Rome. But then there were other parts of the world that questioned and condemned it due to different reasons, such as religion. Religion has always been used as the biggest excuse for discrimination against gay people from the beginning of time. Homosexuality is not a modern phenomenon kick-started by the Western world, as some people like to think.

Homosexuality has existed in all parts of the world and in every culture around the globe from ancient times. Chinese, Indian, Greek, Roman, Persian, and other different parts of the world have a history permeated with homosexuality. Religion, mainly Christianity, started the debate over whether such a way of living is even normal. In ancient times, people did not even differ between homosexuality and heterosexuality. That is why tantra or monks that participated in homosexuality were revered. Sexuality has always been a way for a person to express themselves. In the ancient world, there were different attitudes toward homosexuality but never such hatred or discrimination.

Being at the center of the debate, homosexuality has been facing so much criticism and negative response. In older times, people were more inclined to let people live their lives the way they wanted. The more conservative and religious parts of the society worked the same as they do now. They would not tolerate something they didn't see as 'religiously moral.' They interpreted the Bible according to their own agendas and perspective. Then they preached those interpretations as

---

[110] London, M. O. (2020, July 6). *Were the Romans gay? LGBTQ Londinium*. Museum of London. https://www.museumoflondon.org.uk/discover/lgbtq-roman-london

definite and divine messages from God himself, and people were forced to listen to them. The world has always been at war with sexuality simply due to the fact that it allows women and other gender identities the freedom to express themselves. The world is progressing, but at a slow pace, that needs to pick up if people all over the world are going to get the rights they deserve.

"All truth passes through three stages. First, it is ridiculed. Second, it is violently opposed. Third, it is accepted as being self-evident."

~ *ARTHUR SCHOPENHAUER*

Chapter 12: Who Said That?

Running From Reality

Reality TV has taken over American pop culture. We get our lingo, fashion, and good gossip from most reality TV shows. Reality TV is supposed to be programming where there are no writers, actors, or scripts. But as many of us in the industry learned, most reality TV is scripted. I attended a fundraiser where they were filming a popular reality TV show that shall remain nameless. From setting the scene to influencing the mood and stirring up drama, the producers ran the show. Everything was going fine, and the ladies were having great conversations until the producers got involved. Next thing you know, it was mayhem, drinks being thrown, high heels being slung across the room, security coming out of doors I didn't even know existed. It was crazy. I could not believe this high-end fundraiser turned into this. Amid this chaos, I saw producers smiling, laughing, and high fiving each other. That firsthand experience confirmed for me that most of what we see on TV is not real or fully authentic.

The gag is most people know this. So why are we so glued to reality TV? My guess is it glorifies everything that we want and the life we wish we had. Most of us would love to wake up in a new Bugatti, slap someone every now and again, or live a lavish life of luxury. Reality TV has both its advantages and disadvantages. The huge downfault is it mixes reality with Hollywood make-believe, and many, though they realize something is not quite right, still can't differentiate the real from the fake, the fact from the fiction. Reality TV, among other things, gave us Donald Trump as president. His role on the Apprentice led many to believe he was a strong business leader, while his many failed endeavors proved otherwise.

The upside of reality TV is it gives you insight to truths about life that are not well played out on scripted TV. For instance, The Brady Bunch was a very popular American sitcom created by Sherwood Schwartz that first aired in 1969. The show revolved around a large, blended family with six children. Sure, they had their fair share of problems, but most of them were cookie-cutter simple fixes that always led to a happy ending. That was most of American TV at the time.

The first reality show, broadcast in 1973, cut through all of that. Before the "Real World," before "The Osbourne's," PBS aired a 12-part documentary called "An American Family." The show chronicled the daily lives of the Loud family, who lived in sunny California. The series showcased real family life with real family problems. For the first time, America got to witness marital tensions that eventually led to divorce and the Louds' eldest son Lance's gay lived experience.

The Loud's suffered immense criticism for displaying their real-life problems, especially Bill and Pat's divorce. The Loud's were viewed as a symbol of the collapse of the American family. They argued they fought, they made up, they faced challenges. The Loud's were no different than any typical white American family. So why didn't people overwhelmingly fall in love with them, or did they? A whopping 10-million people tuned in to PBS to watch. Those were big numbers for television in the 70s. TV Guide recognized "An American Family" as the original reality TV series and Lance Loud as the first reality TV star.[111]

If people didn't like them so much, how come they kept tuning in? I think American middle-class life displayed in its rawest form intrigued many. Though they criticized the Loud's for their divorce, divorce rates were steeply increasing in the 1970s, following the

---

[111] *Play It Loud! A Final Visit with "An American Family."* (2021, February 20). International Documentary Association. https://www.documentary.org/feature/play-it-loud-final-visit-american-family

growth of the women's movement and no-fault divorce laws.[112] Doesn't that sound all too familiar, humans criticizing other humans for doing the same thing they are doing?

This was also the same for Lance's life. Lance was the first gay person to appear on television as a vital part of American family life. This reality troubled a lot of Americans. The show was greatly criticized because it featured a gay family member. How many families do you know who've tried to hide gay members of their family? I know plenty, including my own.

Gay life in the 70s was on the rise and gay liberation was booming. The Stonewall Riots kicked off the 70s and exposed just how infused the gay community was in American life. The gay and lesbian community came out of the shadows and began to openly join American politics, activism, and pop culture. The 70s truly represented a remarkable period of transformation for gays and lesbians. It's sad, though, that while the transgender community led the Stonewall Riots, they were still strongly discriminated against by all communities, including their own. I guess you couldn't ask for too much liberation. The 70s gay and lesbian transformation was all about visibility, and this infuriated people. The truth about other people's lives infuriated people. My guess is because many people were dealing with their own identity issues.

I'm sure Lance's presence in 10-million homes also influenced many to begin to explore their truths. Truthfulness is a weird experience. Many people say they want it but can't take it. I think that's why people today dive into reality TV because it helps them escape from their truths while mildly playing with the truths of other people's lives. It's easier to sit back and judge and point and direct

---

[112] Cohen, P. N. (2018, March 20). *The divorce rate has been falling since the 1970s, but we don't want it too low.* Medium. https://timeline.com/divorce-rates-going-down-d85477f83055

from the couch versus doing all that same directing for one's own life.

Generally, the truth counters conventional viewpoints that make us feel superior, false realities that make us feel comfortable, or phony narratives that have been long accepted as the final authority. Scientifically the truth sounds good if it's the truth with which we agree, or that positions us in a favorable light. It's when we hear the truth that doesn't make us feel good or counters our way of life that we start to naturally resist. It's called confirmation bias and cognitive dissonance. Our minds are extremely intelligent and complex but also extremely lazy and presupposing. We are hard-wired to believe what we want to believe and make assumptions off those beliefs, regardless of the facts. Our minds naturally reject anything that is counter to the stories we know or the conclusions we've already made. The lazy part of our mind causes us to override reason and feel really good when we come across information that confirms what we already believe. The mind doesn't want to work hard to learn new information, so it automatically pulls information it already knows and sticks with that. The crazy thing is, all of this happens before thought. It's instant, it's fast, and you can't control it. This is the part of our mind that allows us to recall memories, language, math; it happens with little to no effort.

Confirmation bias happens when a person gives more weight to information that confirms their beliefs and undervalues information that could disprove it. Confirmation bias is the natural way we protect ourselves from ideas that may threaten our social standing in our social setting. Dan Kahan, a law and psychology professor at Yale University, calls it identity protective cognition.[113] Because we are naturally social or tribal, it's more important to protect our values,

---

[113] Kahan, D. M., Braman, D., Gastil, J., Slovic, P., & Mertz, C. K. (2007). Culture and identity-protective cognition: Explaining the white-male effect in risk perception. *Journal of Empirical Legal Studies*, 4(3), 465-505.

beliefs, and relationships in our social settings than risking those connections by adopting new beliefs.

Influential people, powerful people, and most of all salespeople know and understand the power of narrative and the power of persuasion. You find out what people's interests, inspirations, or fears are, and you play on that. The masterminds of great deception also know how to play on those things as well. This is why the truth doesn't matter in most cases because it's all about speaking to what people already believe. So, in a nutshell, when you hear information that you already agree with, your body releases endorphins that make you feel good. When you hear information that you don't agree with, your mind automatically rejects it, and you don't get those feel-good endorphins.

The great conflict comes when belief is met with the truth. This is where cognitive dissonance comes in, which occurs when someone holds two psychologically inconsistent beliefs, attitudes, or opinions that create an unpleasant mental tension.

What I am about to present to you next are all facts and truth. This truth may very well contradict what you believe and what you've been told your entire life. To overcome confirmation bias and cognitive dissonance, you must be willing to face your beliefs, consider the factors that influence your beliefs, and challenge your beliefs with research and facts.

There's a very popular reality TV show that is always making headlines, "The Real Housewives of Atlanta." For the past 13 years, this show has put on display the very posh life of several successful Black women. They argue they fight, they gossip, they backbite, they marry, they divorce, they buy mansions, they open businesses, they travel the world. Many of them became instant pop stars after being on the show. America can't get enough of these beautiful Black women. We make memes, we make fun, we host watch parties, we get one-liners. So much from this show has contributed to pop culture.

There's one episode that actually influenced this chapter. In an episode titled "If These Woods Could Talk," the ladies trek the backwoods of Georgia for a bit of "glamping," (glamorous camping). It really wasn't camping camping as they had hair and makeup, the limobus ride, crystal glasses at dinner, and production setting things up. But I digress. Anyway, one night at dinner Marlo Hampton, who was presumed to be brought back on the show to stir the pot, decided to confront Kandi Burruss about a rumor that had been circulating about her.

"Kandi are you a lesbian?" she asked. Marlo said someone at this table has been talking behind Kandi's back and said, "[Kandi's] a lesbian in the closet."

Sheree Whitfield, Porsha Williams, Kenya Moore, Phaedra Parks all "seemed" to be stunned.

Everyone at the table immediately responded with, "who said that?" including the persons who said it.

You can go check out the episode (Season 9, Episode 13) for the full scoop. I just wanted to get to that famous one-line repeated over and over.

"Who said that?"

Who Said Homosexuality Was a Sin?

What if I told you the word "homosexual" was never meant to be in the Bible? Would you believe me? What was the first thought that came to mind when you read that question? That thought will probably be what you contend with while reading the rest of this chapter. If you aren't already knowledgeable about the topic, it can take you some time to accept the facts because they are counter to what you have been taught about religion and homosexuality.

Ten years ago, if you told me homosexuality wasn't a sin, I would not have believed you. I actually would have rebuked you and called you all types of blasphemous. Why? Because at the time, I was a closeted homosexual who was trying to live up to the standard of being a sanctified "saint." I peddled that same narrative – 'love the sinner, hate the sin.' I had convinced myself and many others that my gayness was the thorn in my flesh that Paul spoke about. It was God's way of keeping me humble on earth so that perfection could never be reached. I thought in order to fulfill God's purpose for my life, I had to suppress these 'feelings' because they were of the flesh.

Today I'm a free man. I'm an LGBTQIA+ advocate and work to free so many others through the knowledge of the truth. I show up to spaces unapologetically and boldly share that I'm Black, gay, and proud. Being bold in all spaces led me to filmmaker Sharon "Rocky" Roggio. She was making a documentary about the LGBTQIA+ Christian experience so that she and her conservative father, Pastor Sal Roggio, could find some common ground. She, like many others, had been expelled from traditional Christian environments because of her willingness to love in public.

Our initial meeting was at a diner, she brought me a burger, fries, and shake for my time. She wanted to share with me her vision for this documentary. I wish she had waited until the food arrived before she started talking because once she did, I was frozen. I think I even stopped listening at one point and had an out-of-body experience. Thousands of thoughts were racing through my mind, years of trauma resurfaced, and I immediately felt enraged. Upset that after all these years, I had been duped and could hold no one responsible. Before she could finish her pitch, I said, "I want in."

Her documentary is a revolutionary new film that chronicles how the misuse of a single word changed the course of modern history. "1946: The Mistranslation That Shifted a Culture" investigates how the word "homosexual" was entered into the Bible, how one man tried to stop it, and how a team of researchers recently unearthed evidence that challenges deeply held beliefs about LGBTQIA+ people and their place in God's kingdom.

At the diner, I learned about Kathy Baldock and Ed Oxford, who put their lives on the line to research the roots of anti-gay theology. You would think uncovering such truths would bring healing, it has brought them tremendous criticism and threats. After years of research, they finally had a breakthrough at Yale University. All the hard work and sacrifice were about to pay off big time.

Uncovered, after searching through 90 boxes of notes from the archives at Yale University, was a letter sent to the RSV translation committee, written by a young seminarian named David S. This letter had been sitting filed away for over five decades.

In the letter, David points out the dangerous implications that could come with the misuse of the word "homosexual." He claimed that it was being mistranslated and, if used, could be weaponized and harm the gay community indefinitely. Dr. Luther Weigle, the head of the translation committee, wrote a letter back to David S. to acknowledge their mistake and commit to correcting their grave error.

It took them 25 years to correct this error.

In 1971, the revised version of the RSV replaced "homosexual" with "sexual perverts." By this time, the damage had been done. The Bible was now an even stronger weapon of oppression toward LGBTQIA+ humans. Other translations of the Bible picked up the mistranslation of homosexuals, and the rest is history. Sidenote, I have no idea what "sexual pervert" means in the context written, which further proves my point that you can't take most of the Bible at face value without due diligence.

Most of the time, the Bible is misquoted and misunderstood by people who think, in the vail of judgment, they are doing God's work on earth. What most fail to realize or don't even want to acknowledge is that the Bible has been translated so many times and in so many languages that the context has become more than a little jumbled.

Over time, people in power and with influence have had the Bible translated according to their own agendas. Whether political, personal, or religious, we have used Bible translations as a tool to further our own ideas and opinions, managing to influence the masses and forming their mentality regarding different subjects.

Originally being written in Hebrew, the language of the Jews, the Bible then got translated into Greek, Aramaic, Gothic, and Latin. The western part of the world followed the Latin Bible translation for thousands of years until it was further translated into Arabic, Spanish, and then English. Martin Luther even translated it into German in 1522, further enabling the transition into Swedish and other European languages. The first time that part of the Bible was translated into English was in 1382. The New Testament was translated into English in 1525-1535. All these English translations led to the King James Version of the Bible. There are multiple versions of the Bible in the world today, each for the Protestants and Catholics.[114]

After being translated into so many languages all over the world and throughout history, it makes sense that some things got lost in translations or were simply mistranslated. Nevertheless, if those things were gravely serious and their mistranslations had a cultural impact all over the world, then what? What if in some of those translations, a few words here and there were mistranslated or

---

[114] *biblical translation.* (n.d.). Encyclopedia Britannica. Retrieved September 10, 2021, from https://www.britannica.com/topic/biblical-translation

misquoted, causing the entire context to be changed? It isn't so hard to imagine because that has happened.

> "Do you not know that the unrighteous will not inherit the kingdom of God? Do not be deceived; neither the immoral, nor idolaters, nor adulterers, nor sexual perverts," 1 Corinthians 6:9 (RSV).

Many conservative Christians have used 1 Corinthians 6:9 as an argument against homosexuality because the previous version of it that was published in 1946 had the word 'homosexual' instead of 'sexual perverts.' Again, the word was very clearly a mistranslation, but the damage had been done. The anti-gay agenda had gained traction and apparent support from religious institutions all over the country.

The original text contained the Greek words 'malakoi' and 'arsenokoitai.' According to experts, the words mean 'effeminacy' and 'sexual pervert,' respectively. However, at the time of the translation and publication, the translating committee decided to use the word 'homosexual' instead. This was the first time that the word had ever appeared in the Bible, and people took that to mean that homosexuality was a sin. There are many Christians who still believe that to be the case. The later translations also used the word, and so the campaign against homosexuality was encouraged.[115] In addition, I question the authors at that time as well. You mean to tell me effeminate men weren't welcome in God's Kingdom? It sounds toxic and cultural to me; it doesn't sound like God at all.

Most conservative Christians use these translations to advance their agenda and idea that homosexuality is a sin, as supposedly described in the Bible. What they don't know is that there is so much more to the stories and verses in the Bible than just what's on the

---

[115] Women Make Movies. (2021, July 29). *1946: THE MISTRANSLATION THAT SHIFTED CULTURE.* https://www.wmm.com/sponsored-project/1946-the-mistranslation-that-shifted-culture/

surface. The original Bible was written in languages that nobody knows or is well-versed with today. The ancient Hebrew and Greek languages are not known today, and so, modern translations of the Bible are all we have to go on. What we need to understand is that there are many things that can be misinterpreted due to cultural, societal, and world differences from then to this day.

One of the biggest weapons used by conservative Christians is Leviticus 18:22 and 20:13, verses that apparently call homosexuality a sin and an abomination.

"You shall not lie with a male as with a woman; it is an abomination." Leviticus 18:22 (ESV)

"If a man lies with a male as with a woman, both of them have committed an abomination; they shall surely be put to death; their blood is upon them." Leviticus 20:13 (ESV)

These are the verses most popularly used to argue against LGBTQIA+ people's rights. However, as with any biblical verse or story, we have to remember that different books of the Bible contain different cultural subtexts. As with Leviticus, it is not talking about homosexuality but rather the acts that are prohibited for the sake of remaining pure. The book talks about commandments and laws that are for the people who need to survive. These verses prohibit the acts of sexual pleasure because the men of the times needed to maintain ritual purity.[116]

As explained by Hebrew scholars, the word 'abomination' is not used here in this context as its literal meaning; wicked, wrong, or vile. The word is used here to translate the Hebrew word 'toevah,' meaning ritual uncleanness. That means that the things listed in this book,

---

[116] Phillips, A. N. (2019, July 16). *The Bible does not condemn "homosexuality." Seriously, it doesn't.* Medium. https://medium.com/@adamnicholasphillips/the-bible-does-not-condemn-homosexuality-seriously-it-doesn-t-13ae949d6619

including the act of laying with another man, are only considered wrong in the context of being impure, for men had to purify themselves before performing any ritualistic acts of worship. In this context, the word abomination simply means not allowed for the sake of remaining clean and pure for ritualistic purposes.

In addition, I always wondered about the rest of the letters in the LGBTQIA+ community. If homosexuality is such a big issue for God, why didn't He address all of the queerness? Most of the text addresses men only. Nothing about the transgender community at all. Most want you to assume that God is lumping all the LGBTQIA+ community in these texts. But if you're going to be a literalist, you can't infer what's being said.

The abominations talked about in the book of Leviticus are all things that people engage in or consume today because it is understood that the time and culture of that era were different as compared to ours. For example, the book also mentions eating pork, shellfish, or having intercourse with a woman who is menstruating as an 'abomination.' In today's world, who considers the act of consuming pork or shellfish as something worth getting executed over? No one. So why do we still focus on homosexuality as the only 'abomination' talked about in the book of Leviticus?[117]

Another verse used by conservative Christians in their debate of damning homosexuality as a sin is Genesis 19:5.

"And they called to Lot, "Where are the men who came to you tonight? Bring them out to us, that we may know them." Genesis 19:5 (ESV)

This is the incident and story that cements the idea of homosexuality being a cardinal sin in many people's minds. The story

---

[117] Crawley, W. (2013, March 26). *BBC - Will & Testament: Have you committed an "abomination" today?* BBC. https://www.bbc.co.uk/blogs/ni/2008/06/have_you_committed_an_abominat.html#:%7E:text=The%2017th%20century%20translation%20of,a%20noun%20which%20may%20be

about Sodom and Gomorrah is what makes people think that homosexuality is so bad that it would incur God's wrath. As the book of Genesis tells the story, people have come up with the resolution that homosexuality was why those people were punished by God. However, the truth is far from being so simple.

Sodom and Gomorrah were sister cities, and Sodom was famous for inhabiting people that were "sinners." Their sins included accumulating excessive wealth and power. The poor were oppressed and weakened by those in power. They were also famously bad at being hospitable. The people of Sodom had done many bad things and committed many sins that warranted the wrath of God. The people were greedy, prideful, and had no regard for the weak and poor. There are many instances in the Bible where even Jesus uses the city of Sodom as an example of the extreme level of wrath that God can incur on His people. So, what was the real reason that God destroyed the cities of Sodom and Gomorrah? People of Sodom were not punished for being homosexual or engaging in homosexual acts. In fact, the decision to destroy the city was made by God well before the men showed up at Lot's door. They were punished because when Lot was keeping two of God's messengers inside his house, the people of the city came to demand him to release them so they could violently rape them. This was customary during that period, violent sexual rape as a punishment.

Lot offered up his own virgin daughters so he could keep protecting the messengers from the sexual violence the Sodomites wanted to incur. This part of the story bothers me so much. How come no one is concerned that Lot offered his daughters to be raped? Why is this acceptable? How is this Godly? The reason why Sodom and Gomorrah were destroyed was due to all the sins they had committed, mainly not having any regard for the weak and poor.[118]

The Impact

The mistranslations and wrong teachings of the Bible have impacted our culture and society in many ways. The people of the LGBTQIA+ community have suffered greatly due to the encouraging propaganda that the Bible condemns homosexuality when there are experts who can prove that that isn't the case. Generations have grown up reading the wrong things or learning the Bible incorrectly. They have been forced to believe that God punishes and prohibits homosexuality. These wrongful teachings have brewed a toxic mentality in society. They use the Bible as their weapon against homosexuality when they couldn't be farther from the truth.

Using the Bible as a weapon against the LGBTQIA+ community has been the conservative group's go-to move. They know that opinions can be changed, but the apparent word of God cannot be argued against. The lack of knowledge about their own faith has made people believe the wrong things and follow the wrong mentality. In doing so, they have caused youth, like me, to grow up with self-esteem issues believing they are not loved in God's eyes. In recent years, society has grown more progressive and started to move towards a more accepting community where LGBTQIA+ people are readily accepted and not discriminated against.

In recent news, the church has also taken a relatively softer stance regarding LGBTQIA+ matters. Following Pope Francis and his statements regarding the LGBTQIA+ community, there is no doubt that the world is facing a shift in its culture yet again. This time for the better. As Pope Francis said, the people of the LGBTQIA+ are also

---

[118] Phillips, A. N. (2019a, July 16). *The Bible does not condemn "homosexuality." Seriously, it doesn't*. Medium. https://medium.com/@adamnicholasphillips/the-bible-does-not-condemn-homosexuality-seriously-it-doesn-t-13ae949d6619

children of God just like anyone else and deserve to have the right to a family of their own; it has brought forth a slew of encouragement and admiration.[119]

Being such a revered and prominent figure in the world, the Christian community faces a transformation. His support for the civil union of LGBTQIA+ people is the sign that times are changing and that the world is moving towards a day where everyone has the same rights and is recognized as an equal citizen, regardless of their sexual orientation. The ministries of the world are following in the footsteps of the Vatican and accepting more and more LGBTQIA+ people in their fold.

They have started being more accepting of same-sex couples and marriages. The main issue that I have is, many LGBTQIA+ people are not permitted to hold leadership positions or wedding ceremonies in these ministries. Gay people are being tolerated but not fully embraced. Even though there is still a lot to be done in the fight for equality for the LGBTQIA+ community, these are signs that we are moving toward the right destination. With growing acceptance and the Pope's affirming words, the world is changing, and so is the church.

Being a gay minister myself, I have seen so much transformation in the Christian community. I can say with an absolute guarantee that the world I see around myself is much better and more accepting than the one I grew up in. Being a teenager, I would have given anything for the Pope to say these words or for the churches to open their doors for gay couples and people a little earlier. Growing up, I had to contend with the fact that I was something that the Bible referred to as an 'abomination.' That is one of the biggest reasons why I, and many

---

[119] Diamant, J. (2020, November 2). *How Catholics around the world see same-sex marriage, homosexuality*. Pew Research Center. https://www.pewresearch.org/fact-tank/2020/11/02/how-catholics-around-the-world-see-same-sex-marriage-homosexuality/

other youths around the world, face depression, anxiety, and other mental issues due to their own identity that they cannot do anything about. I had to live with the fact that God didn't love me or would never forgive me just for being who I am. I had to learn how to deal with that and accept that I would never be allowed into heaven.

However, as I grew to learn more and educated myself further, I learned how wrong the world was. Learning the fact that God never actually said that homosexuality is an abomination, I finally made peace with not just myself but also my faith. The more I learned, the stronger my faith became because I had finally realized that I was not an abomination. I am not someone deserving of God's punishment or wrath just because of my sexuality.

Homosexuality is not a sin, and the Bible does not condemn me to Hell. So please stop saying 'love the sin, hate the sinner' or 'we all sin.' I am not sinning. Who I am is not a sin. That is the biggest lesson I have learned and one that I want to share with every ashamed gay person in hiding. It needs to be highlighted so that the world of tomorrow is kinder, more loving, and more accepting than the world of today.

> "The world is full of angels; if you can't find one, be one."
> ~ *MATSHONA DHLIWAYO*

Chapter 13: Love Thy Neighbor

"Teacher, which is the greatest commandment in the Law?" Jesus replied: "'Love the Lord your God with all your heart and with all your soul and with all your mind.' This is the first and greatest commandment. And the second is like it: 'Love your neighbor as yourself.' All the Law and the Prophets hang on these two commandments." -Matthew 22:36-40 (NIV)

The verses of Matthew 22:36-40 are one of the most important ones in the entire Bible. Many people have asked and still ask me, "Why do you still want to be a Christian?" In response, I always find myself referring to these verses. For it is these very verses that helped me accept me for me and understand God's purpose for all mankind.

It was a chill Friday night, and I was grubbing on some ribs at a nice BBQ spot in Miami. My BMe colleagues and I had just ended a very long work week. We were laughing, reminiscing, having a good time. For my leaders out there, there is no better place to relax people than a BBQ joint. All formality goes out the window when you have BBQ sauce all over your hands and lips. Per usual, the conversation turned philosophical. These things tend to happen when you're having conversations with Trabian Shorters.

I don't remember how we got to talking about evil people like Osama Bin Laden or Adolph Hitler. I just remember saying, "they are burning in Hell as we speak." Trabian responded with a story about his grandfather being a preacher who solely focused on love. He said his grandfather was a representation of his love for his community. He didn't condemn, he compelled. He didn't judge the members of his community for whatever condition they were in, he responded with acts of love and kindness. That's how he operated his ministry. He shared how his grandfather stood on one scripture. Love God and love your neighbor. If you do that, everything else will be alright. That conversation changed my life.

This story in Matthew tells of how Christ taught the Pharisees about the concept of the laws of Christianity. He taught them that the laws are all centered around one thing and one thing only; love. The Pharisees would use the laws to judge and punish anyone who seemed to do wrong, especially if you came from a marginalized community. The tides of racism and bigotry were no different than compared to today. Powerful people using laws and rules to oppress the weaker.

The Pharisee ("separatist") party emerged largely out of the group of scribes and sages during the 400 years of silence between the Old Testament and New Testament. Their name comes from the Hebrew and Aramaic parush or parushi, which means "one who is separated." It may refer to their separation from Gentiles, sources of ritual impurity, or from irreligious Jews.[120] Remember in chapter 10 when I talked about he who controls the scribe controls how history is recorded. Imagine now being superior, and you have the job of interpreting and enforcing scripture and law. Sound familiar?

The Holy Trinity teaches us that Christianity isn't about laws or commandments that are strict rules for living and conducting yourself. It is about unity and love.[121]

'Love thy neighbor' is a commonly known concept of Christianity. However, not many Christians even understand it in its entirety. Goodwill or acts of kindness are simply an extension of the commandment to love your neighbor as you love yourself. So, what does it even mean? Love is one of the most basic feelings that humans have felt ever since we came into being. It is one of the purest emotions that can overtake your heart. It also has many forms, all equally

---

[120] Cohen, S. (2014). *From the Maccabees to the Mishnah*. Westminster John Knox Press.

[121] *The Greatest Commandment (Matthew 22:36–40) | Student Christian Movement*. (n.d.). Movement. Retrieved September 10, 2021, from https://www.movement.org.uk/resources/greatest-commandment-matthew-2236-40

encompasses and devoted.

Our faith is not just about following a set of rules for the rest of our lives, hoping to find redemption and salvation. It is all about opening our hearts and being kind to one another. It implies having love and compassion for all of mankind, just as our Lord Jesus Christ had compassion for all mankind. Even in the middle of grueling pain on the cross did Christ extend love and compassion to us and the thieves hanging next to Him. Love is the biggest weapon of humanity, yet we have not learned to yield it, unfortunately.

When God created the world and then humanity, His intention was to create a united people. He wanted His followers to not just worship Him but be united in their love for Him. Opening our hearts to other human beings is the same as opening your hearts to Jesus Christ. Once you do, you learn empathy, kindness, compassion, forgiveness, and patience – all the essential elements of love. Loving God or humanity means never giving up on others. If one man falls, the other helps him get back up.

Loving your neighbor as you love yourself is a simple concept that many don't practice. One of the biggest reasons why the LGBTQIA+ community is always met with so much judgment and hatred is because humans have lost the concept of 'love thy neighbor.' For most humans, love has become conditional. You are loved so long as you stay in line. Once you step out of line, the love somehow disappears. They simply cannot handle the thought of accepting and loving someone who may have even slightly different opinions, beliefs, or lifestyles. Is that real love? We can see in stories of Christ that even those whom you do not get along with deserve the same love you bestow on yourself. That is what Christianity is about.

Othering

Tribalism is a concept that is as old as time. Tribalism has existed from the time humans lived in caves, hunted, and discovered fire for the first time. It has become an intrinsic part of humanity by now - so much so that we are conditioned to only show love and compassion to those from our 'tribe' or 'pack.'

People settle in groups or communities, forging strong ties that don't allow any outsiders to join. That has given birth to a culture where humans only tolerate those from their community or a community they have similarities with. That is why, no matter how globalized the world becomes, we are still battling with issues like racism, xenophobia, hatred, and more. This is how I give grace and compassion to racists. It's human nature to think your tribe is better than the other. I experience racism from white people while concurrently experiencing bigotry from Black people. But make no mistake, my grace and compassion does not come without accountability. Understanding your journey doesn't mean I continue to let you inflict harm because of your beliefs.

Some Black leaders don't like the way I approach racial equity. I try to get an understanding of where people are on their journey and lead them to a more inclusive, enlightened path. This is because I know oppression is not a white thing only, it's a human thing. White people just so happen to be in power. But what happens when a mob of Black men beats and kills a Black transgender woman. What do we say then? Is it not the same cruelty?

People worldwide have formed their tribes and packs based on such strict rules and traditions that anyone different would never be accepted in. Even though we like to celebrate diversity so loudly, we are still facing an immigrant crisis worldwide. Is that not related to our culture of ostracizing those who are different from us, whether in looks, religious backgrounds, or way of living? We have become prone to fear and hatred when it comes to letting other people inside our communities.

What's worse is that most people use religion as their excuse to do it.

Most Christians who refuse to accept the LGBTQIA+ community and their rights use their faith as an excuse as to why they do it. However, we have learned that the commandment of loving thy neighbor is the one that all other laws and commandments are based on. If we don't love our neighbor, no matter who they might be, are we showcasing our love for God? Because loving God means loving your neighbor, even if their way of living or mentality does not match up with yours.

This is why it has become increasingly clear that religion has just become a tool for people to push their agendas and opinions. Most people, no matter what religion they follow, have biased interpretations of their own religion. When conservative Christians read the Bible, they focus on the parts where women or homosexuals are not liked instead of focusing on the greatest commandment of all, to love thy neighbor. Through my observations, I have discovered that people tend to interpret their religion based on their own life experiences.

If a person grows up in a liberal and loving household, they will interpret the Bible in that way. They'll focus on the messages of love and acceptance because that is what they have been taught and have seen in their lives. On the other hand, when conservative Christians read it, all they focus on are passages like those from Leviticus. They go on to tell gay people that they are Hell-bound. It is all because their lives have been about right or wrong, Black or white, without grey areas. And in most cases, they are right, and you are wrong, even if they are wrong. How can you stand against homosexuals, but you and your whole church is racist? It is all about what you breed; love or hate.

When it comes to raising children, we have two options. We can either force our own opinions and views of the world on them or let them discover the world through their own eyes and form their ideas and opinions. If a family raises their children by teaching them about acceptance and love, the children will go on to be kinder and more tolerant of other people. On the contrary, children born and raised in a hostile and negative environment where they are forced to learn about things according to their parents or communities will most likely go on to spread hate and toxicity.

Love breeds love and hate breeds hate. If a child grows up with conservative, racist parents, we cannot expect them to accept and tolerate people of different races, religions, and backgrounds. They would not know how to, simply because they were conditioned to hate or reject others other than themselves from an early age. A child born with a certain set of values cannot be expected to know anything else. However, that is what religion is about; to learn better and do the right thing, not what we were taught.

I have though, seen in recent years, many cases where children and teens have bucked their parents teaching and embraced a more inclusive way of living. In fact, younger generations are more open and more loving than ever before. This is because of exposure. They are being exposed to "other" in so many ways because of technology and more diversified communities. The more exposure and experiences we have with other "tribes," the better off we will be as a civilization.

Hate is not something people are born with. We are born innocent and pure; it is the world and the circumstances that surround us that fill our hearts with love or hate. If we take the message of love from religion and apply it to our lives, we would find ourselves closer to God. Being judgmental, intolerant, or a misanthropist will never bring peace or contentment to our hearts. People who are strongly intolerant or hateful of LGBTQIA+ people actually fail to learn to love others as themselves. They most likely don't even love themselves. In that case, how can they even call themselves religious? Remember, religion is all about love and compassion; one can never be called religious without these two elements. Christ didn't come to condemn the world but to give us everlasting life. Humans, however, did come to condemn the world and give us everlasting judgment.

Throughout the Bible, we read stories of how Christ responded to hate with love because that was God's way. Why can't humans do the same? We follow every commandment but choose to ignore the greatest one - why? Every religion is founded on a few key elements: the sovereign deity, the evil entity, a sacrifice, creation story, and love. Most religions in the world follow that structure. Christianity, the largest religion in the world, also follows the same structure.

No matter which church they are a part of every Christian should be introduced to the key concepts of our faith; the Holy Trinity, Satan, the crucifixion, and Genesis. We all know that God, the Holy Ghost, and Jesus Christ, our Savior, make up the Holy Trinity and that Satan is the one we have to fight and conquer. We all understand what the crucifixion meant for humanity. Regardless, we ignore the last key aspect of Christianity that love is - the question is 'why?'

Why do we not understand that, at its core, all aspects of Christianity are about love? The Holy Trinity is a unity based on love. Satan refuses to let us love and worship God. Jesus sacrificed himself because of His love for humanity. Christianity is about love; it is the basic foundation of this religion and most other religions of the world. In every corner of the world, you will find people of different religions - the most common ones being Christianity, Islam, Hinduism, Buddhism, Judaism, and other folk religions.[122]

In my entire life and career, with everything that I have read,

---

[122] *These are all the world's major religions in one map.* (2019, March 26). World Economic Forum. https://www.weforum.org/agenda/2019/03/this-is-the-best-and-simplest-world-map-of-religions

researched, and seen, most religions of the world center around one concept; love. We are all meant to love God, regardless of the form we choose to worship and how we do it. Love is what unites humanity and the world at its core. When we follow a religion, the first thing we learn is to love God and the second is to love His people because they were sent by Him. It does not matter which religion you follow; love is the common thread amongst all.

Christianity, Islam, Judaism, and many other religions preach about loving God most of all. Your life should be in servitude to your God because it is what will bring you happiness and peace. You are meant to love other creatures simply because they are all connected to God and you. Most religions teach that you are not put on this earth to serve God and fulfill your desires. You are meant to serve others because in serving them, you serve your God.

To love is a choice. A choice you have to consciously make. The question is, if you can't love – why? What causes you to first judge me and not love me, and you don't even know me. Some would say it takes time to grow to love someone, especially unconditionally. But it took you no time to judge me and send me to an eternal lake of fire. Why is that? Especially when it is counter to the life lived by Christ. Christ loved at first sight. Christ had compassion at first sight. Christ was love at first sight. Are you love at first sight? Do people see and experience the love of God when they encounter you?

Whether you are a devoted Christian or follow any other religion, loving God is not just about worshipping Him in your house of worship or following His commandments. It is also about letting your love for Him extend to those around you. You have to understand that love is the one thing God wants us to learn from religion. Religion, especially Christianity, is not meant to divide people over who gets to go to Heaven or not but to unify people under a single umbrella with one purpose: to love God and spread that love on earth. That is how our

Lord intended it.

    How is your love spreading going?

"I believe that when Black people tell our own stories, we can shift the axis of the world and tell our real history of generational wealth and richness of soul that are not told in our history books."

~ BEYONCÉ

Chapter 14: Before the Atlantic Slave Trade

What Do You Know?

Understanding your heritage ought to be the right of every student in America. It is impossible to create the best possible life for oneself if you have no idea where you came from. Any therapist worth anything will tell you that in order to solve problems of current you have to understand how you arrived at the problem in the first place. This is also why when you're at the doctors describing an unknown ache or pain, the doctor has a bunch of questions that you think have nothing to do with the pain. What did you do today? What did you eat? What did you drink? Try anything new? Where have you been? They are trying to investigate possible contributing factors to the pain.

The summer of 2020 was a perfect example of when you don't know where you come from its impossible to appreciate the essence of who you are. Beyoncé Knowles Carter in partnership with Disney, released "Black Is King" – a visual companion to the 2019 album The Lion King: The Gift. In the film, Beyoncé proclaims that Black is beautiful. Black is glorious. Black is King. The 85-minute film, written, directed, and produced by Beyoncé, was long awaited and viewed by millions on Disney+.

"Black Is King" is inspired by the 2019 remake of "The Lion King". It is filled with powerful imagery that represents different parts of Africa, namely West and South Africa. We follow the story of an African king who is cast out into the world as a baby and grows up to return home to reclaim his throne. We follow him on his journey from shame to glory as he meets people and symbolism that connect him to his history, his family and identity. Beyoncé, who narrates the film as well as does her good singing and dancing, plays his mother figure. She encourages him, thus encourages Black people, to reconnect with our rich royal heritage and not to be defined by the colonial views of Africa.

Adorned with messages of affirmation, Beyoncé really spoke to the heart of Black people:

"Let Black be synonymous with glory."

"The world will always tell you that you're something else, that you're too dark, too short, whatever. We need to show Black men and women are emotional, are strong, are smart, intuitive."

"Be bigger than the picture they framed for us to see."

"King already you know it. It's time to shine."

"The ancestors never left you."

"Look up at the stars. It's been a long time but remember who you are… find your way back."

These messages resonated with all those who are yearning for connection to our African heritage.

Beyond the messages were the beautiful scenes throughout the film. She filmed in locations such as Nigeria, Ghana, and South Africa, showcasing the continent's natural beauty. We saw beautiful cities, mansions, deserts, waterfalls, seas, landmarks, and jungles. It brought tears to so many to see Blackness in such an affirming light. We saw the wealth and beauty that some parts of Africa have to offer. Much different than the traditional western imagery of Africa. She also made sure to feature African musicians such as Wizkid, Yemi Alade, and Tiwa Savage.

Welp, in perfect bigotry fashion, not less than a week after the film's release, you had white evangelical pastors calling the project demonic proclaiming that Black isn't King, Jesus is King. Typical right, no surprises there. Nothing like a good old Black empowerment film to bring bigots out of hiding. The gag is, Jesus was a man of color so technically Black is King, but that's another topic for later in the chapter.

What was surprising was how many Black Christian leaders rebuked the film as well, calling it demonic due to the African symbolism and use of African religions. The imagery features a lot of significant African iconography including horns, masks, cowry shells, snakes, and more. I read so many posts on social media and even had a few conversations where Black people claimed that 'African spiritualism and symbology is demonic.' They even claimed idol worship because Beyoncé was talking to and honoring the ancestors.

Not sure how to even respond, I was grieved. Grieved because after all these years, ignorance and anti-Blackness is still prevailing within our own race. These Black critics skipped over all this Black empowerment to focus on 'the demonic'. It really demonstrated how disconnected some people are and how brainwashed we've been. I always say white supremacy has done a number on Black people.

We've been indoctrinated into believing anything African is bad, demonic, barbaric, and pagan. This includes our skin, our language, our clothing, and even our hair. "That's not biblical" they said. It's impossible for most things to be biblical concerning Black people because the Bible was whitewashed. The only thing biblical in the eyes of colonizers concerning Black people was, "slaves obey your masters." Its humorous how these people can identify and confront demons they can't see but remain silent on the demons they can see in the form of racism, bigotry, and social injustice. Don't write a think piece about the demonic in "Black is King" and you haven't said two words about the demon that occupied the White House from 2016 – 2020.

Thank goodness over the last few generations, the perception of Africa has started to shift with many Black Americans. We are longing to reconnect with roots, culture, and heritage. In 2017, my siblings and I vowed to include one African country in our annual international travel. We started in Egypt 2017, then South Africa in 2018, then Morocco in 2019. Unfortunately, Corona Virus cancelled our Ghana travel plans for 2020.

"Black is King" showcased the affluence and abundance that are underrepresented in media portrayals, and this made people crazy because it was counter to what they have been taught. It's time now to intentionally understand who you are and where you come from.

"The events of 2020 have made the film's vision and message even more relevant," Beyoncé posted on Instagram.

Decolonizing The Colonizers

Colonization is the violent and systematic process where invading people conquer an indigenous population. They lay claim to the land and its resources through acts of violence like rape and genocide. The people who survive this initial purge are placed under systematic oppression and forced to work, their laborers giving fruit to the conquers. In many ways, it is a more refined system from ancient times, where armies would take over and enslave the population they battled. The only difference is that now, the process has been sterilized and turned into an efficient machine, making it all the more deadly and dangerous. Today we call this gentrification.

Colonization is not just limited to enslavement and the theft of resources; it is a process of degradation that destroys the very personhood of the people. Native people are treated as second-class citizens; their language, customs, and traditions are slowly wiped away. The creation of a hierarchy places the oppressed as a lowly and uncivilized beast; everything associated with them becomes taboo. Those who do not die under the physical violence and burden of colonization are subject to psychological warfare. This type of attack is carried out both implicitly and explicitly, going from generation to generation, slowly killing out the qualities that are seen as undesirable. The colonized are trained and taught to despise their own identity. They are made to adopt the colonial mindset, which drives them to propagate this in a self-repeating cycle. The victim becomes the perpetrator, who then continues to make more copies of himself. In this way, the colonizing party simply has to initiate the seeding process and snowball into a greater effort. It is this very paradigm that leaves long-lasting effects, the damage of which can be observed even long after the offending party has vacated the premises.

Decolonization, on the other hand, seeks to empower the oppressed. It does this by first recognizing and calling into question the colonization and then turning said system on its head to gain their independence. Decolonization occurs actively; it is not an organic process that arises from a stalemate or the status quo. Colonization is a sin that can only be remitted when action is taken against it. Unlike the destructive process, the healing part can take much longer. It has to reverse the damage that has been done, often through several generations. Sometimes, the greatest resistance can come from the very people that are being decolonized.

The Atlantic Slave Trade

The transatlantic slave trade was part of the global slave trade between the 16th and 19th centuries. Millions of Africans were stolen, captured, and sold to be transported to colonies in America. It is estimated that around 12 million Africans were enslaved and sold to the Americas during this slave trade. The Portuguese, Spanish, Dutch, English, French, and Americans were the majority of slave owners and traders who participated in this activity. The slaves were then sold to plantation, industry, mine, and field owners for economic purposes.

There were so many devastating effects of the trade on not just the

African economy but also the people and their culture. Young men and women were captured to be sold into markets as trade goods, while the more dependent or disabled people were left behind in Africa. The impacts of this slave trade meant the captured Africans had to leave behind their entire lives. The transportation of the slaves aboard ships crossing the Atlantic Ocean included brutalities not just in terms of physical abuse but also in the stripping of the Africans' traditions and customs.[123] This was done to prepare them for the "re-education" that would follow.

African American culture, mostly referred to as Black culture, is very much rooted in African cultures that have trickled over time from the sub-Saharan African and Sahelean cultures. Slave trading did not just seek to demolish the economic and financial development of Africans but also to undermine their culture. Slave owners made sure to repress Africans by controlling them and forcing their traditions and culture on them. The slave trade managed to strip the Africans of most of their culture but not entirely.

To control the African slaves and not let any rebellions take place, the slave owners did not allow the slaves to be educated. By refusing to provide them with basic education, the slaves were reduced to passing down their traditions orally. Isolating the Africans and cutting them off from their home Africa damaged most of the African culture. Slave owners sought to force their own culture on their slaves so that they could continue to repress the original African culture. They knew that if allowed to practice their customs, the Africans could grow independent and rebel. [124]

It wasn't just the customs and culture that the slave owners forced

---

[123] *transatlantic slave trade | History & Facts.* (2021, August 18). Encyclopedia Britannica. https://www.britannica.com/topic/transatlantic-slave-trade

[124] *AfricanAmericanHistory.* (n.d.). Hmpcl. Retrieved September 10, 2021, from https://guides.hmcpl.org/AfricanAmericanHistory

onto the Africans. By refusing to provide them with education, slave owners would force their slaves to practice Christianity because of the common notion that almost every Christian had at the time: their religion is superior. The North and South American slave owners weren't very educated about African spirituality, so they considered it as their 'duty' to educate them about Christianity, the superior religion.

That idea was born out of the Doctrine of Discovery. Pope Nicholas V expressed in the papal bull "Dum Diversas" of 1452 that colonizing and capturing the property or assets of non-Christians was justified. This doctrine was used to capture many lands and colonize indigenous people around the world, including Native Americans and Africans. Many of the colonists believed their efforts to be in line with doing God's work. The concept would later be refined in the 19th century as manifest destiny. It was seen as the "burden" of the white man to pass on his superiority to the inferior natives. Strip them of their own identity and fill them up with your ideas and beliefs, and you will have made a civilized man out of a savage. In time, the newly molded mind would rebel against itself and perpetuate the ideas forced into it; the oppressed would become the oppressors.

The doctrine is still being used to drive the campaign against non-Christians in the United States. This promotes the idea that Christianity is superior to other religions and that non-Christians deserve to be colonized and have their religion oppressed.[125] The core of the problem lies in a great misunderstanding or complete lack of recognizing the values of African spirituality. This harmful idea perpetuated that the colonizers brought monotheism to Africa. In reality, such a perspective was already quite saturated in the

---

[125] Miller, E. M. (2018, December 31). *Denominations repent for Native American land grabs*. Religion News Service. https://religionnews.com/2018/08/22/denominations-repent-for-native-american-land-grabs/

population, possibly even before Christianity came into existence. Then why is this idea so prevalent? One, it served the narrative of the savior colonizers bringing redemption to the so-called savages of the land. Two, it allowed for the creation of the "other," which made it much easier to compartmentalize and justify the atrocities being committed against the indigenous population.

African slaves were forced to learn and practice a religion that was not their own. African spirituality is more nuanced than Christianity and not as fixed in the creed. Different ethnic groups have different spirituality. For African slaves, it was a unique idea to worship one God, follow a book of guidelines, and conform to such strict rules. African spirituality has always been more varied and encompasses a person's entire life. It would come as a shock to the outsiders who compartmentalized their lives; religion is a rulebook, and Sunday is for the church.

African spirituality does not have the simplistic approach of having one God, a set of commandments, or a book that tells the story of Genesis. African spirituality is all about how one lives. It is about the different aspects of life, such as economics, politics, diet, how to dress, death, and marriage. This would have stood in stark contrast to the colonizers' simplistic view of the world. In a dramatic twist of irony, those who claimed to be superior employed a more primitive approach to something that their lives supposedly revolved around. For Africans, religions and spirituality were an inherent part of life. For the colonizers, religion was like a swappable part that could be turned on or off as needed.

Indigenous African spirituality has the approach that religion is not a separate aspect of one's life. It is the way of living one's life. Its customs and practices are in accordance with all aspects of a person's life like eating, behaving, communicating, or spending their money, etc. It does not bind you to one certain rule but allows you to explore things in your life according to the ancestors' words.

All the slave trades that Africa had to experience, including the Christian and Islamic colonization of the continent, made the indigenous African religions suffer in widespread dominance. What was once the majority of the continent's religion and spirituality is now only practiced by about 10% of the population. The loss of such spirituality speaks volumes about how much the African continent has suffered throughout the centuries.[126] The true extent of the destruction is hard to calculate. There is no doubt that unique and valuable perspectives have become lost to history as a result of this consistent culling, something that may never be recovered in its entirety.

African Spirituality

African spirituality is one of the main pillars of African cultures, a springboard to everything else in their lives. They exercise and give power to their spiritual beliefs through their daily actions, such as evoking the creator's names. The creator plays a constant role in the lives of both the community and the individual, from the morning when they rise to the time they go to bed. The night marks giving thanks for the blessing of the day, and the day marks the safety afforded throughout the night. This culture created a relationship between the individual, the community, and the environment. This was more implicit and was not externally displayed.

There is this idea presented that everything within the cosmos is connected at an inherent level; invisible bonds tie everyone together. As this spiritual connection is so deep, it acts as a perceptive lens for the people and gives them a way to think about their existence and place in the world. One becomes aware that they are part of a greater

---

[126] Chiorazzi, A. (2015, October 6). *The spirituality of Africa*. Harvard Gazette. https://news.harvard.edu/gazette/story/2015/10/the-spirituality-of-africa/

system and do not possess full agency or control over what can happen. Unlike the western world, spirituality is not such a contested idea or concept for the African people. While views may differ on the spirit and spirituality, there is an inherent common recognition of *spirit* being very sacred; it is a part of everything and should be cherished.

What is essential to understand here is that religion is seen as the practical part of spirituality, something that forms in relation to civilization. This is in contrast to the west, where the two are seen as separate entities, with spirituality being a more personal endeavor unique to each individual. There is also an increased focus on community and the way it gives validation to the person. *Ubuntu*, while hard to translate accurately, states the existence of a person hinging on other people. That is, one is only who they are because of the involvement of others.

For most Africans, spirituality is inherent to life and is passed on from one generation to the next. Their way of life recognizes the existence of a higher supreme being that is pure spirit and the source of everything that exists. The African people believe in one unique and divine being but attribute many symbols to the entity. This may be a possible reason that outsiders have so misunderstood their beliefs. What is even more interesting is the lack of the dichotomy between good and evil. Instead of there being evil, there is the absence of love and good qualities associated with *ubuntu*.

The body and spirit are seen as reflections of one another. What happens to one affects the other. In the same way, the individual reflects the community. When one is sick or injured, it reflects the whole. This is in stark contrast to the individual mentality that the colonizers have used. This clash of perspectives has been the root of many misunderstandings, some even leading to the label of the indigenous people being savages.

What Is Colonization? What Is Decolonization?

Colonization is the violent and systematic process where invading people conquer an indigenous population. They lay claim to the land and its resources through acts of violence like rape and genocide. The people who survive this initial purge are placed under systematic oppression and forced to work, their laborers giving fruit to the conquers. In many ways, it is a more refined system from ancient times, where armies would take over and enslave the population they battled. The only difference is that now, the process has been sterilized and turned into an efficient machine, making it all the more deadly and dangerous. Colonization is not just limited to enslavement and the theft of resources; it is a process of degradation that destroys the very personhood of the people. Native people are treated as second-class citizens; their language, customs, and traditions are slowly wiped away. The creation of a hierarchy places the oppressed as a lowly and uncivilized beast; everything associated with them becomes taboo. Those who do not die under the physical violence and burden of colonization are subject to psychological warfare. This type of attack is carried out both implicitly and explicitly, going from generation to generation, slowly killing out the qualities that are seen as undesirable. The colonized are trained and taught to despise their own identity. They are made to adopt the colonial mindset, which drives them to propagate this in a self-repeating cycle. The victim becomes the perpetrator, who then continues to make more copies of himself. In this way, the colonizing party simply has to initiate the seeding process and snowball into a greater effort. It is this very paradigm that leaves long-lasting effects, the damage of which can be observed even long after the offending party has vacated the premises.

Decolonization, on the other hand, seeks to empower the oppressed. It does this by first recognizing and calling into question the colonization and then turning the system on its head to gain their independence. Decolonization occurs actively; it is not an organic process that arises from a stalemate or the status quo. Colonization is a sin that can only be remitted when action is taken against it. Unlike the destructive process, the healing part can take much longer. It has to reverse the damage that has been done, often through several generations. Sometimes, the greatest resistance can come from the very people that are being decolonized.

Whitewashing Christianity

There's almost little to no white people in the Bible. Namely not Adam, Eve, or Steve, and especially not Jesus. I could end this section right here but I'm sure you'd like to know more about this scathing new intel. When it comes to culture and religion, Europeans have had the advantage, using their religion to oppress others. As evident in the Doctrine of Discovery, Christians thought it was their divine right to be the superior race and culture. What that mentality gave birth to is a form of white supremacy that we see prevalent nowadays. Perhaps the biggest example is the common depiction of Jesus Christ as a white man with long blond hair, pale skin, and blue eyes.

This is shown through many paintings and artworks by artists of the world, such as da Vinci or Warner Sallman. Their paintings and depictions of Jesus Christ as a white man has promoted the idea that Jesus was white. The Bible itself does not have much in the way of the physical description of Jesus, leaving historians to piece together history, geography, and the hints from the Bible to come up with a rough idea of what he looked like, which was not white.

Depicting Christ as a white man, especially in the face of minorities and oppressed ethnicities, portrays the idea of white supremacy. It perpetuates the belief that the European race is superior since it was the race of God's son himself. It also promotes the idea that since Jesus was white, he sides with the ideas and behaviors of white people. It shows the subtle yet pronounce claims of white people being the better race.

Thinking that Jesus was white would, for instance, make Black people think that they were enslaved by men that looked like the God they worship. Throughout history, the Bible has been the victim of whitewashing because of such practices. When looking at da Vinci's paintings, though, people have been made to consider more things about the artist himself. The painting of Jesus by the artist is even thought to be inspired by his male lover. Over the years, people have wondered about the sexuality of the Renaissance painter. Stories and paintings by the painter himself have brought about the debate as to whether Leonardo da Vinci was gay or not. Some experts argue that he most probably was. The basis provided is that he lived in Florence in an era when homosexuality and adult men having sexual affairs with younger boys was common.[127]

The debate is provoked by the claims that some of da Vinci's paintings are depictions of his gay lover, Salai. The famous painting of St. John the Baptist is claimed to be inspired by the boy and depicts the beauty of the young male.[128] However, the debate points out that da Vinci's lifestyle and his close relationship with the church itself were proof of the tolerance of homosexuality in the early ages. Ironically, the era people base their supposed ideas on is one with values that go against the very thing they perpetuate. In a classic case of cherry-picking, one merely chooses a conclusion and then shops for supporting information while ignoring everything else.

As for the whitewashing of the Bible, the proof lies in the pudding. Leonardo's Jesus, Michelangelo's David, depictions of Moses, Paul,

---

[127] Judah, H. (n.d.). *The men who Leonardo da Vinci loved.* BBC Culture. Retrieved September 10, 2021, from https://www.bbc.com/culture/article/20191107-the-men-who-leonardo-da-vinci-loved

[128] Visions, N. (2018, April 17). *Was Leonardo Da Vinci Gay? - Dose.* Medium. https://medium.com/dose/was-leonardo-da-vinci-gay-e0871f31a666

Mary, and Joseph all tell the tale of how characters of the Bible have been portrayed as white. None of the people were European, so why is it that they are depicted as them? There aren't many instances where white people make an appearance in the Bible. So, why is the Bible so whitewashed? The answer is quite simple. As evinced by the Doctrine of Discovery, Christian Europeans have always thought themselves to be superior. Being in a position of power and influence throughout history, they were able to drive the idea of white supremacy. In recent years, people have spoken up and questioned the authenticity of such claims as to whether Jesus was white or not. It is controversial and not commented on by the church because it proves that earlier Christianity campaigned for white supremacy.

If people were to actually read the Bible, they would realize that there are barely any descriptions of what Jesus looked like physically. Revelation 1:14-15 is considered to hint at what Jesus looked like. It mentions that his skin was a darker color while his hair was white. There are many instances where it is described that he was an average-looking man, never standing out of the crowd because of his physical features. That means that he looked just like any first-century Palestinian Jewish man in his thirties. It may not ever be clear as to what exactly Jesus looked like, but we can say for sure that he was not white.[129] Why should his appearance have a matter in the first place? The focus seems to be placed on incidental details, while the core message and philosophy, the actual point, seems to get glossed over.

Decolonizing Jesus Christ

The figure of Jesus Christ has been most commonly referred to and

---

[129] Pruitt, S. (2021, March 22). *The Ongoing Mystery of Jesus's Face*. HISTORY. https://www.history.com/news/what-did-jesus-look-like#:%7E:text=For%20many%20scholars%2C%20Revelation%201,refined%20as%20in%20a%20furnace.%E2%80%9D

presented in the media as a construct of the west. Indeed, in many ways, the west and Christianity are presented as being synonymous with each other. In the same territory comes the idea of Jesus being a white savior. The reality of the situation is that the idea of Jesus has been embraced and present in many different cultures and societies. For some, Jesus has been part of their lives long before modern western civilization was established.

One of the most prominent positions of reverence that of the prophets is afforded to Jesus in Islam. Islamic literature extensively features Jesus. He is seen as one of their own instead of a foreign entity that is exclusive to just one group of people. Even in Asia, Jesus and Christianity play a vital role in the lives of the local population. Yet still, there is this mainstream idea of Jesus being a white man tied to the colonizers. For one, the idea of Christ being a white man was perpetuated to brainwash the Blacks into thinking they were an inferior people. As Christianity was forced onto the indigenous people, they were made to see themselves as being second-class citizens. After all, if Jesus was white, then what chance did they stand at salvation. Case in point, the perpetrator of the colonization could use their supposed association with Jesus (race) as an excuse for their colonial practices.

Decolonizing Christianity

Unbeknownst to so many Christians today, Christianity was the tool used to build the colonial empire. Rather than seeking equality amongst men, colonizers used their supposed spiritual superiority as a tool of oppression. This narrative of Christianity being the superior religion has led to polarizations wherever the gospel was spread. It created an "us" vs "them" mentality and because "us" is better they can treat "them" anyway they want. Those who fall within the circle of Christianity are accepted; those who are outside it are beaten into submission. Case in point, the violent colonization of Native

Americans. The United States government built boarding schools and then forcibly placed the indigenous people in them to be brainwashed. They were stripped of their customs and beliefs, forbidden to speak their language, and forced to learn the Bible. They were to be civilized from their savage state.

The colonization of Christianity has pushed the narrative and values of the oppressors, presenting them as one and the same. The decolonization of Christianity occurs when the faith is viewed no longer as the property of western nations but instead as a faith of all peoples. Christianity is not a white religion. It's a history book full of stories of middle eastern and African people. There is major work needed to separate the white narrative from the work of Christianity. For one, traditions, thoughts, and perspectives about life that stem from a white societal perspective have to be detangled from the faith. This is a complicated process because colonizers in the past have used their extensive influence to push their own ideas under the guise of Christianity. This has left a deep mark that will take several generations to correct.

Colonialism And Its Impacts on Different Religions and Cultures

White supremacy is not just affecting the United States but most parts of the world. White supremacy led so many European and American conquerors to forcefully take the land of different regions in the world. Asia, Africa, Australia, South America and other indigenous lands suffered at the hands of white supremacy. White Christian leaders felt it was their divine right to conquer non-Christian lands and force them to practice Christianity or face mortal danger.

The transatlantic slave trade is just one example of white supremacy impacting the religions of Africans and Native Americans. The East India Trading Company is another such example where white

Christians felt it was okay to conquer non-Christians and make them suffer through their brutalities just because they weren't of the same faith.

Indigenous people that have been affected by colonialism have also suffered losing parts of their history about sexuality and gender. The world that we see today has a very controversial view about sexual orientation other than heterosexuality. In earlier centuries, before the Western world colonized the continent, Africans had a common practice of gender queerness and female husbandry. The most famous example is of Queen Njinga Mbande, who ruled the Mbundu people. The region now called Angola was home to female husbandry and queerness. The Queen would practice gender queerness and had wives, which was allowed for people of high status and economic standing in society. Even today, some regions have a similar practice but only for those females who are wealthy or influential. After the Western colonizers came to dominate the continent, they also brought their customs and religious practices of heterosexuality and monogamy. The colonialism of Africa forced people to accept the customs of Christianity and adhere to homophobic rhetoric.[130]

The notion of a male-female relationship and conforming to gender stereotypes is an idea that was perpetuated by Western colonizers based on their knowledge and interpretation of Christianity. So, if people claim that homosexuality is a Western phenomenon, it is incorrect. That's because homosexuality has existed long before colonialism. Rather it was the homophobia that was brought forward by the Western people.

Native Americans, according to the reports of European colonizers, were also in the habit of practicing gender fluidity. Before colonialism

---

[130] *Queer Africa - Essay.* (n.d.). Albany. Retrieved September 10, 2021, from https://www.albany.edu/faculty/jhobson/middle_passages/queerafrica/essay.html

attacked and forced them to either give up or hide their practices and customs, Native Americans exhibited gender-bending practices and homosexuality. There are many accounts and stories of Native American tribes where men were married to men and even the existence and acceptance of the third gender. There were people who were proclaimed male after birth but went on to live life in with feminine roles. Not all tribes celebrated sexual and gender diversity, though, because most of it was forced upon the conquered warriors. The acceptance of Two-Spirit and third genders was fairly common in many Native American tribes. It was only after Christian Europeans colonized them that the ideas and notions of these things came to be known as something that was not right or natural. The idea of people not conforming to their gender roles, engaging in homosexual or polyamorous relationships are all notions that Christian colonizers brought with them. It was a tactic that these colonizers used to dehumanize the indigenous peoples, Africans, or Native Americans. They would use these practices to label them as 'sinners' or 'sexual beasts' to provoke a general hatred of them so that when they forced their cruelties on them, it would seem as acceptable and almost deserved.[131]

In the United States, serious issues, such as racism, still exist today even though we consider ourselves progressive and modern. Black people in America have been forced to go through an identity crisis that makes us dislike our own culture because of the stigma attached to so many aspects of it. Whether it is our skin color, how we make music, our hairstyles, or even our art and diet are all known to be criticized because of racism. There is a reason why a Black man walking down the street at night is immediately considered suspicious, especially if he is wearing baggy clothes, has dreads,

---

[131] *Two Spirit and LGBTQ Idenitites: Today and Centuries Ago.* (2020, November 23). HRC. https://www.hrc.org/news/two-spirit-and-lgbtq-idenitites-today-and-centuries-ago

listening to rap music loudly, or looks like he is from the 'hood.' These are all effects of colonialism that have trickled down to society today. However, as 2020 has shown us, people are ready to destroy colonialism and its impacts on society today. The movement against racial injustice has proven that people are decolonizing a country that has been plagued with colonization for centuries. People are learning more and more about their roots and culture. They are rewriting the perspective of their culture from a non-colonialist lens. They are bringing awareness about their culture and taking back the reins that have been in the hands of white Christian leaders too long.

By reconnecting with their culture and roots, Black people and Native Americans are celebrating their uniqueness. By allowing yourself to proudly portray your Black heritage and culture, you can decolonize your society. It will also help you reconnect with African spirituality by not giving in to the pressure of white supremacy and following a faith that you do not connect with. Many Black people accept Christianity with their whole hearts, and that is alright too. However, the beauty of African spirituality should be kept alive and celebrated for its exclusive and unique customs and practices.

It is evident that we can conclude that colonialism and white supremacy was the evil that destroyed and disrupted indigenous love and spirituality in most parts of the world. Thus, greatly disconnecting humanity from spirit. The full impacts of these atrocities we may never know.

Did Africans Know Jesus Before the Slave Trade?

The idea of Christianity as the white man's religion has led to the approach of the faith being viewed from a European perspective. It would be false to state that it was brought into the region by the colonizers, who saw their efforts as a service to good. Indeed, Christianity was introduced to North Africa less than 150 years after the death of Jesus. This was far earlier than the conquest and pillaging that would come in the later centuries. It is quite possible that Christianity came to Africa before it reached the Britons, something that is quite ironic in retrospect.

Furthermore, concepts like the Trinity found their origin in Africa. It was Tertullian who coined the term, something that would become a key part of faith for colonizers. Augustine of Hippo authored several key texts on the faith, works that are highly revered and have influenced Western Christianity and philosophy. Without the contribution of these great African thinkers, modern Christianity would have been deprived of several key concepts and ideas that are so prevalent today.

Christianity found a firm home in Egypt because its ideas were not perceived as being overly foreign. In Memphis, there was the concept of a trinity between Isis, Osiris, and Horus, all combined into one. A branch of the faith developed in Egypt was named after the language of the land, Coptic. The terms from this time and region are still in use in modern-day churches.

As such, it would be false to state that Africans were unaware of Jesus before the colonizers supposedly introduced them to the faith.

African Spirituality Today - The Great Return

With the growing recognition and realization of the effect colonization has had on the faith and spirituality of African people, there has been a movement to go back to the roots. For one, African spirituality offers Black believers a decolonized version of the faith. People like Rev. Lyvonne Proverbs Briggs embrace the spiritual practices of the African ancestors and bring them into the faith as an integral part of the decolonized faith. There is a movement from the traditional approach of good and evil, as based on the African approach of love and a lack of love. People are keener to explore and question their faith and life, challenging previously held notions of what it means to be a person.

Increasingly more concepts are being brought from African spirituality in the application of faith, as Black people try to reconcile and repair the damage left behind by colonization. Ancestral veneration has increased, and there is a focus on individual intuition. The blind application of faith is rejected in favor of learning from it and then applying lessons based on the circumstances in which one finds themselves.

Many individuals struggle to find the right words for their new approach to faith, saying it still felt "churchy." However, the idea of being true to oneself and the application of African spirituality as outlined in the previous parts has become more prevalent. While it may not reflect the entire approach used in the past, it represents a shift in thought that is a good move towards decolonizing the faith and the people who subscribe to the beliefs.

> "When I was perceived as a Black man I became a threat to public safety. When I was dressed as myself, it was my safety that was threatened"
>
> ~ *LAVERNE COX*

Chapter 15: Queer is the New Black

The Heart of The Matter

My, how far we've come but oh how far we've yet to venture. Each generation, since the Emancipation of Black slaves in America, has led to the progressive dismissal and desertion of harmful beliefs and behaviors within the community.

Just as Black skin was brought out of an age of intolerance, so too are we slowly shedding light on being queer. When I say queer is the new Black, it means that the idea is undergoing the same process that applied to being Black. First, they feared it because they did not understand it. Then, they "othered" it so they could feel good about mistreating it. And then they developed a hatred that had to be slowly broken down by awareness, love, and consideration for other human beings.[132]

As more people gain an understanding of what it means to be queer, those who were previously seen as deviants are freer to express and show themselves in public. This openness reveals parts of society that were once shunned, mocked, and attacked.[133]

People now have more choices and avenues to participate in their interests than ever before. The presence of Black gay culture in American culture is quite extensive. This is because race relations in this country have significantly improved.

While race relations are not entirely perfect, Black people today enjoy a much better position than they did in the past.[134] There is considerably more acceptance of Black people and their position in

---

[132] Walcott, R. (2007). Somewhere out there: The new Black queer theory. *Blackness and sexualities*, 16, 29.
[133] Johnson, E. P. (2014). To be young, gifted, and queer: race and sex in the new Black studies. *The Black Scholar*, 44(2), 50-58.
[134] Thernstrom, A. T. A. S. (n.d.). *Black Progress: How far we've come and how far we have to go*. Brookings. https://www.brookings.edu/articles/Black-progress-how-far-weve-come-and-how-far-we-have-to-go/

society, particularly in urban areas, like California in the west and New York in the east. Tragic events like the death of George Floyd have only opened the gates for an increased focus on taking steps to ensure that racism and intolerance are fought at a systematic level.[135]

In general, there is greater recognition of the need to address systematic issues that lead to the initiation of inequality. Such an approach is not entirely novel and has been observed by scholars in the past. In his works, The Philadelphia Negro (1899), and The Negro American Family (1908), W.E.B. DuBois asserted that the problem of race relations could not be resolved without first coming to an understanding. The understanding would have to contextualize the historical, cultural, social, economic, and political forces in play.[136] In part, the presence of racism was not an inherent quality but rather a product of inequality in the system that recognized no color, race, or ethnicity. The "negro" problem, as DuBois put it, was caused by several coinciding factors and elements that fed into the larger problem of racism. These complex systems that gave rise to inequality were based on the perception of the people and the perpetuation of these beliefs.[137] As laws and systems are derived by the people, it was necessary to change not just the system but the minds of the people.[138]

This is why I am writing this book, and this is why I fight every day to raise a standard of equity for all. The "gay" problem in America and around the world goes beyond the religious laws and doctrines that encourage intentional discrimination. Before we can have meaningful dialogue about homophobia, religious dogma, and discriminatory laws, we must contextualize the historical, cultural, social, economic, and political forces at play. Laws and religious dogma are just part of

---

[135] Lambert, D. (2020). *California schools chief launches a campaign against racial bias*. EdSource. https://edsource.org/2020/california-schools-chief-launches-campaign-against-racial-bias/633134

[136] Hunter, M. A. (2013). *Black city makers: how the Philadelphia Negro changed urban America*. Oxford University Press.

[137] Feagin, J. (2013). *Systemic racism: A theory of oppression*. Routledge.

[138] Salter, P. S., Adams, G., & Perez, M. J. (2018). Racism in the structure of everyday worlds: A cultural-psychological perspective. *Current Directions in Psychological Science*, 27(3), 150-155.

the problem but not the source. The source of the problem is people. The Bible tells us to literally stone our disobedient children and to kill married women who commit adultery. You don't see much of that as common practice in America, and that's because our society has collectively rejected those religious rules. American Christians even criticize the small percent of Muslim culture that still practices such harsh atrocities. The only difference between them and us is, we decided not to continue the inhumane practices that come from our religious rule book. Rules don't have true power, people do.

It's so important that we check the sources of our beliefs. You weren't born thinking homosexuality was wrong, you were taught that. White people weren't born thinking Black people grew tales like monkeys, and they were taught that. And how silly they must have felt when they found out it wasn't true. I would imagine it felt like how homophobic people will feel if and when they make it to the pearly gates and see all us gays swimming in milk and honey having a marvelous time.

Humanity is always advancing, slow to advance, but still advancing. We have overcome silly beliefs, harmful practices, and dangerous laws. The only way to truly become harmonious humanity is to push relentlessly toward evolution that surpasses our prejudices. We honestly can't evolve without understanding where we came from. History unexplored is often repeated. That is why I thought it was important to speak to the cultural advancement of Black Americans and follow the story of our perceptional evolution internally and externally.

Since our African ancestors were stolen from their homeland and brought to foreign shores, we have been fighting for our God-given right to be treated as equals. Still today, we fight against narrative and law that allows us to be treated less than. Over the centuries, many internalized the narratives and accepted the laws as the way of life while others rejected the narratives and fought 'til their dying day to dismantle the laws. We are here today because of those freedom fighters. All of society has benefited because of the sacrifice made by those who believed Black people should be treated equally and fairly under the law. They fought against doubt, fear, harassment, lies, hatred, violence, and some of that coming from their own people. They fought for a life that they could only dream about, many not living long enough to see the fruit of their labor. Their fight is no different than my fight as a Black LGBTQIA+ advocate. Every day I fight against doubt, fear, harassment, lies, hatred, violence, and most of that coming from my own people. I am fighting for a life that I might not see. But that doesn't mean I'm going to stop fighting.

The real story of Black America's fight for equality is often mistold, romanticized, or not told at all. It wasn't until the opening of the new National Museum of African American History and Culture in 2016 that America got a national museum dedicated to the full breadth of the Black experience. The fact that it took more than 150 years after Emancipation for this museum to open speaks to Black people's long-standing fight for acknowledgment and respect. Over 400 years of struggle, oppression, pain, mental warfare, abuse, murder, liberation, recognition, achievement, and victory are packed into the 400,000-square-foot museum. I strongly recommend everyone visit the museum in person. The experience from top to bottom is like no other. And what I appreciate most about the museum is that it includes the contributions of Black LGBTQIA+ history makers.

The LGBTQIA+ objects and archival collections at the museum focus on the familiar, untold, and unknown stories that have shaped America. There is no America without the contributions of gay Black Americans – in culture, arts, politics, civil rights, entertainment, medicine, education, and the list could go on. I'm most excited about the museum's mission to promote a greater understanding of

LGBTQIA+ identities and contributions by exploring the lives and artifacts of queer Black people who have changed the course of history. The museum's website is full of Black LGBTQIA+ history that is not taught in our grade schools.

We are entering a phase in American life where accepting the many identities that come with being Black is becoming mainstream. This includes being queer and Black. More and more people are loving our Black queerness and acknowledging our lived experiences. This is different from how the Black queer experience was valued and appreciated in the '70s, '80s, and '90s. This period was one of the most devastating for the LGBTQIA+ community, especially in the Black community. On top of fighting police brutality, discriminatory laws, drugs distributed by the government, gun violence, injustice in the justice system, and poverty, Black queer people had to fight against homophobia at home, all on top of the AIDS crisis.

The normal outlet for refuge during hard times in the Black community is generally the Black Church, but I think we can all conclude why that wasn't a good idea for queer Blacks in the '80s. The only outlet most Black queer people had was a creative expression and using that expression to make safe spaces, fight oppression, and find community. They created art that valued the essence of who they were. They created experiences that allowed for authenticity no matter how it showed up, so long as it was loving and accepting. In the face of great pain and tribulation, Ball culture was established.

Ball culture, also known as House Balls or Drag Balls, represented a variation on the classical fashion show. Ball culture found its roots in necessity and defiance, a key quality that ensured that the oppressed could survive and pave a brighter future for those that came after them.[139]

The amazing documentary *Paris is Burning* gave us great insight into the Black queer experience of the '80s and '90s. The documentary showed how different dimensions of queer life could come together to make families for those who were discarded by society. These families existed in the shadows and underground of society.[140] The expectations and the freedoms afforded by this new art form allowed those discarded from marginalized communities to explore their personality and experiment.

Out of these dark places rose an art form called voguing that transcended cultures. From underground Ballrooms to mainstream television, voguing became a hit in homes across America. Voguing, a highly stylized, modern house dance that includes a sequence of stylish poses, with linear and angular movements that originated in the late '80s but evolved out of the Harlem ballroom scene of the '60s. And much like Black culture, white people loved what was created but didn't love the creator.

This unique and special part of the Black queer culture was stolen, appropriated, and prostituted. Pop-Artists like Madonna and others made money off Black queerness and culture but never acknowledged or valued the lived experiences of the culture. In addition to the dance moves, many of the terms used in modern linguistics, such as "yass queen" or "shade," originated from Ball culture.[141]

I believe today's acceptance and appreciation for Black queer culture in the mainstream isn't because white culture loves us. They mostly love the money they can make from parading us. Black

---

[139] Edgar, E. A. (2011). Xtravaganza!": drag representation and articulation in" RuPaul's Drag Race. *Studies in Popular Culture*, 34(1), 133-146.
[140] Feldman, Z., & Hakim, J. (2020). From Paris is Burning to# dragrace: social media and the celebrification of drag culture. *Celebrity Studies*, 11(4), 386-401.
[141] Green, J. (1993, April 18). *Paris Has Burned*. The New York Times. https://www.nytimes.com/1993/04/18/style/paris-has-burned.html

queerness on TV is a money maker. Black queerness on brands is a money maker. Authenticity is a money maker.

So how do I now take this acceptance and brandishing of Black queer culture and use it for good? How do we use this moment to move a culture? We must change hearts and minds. Sometimes this is done through reasoning and understanding. The Black community is very relational; thus, building relationships and helping people understand their why is important.

I'm going to lay out a very high-level narrative that explains Black progress from Emancipation until now. We'll explore the struggles of being accepted and accepting ourselves and the years of heartache and oppression that have decreased but continue today. I strongly recommend pursuing your own studies on Black evolution. In the past 150 years, we have evolved in ways the previous generations could only imagine. Shall we now continue in the vein of the days of old and oppress our own people because we represent our Blackness differently?

Since Emancipation

Emancipation required that Black people be viewed as equal in both the eyes of the system and of the people that fell under it.[142] The problem for Black Americans after Emancipation was figuring out how in the world do they live as "free men" with absolutely no resources. No land, no housing, no money. In fact, slave owners were paid by the US Government to make up for the lost labor. Money that should have gone to slaves to get them acclimated to society actually went to their slave owners. Slave owners got reparations. Black people were already starting out on unequal footing. Free but not free at all. In fact, many didn't even know they were free. Some slave owners refused to share

---
[142] Achebe, C. (2016). An image of Africa: racism in Conrad's Heart of Darkness. *The Massachusetts Review*, 57(1), 14-27.

the news or let them free. And many slaves had no choice but to stay on the plantations and work for nothing, and it was the only land they knew.

Secondly, Black Americans had to navigate life in a society full of white people that could legally treat them unfairly with no repercussion. How did they go on from there? Three extraordinary Black visionaries offered different solutions to the problem. All of them have different pieces of the puzzle but could not seem to come together on a path forward. This division was used against them to stifle the progress of Black Americans.

Booker T. Washington argued for Black Americans to first improve themselves through education, industrial training, and business ownership. Equal rights would naturally come later, he believed. W. E. B. Du Bois agreed that self-improvement was a good idea but that it should not happen at the expense of giving up immediate full citizenship rights. Du Bois wrote, "We want to be Americans, full-fledged Americans, with all the rights of American citizens." He envisioned the creation of an elite group of educated Black leaders, "The Talented Tenth," who would lead Black Americans in securing equal rights and higher economic standards. Another visionary, Marcus Garvey, believed Black Americans would never be accepted as equals in the United States. He pushed for them to develop their own separate communities or even emigrate back to Africa.[143]

Ultimately to adequately address the issues that existed, change had to come from within and without. Du Bois focused on what to do about white people and the unjust systems they enforced. It is only by winning the war on the hearts and the minds of the decision-makers and/or general population that true change can occur. This applies in

---

[143] *Three Visions for African Americans*. (n.d.). Constitutional Rights Foundation. Retrieved September 10, 2021, from https://www.crf-usa.org/brown-v-board-50th-anniversary/three-visions-for-african-americans.html

practically all cases of systematic oppression, and not just in the United States. While seemingly an obtuse approach, it tackles and underlines many of the key problems that could not be erased by working from the bottom up. For one, the presence of a system can only enforce certain paradigms in a formal setting. Individual, and on a more intimate level, people can still create figurative walls to segregate themselves from what they see as the "other."

Washington focused on Black people and what should be done to equip them for the next phase of life in America. Black Americans had never been free before, most were uneducated, and they were never able to unify as a body, so to collectively advocate for anything at this point was foreign. In addition, any forward motion toward equality was met with life-threatening resistance from white people. There were constant lynching's and riots against Black Americans, sometimes in response to progress, other times just for sport.

This caused many Black leaders to flee to Canada just to have meetings. One of the first major meetings being the Niagara Movement gathering in 1905. A group of prominent Black intellectuals led by W.E.B. Du Bois met in Erie, Ontario, near Niagara Falls, to form an organization calling for civil rights for Black Americans. The meeting forged many relationships and mobilized Black leaders to get organized in America. Eventually, the movement died out but from that initial meeting grew Black fraternities and sororities, associations, and other movements. The first fraternity being Alpha Phi Alpha Fraternity, Inc., founded in 1906, and the first major association being the National Association for the Advancement of Colored People (NAACP), founded in 1909.

The concepts of Washington, Du Bois, and Garvey could not secure the future of Black Americans in the immediate. But their work spawned the era of Black liberation in America. New leaders took the ranks like Martin Luther King Jr., who led strategy to overcome segregation in the South; Thurgood Marshall, who pushed forward legal cases to end segregation; Malcolm X, who advocated for justice by any means necessary; Huey Newton, Bobby Seale and The Black Panthers who started community programs and revolutionized the movement. And the list could go on.

Artists and entertainers also helped in the pursuit of Black liberation. The Harlem Renaissance represented one such movement.[144] The proliferation of Black culture, art, theater, song, and performance led to cultural integration and a representation of the minority.[145] It allowed Black people to express their individuality and contribute to the melting pot of culture that was the United States of America. For some people, this never ended and ties back into how Black people are empowering themselves by decolonizing practices and reclaiming our rightful heritage.[146]

The world can thank trailblazers like Langston Hughes, who made his mark by using his art to show the universal experience of the Black community. Zora Neale Hurston was an author, playwright, and filmmaker who celebrated the culture of the Black rural South. Louis Armstrong is known as one of the founding fathers of jazz who revolutionized the genre. Aaron Douglas, called the "Father of African Art" thanks to his impactful paintings that were shaped by the pillars of the Harlem Renaissance. Countee Cullen, the 15-year-old pastor of Harlem's largest congregation, who explored modern racial injustice using the classical structures associated with white poets. Bessie Smith who became known as the "Empress of the Blues" thanks to her captivating and powerful vocals. Sterling A. Brown, critically acclaimed author and poet, whose writings mused on race and class in

---

[144] Krasner, D. (2016). *A Beautiful Pageant: African American Theatre, Drama and Performance in the Harlem Renaissance*. Springer.
[145] Smethurst, J. (2011). *The African American Roots of Modernism: From Reconstruction to the Harlem Renaissance*. UNC Press Books.
[146] Rabaka, R. (2011). *Hip hop's inheritance: From the Harlem renaissance to the hip hop feminist movement*. Lexington Books.

America. Alice Dunbar Nelson, who was born to mixed-race parents in New Orleans, set the tone for the nuanced take on race, gender, and ethnicity[147]

Lastly, Alain Leroy Locke, who was a major advocate for artists and one of the greatest supporters of the Harlem Renaissance, wanted Black Americans to understand that their contributions to American society and the world were great. Locke's work as an educator and advocate for artists, as well as his published works, all provided inspiration for Black Americans during the Harlem Renaissance. Langston Hughes argued that Locke, Jessie Redmon Fauset, and Charles Spurgeon Johnson should be considered the people "who midwifed the so-called New Negro literature into being.[148]

These artists and so many others paved the way for increased acceptance of Black people and Black culture into the mainstream. And it wasn't an easy feat. Many of them had to travel in secret, were mistreated on the road, and faced sudden death. Some were even arrested for performing for integrated audiences. The progressive normalization of Black culture began to slowly ease the tensions that existed between Blacks and whites.[149] For some, it represented a struggle to gain a foothold in the community. For others, it was a chance to reclaim their individuality and heritage, giving way to reclaiming the history of their people.

Overcoming Negative Cultural Norms and Discriminatory Laws in America

The position enjoyed by Black people today is a huge achievement, akin to a victory after a lengthy conflict or war. Because the truth of our fight and contributions are lost in lack of historical knowledge and

---

[147] Russian, A. (2021, July 27). *9 Key Figures of the Harlem Renaissance*. Biography. https://www.biography.com/news/harlem-renaissance-figures
[148] *5 Influential Leaders of the Harlem Renaissance Movement*. (n.d.). ThoughtCo. Retrieved September 10, 2021, from https://www.thoughtco.com/leaders-of-the-harlem-renaissance-45321
[149] Widener, D. (2010). *Black arts West: culture and struggle in postwar Los Angeles*. Duke University Press.

intentional cover-ups, many don't appreciate our current state. You have mainstream Black rappers who say they don't see racism. Cultural icon Kanye West, said, 'slavery was a choice,' and 'Harriet Tubman didn't actually free slaves.' These people have millions of followers and impact young impressionable minds in such a huge way. The issue is they are judging history from a present state point of view. Not acknowledging all the factors of the past that are no longer present today.

Figures like Fannie Lou Hamer, James Baldwin, Jesse Jackson, Rosa Parks, Bayard Rustin, Al Sharpton, John Lewis, Joseph Beam, Brother Grant-Michael Fitzgerald, Nina Simone, Harry Belafonte, Ella Baker, Marsha P. Johnson, and so many others led Black people in overcoming discrimination and advancing as a people.

Black people were, for a large part of American history, considered to be inferior beings, often treated like animals kept for their labor. Even after the abolishment of slavery, steps were taken to ensure that Black people would still be treated as inferior[150] The infamous Jim Crow laws, enacted on a state and local level, enforced racial segregation.[151] Almost all aspects of society, interaction, and public affairs were influenced in one way or another. The general theme that followed the approach was segregation in every sense of the word. It was meant to establish the supposed superiority of whites over Black people.[152]

Black people were not allowed to use the same public facilities as whites, nor could they walk on the same side of the street. Black people had to degrade themselves and look down as a show of respect; they were not allowed to look white people in the eye.[153] Even their

---

[150] Hannah-Jones, N. (2019). America wasn't a democracy until Black Americans made it one. *The New York Times Magazine*, 14-26.
[151] Tischauser, L. V. (2012). *Jim crow laws*. ABC-CLIO.
[152] Fremon, D. K. (2014). *The Jim Crow laws and racism in United States history*. Enslow Publishing, LLC.
[153] Chafe, W. H., Gavins, R., & Korstad, R. (Eds.). (2011). *Remembering Jim Crow: African Americans tell about life in the segregated South*. The New Press.

movement was restricted, as they were not allowed to be outside after sundown. This greatly hampered their social community; as such, this would place an unfair restriction on their conduct and their ability to form solidarity within their own community. Moreover, the facilities offered to Black people were inferior to the ones offered to whites.[154] More often than not, the utilities or offerings barely passed the minimum for what could be considered acceptable.

Black people were pit against one another, and whenever there was unity, you can believe harm was sure to follow. This division began to be embraced by the Black community. Black publications released articles comparing light skin vs. dark skin, good hair vs. bad hair, the educated negro vs. the ghetto negro. And whenever Black people were successful in building their own communities', terror was soon to follow. We often hear about the Black Wall Street massacre, where thousands of Black people were killed and terrorized just for being successful in Tulsa, Oklahoma. They had their own schools, bank, restaurants, tailors, and the list could go on. All were destroyed because of no other reason than envy and hatred. And this was just one of the hundreds of Black successful communities and businesses destroyed at the hands of hateful white people.

Black people were considered inferior in both body and mind. Thus, it would stand to reason that they were not capable or had the right to enjoy the same quality of life as the white people. Even when Black people were considered as being "human," their representation counted as 3/5th of a person.[155] This legal state applied to all areas, whether it be for voting or eligibility for other services.

This was all permitted not because of evidence or real data that demonstrated that Black people were inferior. These harmful actions

---
[154] Highsmith, A. R., & Erickson, A. T. (2015). Segregation as splitting, segregation as joining: Schools, housing, and the many modes of Jim Crow. *American Journal of Education*, 121(4), 563-595.
[155] Flynn, J., & Jackson, D. (2020). Extraordinary Rule (Three-Fifths Compromise). In *Encyclopedia of Critical Whiteness Studies in Education* (pp. 198-203). Brill Sense.

were permissible because of discriminatory doctrine and narrative that basically said white was right and Black was wrong. Sound familiar? There is no evidence or real data that says being gay is wrong, yet people strongly believe it is. Why? Because of discriminatory doctrine and narrative that says straight is right and gay is wrong.

One of the biggest hurdle Black LGBTQIA+ people had to overcome was the AIDS crisis of the 80s and 90s. White gays were already being treated terribly and disregarded by their own people; can you imagine how Black gay people were treated? HIV and AIDS devastated the Black community and still are. Black men but moreover, Black women contract HIV at higher rates than any other racial group. On the early onset, people were discarded and left to die. Activists did the best they could to mobilized to fight the epidemic, but the task was extremely hard. While activists were fighting for resources, their friends were dying left and right. People literally got sick one day and were gone the next. Because the Black queer community was already discarded, it became hard to get resources to the community and help those who needed them. Imagine being a teen thrown out of your parent's house because you're gay, and you land into a world where an uncontrollable deadly disease is killing people at alarming rates. Many people today are still suffering from the mental trauma of the AIDS crisis. In fact, advocates are still fighting the stigma attached to HIV and AIDS. So many won't get tested because of the stigma. Even still, when I mention I'm gay in non-gay environments, some people still automatically think of HIV and AIDS. Attaching a deadly disease to whom I am as a person further gives you the impetus needed to discard me.

Luckily today, there are so many resources available to help people get tested or help positive people stay healthy. More and more people are willing to talk about their experiences, and the shame of being positive is slowly lifting.

A Change Always Comes

Fortunately, in the modern era, there has been a reversal on many of the conditions from the times of Jim Crow. An example being interracial marriage, which was outlawed in many parts of the country and is now generally tolerated and celebrated in the United States.[156] While there may be opposition to such a movement on a more individual level, systematically, the issue has been virtually resolved. We are even seeing more and more nontraditional families in advertising and marketing to include gay dads and lesbian moms.

As we think about how African slaves were stripped of their heritage and culture, we must recognize and celebrate Black America's ability to freely explore African culture. In fact, one such celebration has become mainstream in America. Maulana Karenga, professor and chairman of Black Studies at California State University, created Kwanzaa in 1966. After the Watts riots in Los Angeles, Dr. Karenga searched for ways to bring Black Americans together as a community. Kwanzaa is a celebration of African American culture that occurs yearly, from December 26 to January 1.[157] It was derived from African harvesting festivals, and is meant to be a modern rendition, a twist and upgrade on the ways of the old while recognizing the changes of the present. The cornerstones or principles that follow this celebration represent strong pillars that helps the Black community sustain itself.

Each of the seven days stands for one quality out of many that are part of the African heritage. Day one celebrates unity. This solidarity applies to all levels of society, whether it be the family, the community, the nation, or the race. The second day celebrates self-

---

[156] Qian, Z., & Lichter, D. T. (2011). Changing patterns of interracial marriage in a multiracial society. *Journal of Marriage and Family*, 73(5), 1065-1084.
[157] Anderson, S. (2010). *Kwanzaa*. ABDO Publishing Company.

determination. Here, the importance of naming and self-discovery is emphasized; one must be able to create and speak for themselves and make their voices known.

The third day stands for collective work and responsibility, calling for people to build a better community for their fellow brothers and sisters. The fourth day celebrates cooperative economics, that is, the establishment of businesses and shops that share their prosperity with each other. The fifth day celebrates purpose, one of improving and developing the community in an effort to restore traditional greatness. The sixth day celebrates creativity, encouraging people to exercise their minds and work towards improvement. The people are supposed to leave their position in a better, more beautiful state than when they arrived. This creates the incentive to paving the way for the future generation, planting the seeds so that the next people can benefit from the labor of the current generation. Finally, the last and seventh day celebrates faith. This faith falls on the people, the community, leaders, and the righteousness of the struggle and victory of the collective.[158]

Black Is the New Black

Integration of practices and lifestyles that were once seen as exclusive to the white community illustrates the normalization of Black people in American culture. You see more and more Black people surfing, exploring nature, taking yoga and pilates, and so much more. The emphasis of this cannot be overstated, as it represents the dissolution of boundaries, both figurative and literal.

For example, yoga, though not a European practice, was seen as an affluent activity that was done by white people. It was associated with leisure and status, in part, because of its association to the "superiority" of white people. It was also seen as demonic and anti-

---

[158] Saba, M., & cha Umoja, K. How to Celebrate Kwanzaa.

Christian by a lot of Black Christian households. Ironically, the practice of yoga is founded and derived from Asian origins. Now, yoga is being widely embraced by Black families who see it as just another part of their life. Instead of being an exclusive and walled of "activity" that was seen as "demonic" or a "white people thing," yoga has been decolonized.

What does this mean for the Black community living within the United States? Two major points can be ascertained; one, that there is now a recognized acclimation of Black culture into the larger collective. That is, Black culture is slowly being recognized as an integral part of the American way of life. There is no American culture without Black culture. In fact, American culture is Black culture. America's personality comes from Black people. What the world marvels about America and often imitates is Black culture. It's been this way since the Renaissance, but Black culture was never credited and always appropriated.

But what this shows us is that being Black, and being American, don't have to be clashing qualities; they can exist side by side without conflict.[159] There is no "going back to Africa." Black people-built America literally and figuratively. This is our country. America could not go 24 hours without an invention or product of Black labor. The country would not survive. Two, Black people recognize the importance of our heritage and embrace our African origins without shame, from within or without. As a result, we can still display our individuality while still participating in the life of the larger collective. It is a balance between being a citizen of a country and belonging to an ethnic group, given reasonable credibility to both aspects without letting one overpower the other.[160]

---

[159] Taylor, Q. (2011). *The Forging of a Black Community: Seattle's Central District from 1870 through the Civil Rights Era*. University of Washington Press.
[160] Meskell, L. (2011). *The nature of heritage: The new South Africa*. John Wiley & Sons.

Black people are more confident than ever when traveling abroad.[161] For one, we have the freedom to move from one place to another without having a fear of being attacked or restricted, as was the case with Jim Crow laws.[162] Increased financial and spending power has enabled us to enjoy aspects of life that would have once been seen as luxuries.[163]

Moreover, certain parts of life, such as therapy, have become a basic necessity for the mental well-being of the Black community. Therapy, traditionally, was seen as something that white people used to talk about their troubles while Black people could only rely on each other to destress. A great example of this is barbershops or other frequently visited spots where Black people would have social gatherings. These hangouts act as venues where Black people could get together, and discuss their problems, confide in one another, and host general discussions about daily matters in their lives.[164] Family therapy was either seen as a foreign concept or something that was too expensive for Black people. There was a general stigma surrounding the idea of going and paying a person to listen to you talk; Black people could do that for free at their hangouts. However, increased education and the dissolution of separating societal walls have helped Black people see that therapy can be incredibly beneficial. It makes total sense when one considers the historical context of what Black people have been through.

The colonial impression that has been imprinted across the generations has left deep marks that can only be solved by consistent and dedicated efforts to heal the wounds of the past.[165] Black families

---

[161] Panayotou, T. (2016). Economic growth and the environment. *The environment in anthropology*, 140-148.
[162] Purnell, B. (2013). *Fighting Jim Crow in the County of Kings: the congress of racial equality in Brooklyn*. University Press of Kentucky.
[163] Cargill, J. (2010). *Trick or Treat: rethinking Black economic empowerment*. Jacana Media.
[164] Akinyela, M. (2002). De-colonizing our lives: Divining a post-colonial therapy. *International Journal of Narrative Therapy & Community Work*, 2002(2), 32.
[165] Wilson, L. L., & Stith, S. M. (1991). Culturally sensitive therapy with Black clients. *Journal of Multicultural Counseling and Development*, 19(1), 32-43.

are embracing therapy, both as a means of healing themselves and their collective community. I also suggest that white people, especially leaders, get therapy to help them recognize and overcome the behaviors, patterns, and belief systems that perpetuate white supremacy. Such an act is important and plays a vital role in decreasing the cycles of violence and injustices that arise out of the heritage of colonization. While the process is no doubt long, the efforts made by the Black community and white allies today will no doubt help future generations avoid the same issues as their parents.

The Evolution of Black Church

The creation of an autonomous Black church marked a major achievement and reflected a figure of freedom for those who were liberated from their chains. The church played an important role in the community, both before and after the Emancipation took place. Prior to the civil war, Black people had two choices when it came to religious congregations.[166] They could hold informal meetings and gatherings away from their owners or go to the church of their slave masters.

In the latter, Blacks would be forced to sit in the rows behind whites, signaling their supposed inferiority to the latter.[167] Both instances were a sign of the degrading position that Black people were subject to at the time; even in faith, they were given a disadvantageous position.

Furthermore, the church of the old held strict views; one had to practice propriety and demonstrate themselves as a "civilized man." Though the church is supposed to be a place where you can come and get fixed up, many were forced to pretend to be perfect. This attitude is likely the result of the mark left behind by the colonial mindset. In

---

[166] Turner, N. M. (2021). BLACK CHRISTIANITY AFTER EMANCIPATION. *A Companion to American Religious History*, 206-222.
[167] Lincoln, C. E., & Mamiya, L. H. (1990). *The Black church in the African American experience*. Duke University Press.

essence, the freedom to be and express oneself genuinely was seen as a mark of savagery and being a primitive being. In line with this "proper" attitude, there was a strictly enforced dress code. One had to dress up in their "Sunday best" if they wished to approach the House of the Lord.[168][169] That former standard still impacts how some Black people show up for church today.

Once Black people were free to move away from the confines of the white church, they were able to express their faith in their own unique way. For one, their animated interaction was no longer suppressed; instead, it was seen as a mark of their passion and dedication. As the church is a major communal point for people, it created a sense of solidarity amongst Blacks. Churches were not just a temple of worship but also housed schools, social events, and even political events.[170] This variable usage of the church represents a bittersweet point. On the one hand, this central location united the community. On the other hand, it showed how social structures and institutions were not yet in place to cater to the unique needs of the Black community.[171]

Though the Black Church found liberation in their own gatherings, they still carried over mindsets from the colonial structure. Women could not wear pants or make-up and had to style their hair in certain ways. Women were also not permitted to speak in church and sometimes had to sit in certain sections.

Men commanded the pulpits of the Black Church while also dominating church power and politics. Women had to find other ways to participate in church life. Women mostly organized missionary societies, social services, and book clubs. Though they weren't

---

[168] Tamney, J. B., & Johnson, S. D. (1998). The popularity of strict churches. *Review of Religious Research*, 209-223.
[169] Dudley, R. L. (2000). *Why our teenagers leave the church: Personal stories from a 10-year study*. Review and Herald Pub Assoc.
[170] Littlefield, M. B. (2005). The Black Church and Community Development and Self-Help: The Next Phase of Social Equality. *Western Journal of Black Studies*, 29(4).
[171] McCray, C. R., Grant, C. M., & Beachum, F. D. (2010). Pedagogy of self-development: The role the Black church can have on African American students. *The Journal of Negro Education*, 233-248.

permitted on pulpits, women fought for suffrage and demanded social reform in whatever other ways possible. They wrote for religious periodicals, like the crusading newspaper reporter Ida B. Wells. They protested racial injustice, lynching, violence and confronted the male-dominated pulpit. In 1920, Nannie Burroughs, who served as the corresponding secretary of the Woman's Convention of the National Baptist Convention, in a major address to the convention, chastised Black ministers:

"We might as well be frank and face the truth. While we have hundreds of superior men in the pulpits, North and South, East and West, the majority of our religious leaders have preached too much Heaven and too little practical Christian living. In many, the spirit of greed, like the horse-leach, is ever crying, "Give me, give me, give me." Does the absorbing task of supplying their personal needs bind leaders to the moral, social and spiritual needs of our people?"

Men, she argued, must welcome women into the affairs of government. Women must organize and educate. "There will be protest against politics in the Church," she predicted but insisted, "It is better to have politics than ignorance."[172]

It's only in the last 50 years that women have been given free rein to found, build, and preach in a Black church. So much has advanced in church culture. The Gospel music we enjoy today would have been blasphemous 40 years ago. In 1983, Dr. Mattie Moss Clark, who was the International President of the Church of God in Christ's music department, was sat down and stripped of her title because of her participation in the 1983 Grammy Awards. Her and her daughters, the Clarke Sisters, gave a rousing performance that had the entire auditorium on their feet. This was a major breakthrough for gospel

---

[172]American Experience. (2019, May 13). *The Black Church*. American Experience | PBS. https://www.pbs.org/wgbh/americanexperience/features/godinamerica-Black-church/

singers. But back at home, the male-dominated leadership of the COGIC Church was not pleased.

Today Bishop John Drew Sheard, who was an executive producer of The Clark Sisters and who's currently the Presiding Bishop in the COGIC church, said the move was a mistake. "Even as Christ followers, we're supposed to be fishers of men, spreading the gospel and not just in the church. So here you had this Black woman, who was this strong and effective and powerful leader in the church," Sheard began. "It's even kind of risky that I say this, but she was more effective than some men in the church."[173] These days, Gospel artists would kill to perform at such a prominent event. This shows the migration of attitude, from one of restriction to one that embraces human values and social interaction.

Gospel music today can also thank the pioneers of freedom of expression dating all the way back to the early 1900s. During the Great Migration, millions of Black people left the South and headed to Northern cities. They brought with them a more emotional style of worship; Southerners imbued churches with a "folk" religious sensibility. The distinctive Southern musical idiom known as "the blues" evolved into gospel music.[174]

Gospel music has certainly evolved over time. In the early 2000s, when I was a Gospel DJ on WANM 90.5FM in Tallahassee, I started playing Gospel Hip-Hop on Friday mornings. The older saints were upset with me. Calling into the station rebuking me and denouncing the music. One time someone called speaking in tongues rebuking the devil. I kindly hung up in Jesus' Name. Every Friday, I had to remind people that, one, this was a college radio station, and two, this was our

---

[173] McKenzie, J. (2020, April 12). *Kierra Sheard Talks Aunjanue Ellis Portraying Mattie Moss Clark In 'The Clark Sisters.'* Essence. https://www.essence.com/feature/aunjanue-ellis-mattie-moss-clark/
[174] American Experience. (2019, May 13). *The Black Church*. American Experience | PBS. https://www.pbs.org/wgbh/americanexperience/features/godinamerica-Black-church/

style of Gospel music. The request lines would blow up with students and young adults requesting to hear the latest Holy Hip-Hop. I knew I was on to something, and I wasn't going to let those who were stuck in the past keep me there.

The one thing that remains constant in mainstream Black Church is the 'don't ask, don't tell rule.' Black LGBTQIA+ people have influenced church culture since Black Church started, especially in the pulpit and music departments. Everyone gossiped about the gay choir director but never said anything. Everyone knew the drummer was sleeping with everyone, but no one said anything. Pastors and evangelists would often preach against homosexuality and promiscuity but rarely called their favorites out. You could be gay so long as you kept it a secret. As long as you were bringing in the money or had the choir hopping, you could be as gay as Billy Porter in Kinky Boots. Just keep your gay life to yourself.

In a dramatic, though non-surprising, twist of irony, many of the pastors that heavily condemn homosexuality have pews filled with the very people they are so quick to dismiss. Or, as in most cases, they are struggling with their identities as well. As a teen, I would speak against homosexuality and promiscuity all the time and preach perfection and holiness. One of my mentors pulled me aside once and said, "son, generally what you preach against the most, you struggle with the most." I kindly shut myself right on up.

I'm so thankful for Black trailblazers like Bishop Yvette Flunder, Rev. Dr. William J. Barber II, Rev. Naomi Washington-Leapheart, Rev. Frederick Davie, Rev. angel Kyodo Williams Sensei, Imam Daayiee Abdullah, Bishop Allyson D. N. Abrams, Rev. Cedric A. Harmon, Bishop Tonyia M. Rawls, Rabbi Sandra Lawson, Rev. Rodney McKenzie, Jr., Rev. MacArthur H. Flournoy, Rev. Verdell A. Wright, Bishop O.C. Allen III, Twiggy Pucci Garçon, Darnell Moore, David Johns and so many others - who I am probably going to get in trouble for not mentioning.

These wonderful humans work every day to make spaces for Love, God, and the LGBTQIA+ community.

Queer, Black, And Woke

Black people have had an increasing role in American politics. Going all the way back, we can thank pioneers like Hiram Revels of Mississippi, the first Black U.S Senator in 1870, Louisiana's Pinckney Benton Stewart Pinchback, the first Black Governor of a US State in 1872, Shirley Chisholm, who was the first Black woman to campaign for the Democratic Party presidential nomination in 1972, Barbara Jordan the first openly gay Black person elected to the Texas Senate in 1966, and the first Black person elected to Congress from Texas in 1972, and former Palm Springs Mayor Ron Oden, the first openly gay Black man elected mayor of an American city in 2003. Efforts and strides by these Black politicians eventually made way for the first Black president of the United States, Barack H. Obama, in 2008.[175]

These reformers also made way for openly Black LGBTQIA+ politicians to take space and be supported. Many of these leaders are my friends or associates, and I could not be prouder. Andrea Jenkins made history in November 2017 by becoming the first openly transgender Black woman elected to public office in America. Malcolm Kenyatta, a North Philadelphia native, became the first openly gay Black man to join the Pennsylvania Statehouse. Lori Lightfoot, a former prosecutor with no experience in elected office, swept all 50 of Chicago's wards in 2019 to become the city's first-ever Black female mayor and its first openly lesbian mayor.

The year 2020 was also the year for the queer politician. So many members of the LGBTQIA+ community took office, breaking glass ceilings and paving equitable paths. New York Congressmen Ritchie Torres and Mondaire Jones made history as the first openly gay Black

---

[175] Marable, M. (2016). *Beyond Black and white: From civil rights to Barack Obama*. Verso Trade.

men to hold positions as members of Congress.

LGBTQIA+ politicians also swept up in statehouses, some in very conservative states. In Florida, Shevrin Jones became the first gay representative in Florida's Senate, while Michele Rayner became the first Black queer woman to win a seat in the Florida legislature.

Jones and Rayner are also joined by Kimberly Jackson, who became the first openly lesbian state senator in Georgia history, and Jabari Brisport, the 3rd-generation Caribbean American who became the first openly gay person of color elected to the New York State Legislature. Mauree Turner broke barriers in Oklahoma's statehouse as the first Muslim in the Oklahoma Legislature and the first nonbinary legislator in America. And not to be outdone, California Gov. Gavin Newsom nominated Judge Martin Jenkins, the first openly gay Black man, to serve on California's Supreme Court.

While there is no presence of a majority within political circles when it comes to openly queer Black people, there is a trend towards increased acceptance. This is in stark contrast to the narrative that is out there concerning support for LGBTQIA+ politicians. Black people are willing to believe that an individual should be judged for their merit and not their sexual orientation.[176] In fact, research shows that Black people supported candidates from marginalized groups, including LGBTQIA+ people, more than their white counterparts in the 2020 election.[177] More Black people supported LGBTQIA+ candidates than ever before.

Long Journey Ahead

Before, being Black anything was like marking yourself as a target.

---

[176] Jones, B. E., & Ferguson, A. (2020). Black and gay: A historical perspective of Black gay men. *Journal of Gay & Lesbian Mental Health*, 24(4), 336-359.
[177] Arceneaux, M. (2020, September 10). *Black Voters Don't Need Lectures, They Need Empathy*. Medium. https://level.medium.com/black-voters-dont-need-lectures-they-need-empathy-313618777486

As a matter of fact, just being Black was a target. If you tried to represent Black people in any political capacity, you were targeted for attacks and assassinations. Black people are no longer afraid to be themselves; we have developed the courage to stand proud and be who we are without an ounce of shame or guilt.[178]

Black people have taken the courage and the power to own their Blackness. We value who we are, what we are, and what we represent as a people and as a collective. Black people are no longer ashamed to claim their race and use this as a cause for celebration instead of grief. We use our position to establish our own rights within the community. We see ourselves as a people and a cause, in and of ourselves, instead of a transition or a stage that has to be passed to reach an ultimate goal of becoming another people. This milestone represents a major cultural shift from colonial times. Before, Blackness was seen as something that had to be gotten rid of if one wanted to join "civilization" and leave their supposed primitive qualities behind.

Black people have broken through a generational brainwashing effort that had us see our own persons as something animal-like or barbarian in nature. People proudly proclaim their Blackness and use it as a point of solidarity. This asserts our position within society and also encourages those who might still be in a colonial mindset to think without such biases in their perceptual framework. Despite the advances that have been made in the last century, America is still a relatively young civilization. It does not yet possess an established history that many European nations enjoy. However, what is unique about America is the large range of diversity one encounters across the states. People have managed to create a balance between retaining their individuality while still being a part of the greater whole.

The United States is unique in this way; it is a melting pot of

---

[178] Reed, A. (2020). State of Pride.

cultures and experiences. Everyone can express themselves and take the chance to learn from others. Few places in the world can offer such a diverse learning experience. However, as the election of Donald Trump as president has shown us, there is still much to be done to repair and unify the country.

Moving towards a more tolerant and accepting America, we must make a place for those who are oppressed and marginalized. We must stand as a people, equal in worth and value. Being anti-racist or anti-whatever is not enough. One has to demonstrate that they are willing to actively fight, protest, and stand against those who seek to establish tyranny and dominance over other people. Good can only prevail when good people are willing to act and fight against evil.

We must all develop a sense of spirituality, regardless of our sex, race, or ethnicity. To be spiritual is to recognize the immaterial qualities and the abstract notions of the values that we hold dear. By thinking in terms of intangibles, we can better define ourselves and think about the values that we want to promote.

Every individual carries within them ideas that want to bloom, emotions that beg to be expressed, and the reality of looking at the world entirely unique to them. Only by getting in touch with our inner selves can we realize who we are as a person. Spirituality can enable us to tear off the shackles that society puts on us. We do not have to go by the rules, notions, and restrictions of other people; we can be free to be who we really are.

The journey we go through shapes us and the perspectives that we hold, which is why mindfulness is so important. Not everyone holds the same values as you do, and I want you to focus on this concept. Think about it every time that you want to make a change within the world. Every conversation or debate you have, think of how the other person does not share the same headspace as you.

If you were in their position, it is likely that you would spout the same bigoted or limited view. Think from their angle, and then consider how you would have preferred someone else approach you when trying to remove your ignorance. I often take myself back to the days when I bashed homosexuals. What was I thinking? What was my motivation? Why was my hate so strong? Contemplating these thoughts help me to reason with those who are still of that mindset. This is the only way that our message of love and tolerance can cross the barriers that people build around themselves.

Lastly, change takes time. No matter how hard we try, we cannot change the minds of everyone we encounter. Progress is made in the hearts and minds of the people, not in the superficial social construct that we employ when interacting with each other. Sometimes, it can happen quickly. Other times, it may require several generations before progress is made. We may not see the fruits of our labor, but we can work to try to ensure that our children will enjoy the love, respect, and acknowledgment that we are so eager to receive.

I'M BLACK, I'M A MINISTER, AND I'M GAY

"Black and Third World people are expected to educate white people as to our humanity. Women are expected to educate men. Lesbians and gay men are expected to educate the heterosexual world. The oppressors maintain their position and evade their responsibility for their own actions. There is a constant drain of energy which might be better used in redefining ourselves and devising realistic scenarios for altering the present and constructing the future."

~ AUDRE LORDE, SISTER OUTSIDER: ESSAYS AND SPEECHES

Chapter 16: Labels – Are They Needed?

Since the dawn of time, humans have used labels to help identify things. It's not because someone woke up one day and said, 'hey, let's start using labels'; it's because our minds can't function without them. Our brains are somewhat lazy. Actually, I take that back; our brains are extremely lazy. We unconsciously process so much information per minute, per hour, per day, that our brains naturally develop mechanisms to help us process information quickly and with minimal effort.

We as humans do not respond to information or experiences the same way or see the world through the same lens, but we all have a similar introductory process to information. Our brains, without conscious thought, look for patterns, makes connections, and categorizes all information that comes our way. It's part of our innate survival techniques. These are mental shortcuts that help us filter the amount of information we process per day. According to the National Science Foundation, an average person has about 12,000 to 60,000 thoughts per day. Of those, 80% are negative, and 95% are repetitive thoughts.

Grouping people based on 'likes': race, gender, politics, etc., is innate within all of us. The part where we insert our individual will is when we decide what to do with the information. Some people will take the differentiating information to create 'us vs. them.' They will side with and prefer elements that are 'like' them and disregard or judge anything that is not 'like' them. And unless we take the extra step to explore our 'likes' and 'biases,' this part of the information process can happen naturally without thought as well.

The unconscious part of the brain processes everything associatively rather than logically or analytically. Associative thinking, 'like vs. like,' is fast and nonlinear. The conscious part of our brain is logical; it's slow, effortful, and unaware that it's being primed by the unconscious part of the brain. Meaning the unconscious part of the brain is telling the conscious part of the brain what to do or how to interpret. 'Stay away from that dog,' 'Guy in a hoodie means danger,' 'Queer equals pervert,' 'The Black one is lying.' There are so many factors that contribute to our unconscious thinking – narrative, experiences, what your momma told you, media, music. It isn't until we face those thoughts that we can change how we interpret that information. We can only expand our minds by confronting our ignorance.

As our minds have grown, so have the words that we use to describe different subjects. As we are in a space where exploring sexuality, gender, and orientation is becoming mainstream, our brains are working to process it all. How do we categorize this new data and interpret these new stimuli and experiences? The process advances the more we learn about ourselves and the environment.[179]

Our discrete thoughts have given way to specialized language, and the latter has given way to recognition and awareness. For example, instead of just seeing blue, words enabled us to identify aquamarine, teal, and azure. As humans, once we realize something, we have to give it a name. In doing so, we recognize its existence, and our linguistics evolve to represent that progression. This is important because language represents a marker for our growth.[180]

Sexuality and gender used to be seen as concepts that existed within the bounds of duality, man vs. woman. While intersex people existed, they were seen as an exception. This exception was used to further fuel support for heteronormative mindsets.[181] The incapability

---

[179] Lieberman, P. (1993). *Uniquely human: The evolution of speech, thought, and selfless behavior.* Harvard University Press.
[180] Harnad, S. (2003). Categorical perception.
[181] Geller, P. L. (2009). Bodyscapes, biology, and heteronormativity. *American Anthropologist,* 111(4), 504-516.

or unwillingness to give intersex humans recognition showed that we were unwilling to move on.[182]

What Does Each Letter of LGBTQIA+ Stand For?

The LGBT terminology started out as a way of increasing inclusion, to broaden what was then as just being "the gay community." As we have started becoming more inclusive, we have begun to recognize and label the nuances that exist between people, their sexuality, and how they express themselves. Therefore, it was only fitting that LGBT is expanded to contain letters that further encapsulated the diverse spectrum. Each letter pointed out another color in the rainbow, allowing us to identify and talk about something that may have been invisible to the general public. Furthermore, the terms gave way for people to use specific words and a means to express what might previously have been ambivalent.

The term "homosexual," coined in 1869 by the Hungarian doctor Karoly Maria Benkert, who wrote under the pseudonym K.M. Kertbeny, was not in popular usage till the early twentieth century. And until the 1990s, "gay" was often used as a shorthand to refer to the entire spectrum of sexual and gender minorities. This usage shifted with the rise of bisexual, transgender, and queer movements, giving birth to the four-letter LGBT initialism, which was seen as more inclusive than broadly referring to the community simply as "gay."[183]

Lesbian

Lesbian can be used as a noun and an adjective. It is the term used to refer to women who are attracted to other women. The term "lesbian" comes from the Greek island of Lesbos, associated with the

---

[182] Ferguson, R. (2000). The nightmares of the heteronormative. *Journal for Cultural Research*, 4(4), 419-444.
[183] Iovannone, J. J. (2019, May 30). *A Brief History of the LGBTQ Initialism - Queer History For the People*. Medium. https://medium.com/queer-history-for-the-people/a-brief-history-of-the-lgbtq-initialism-e89db1cf06e3

poet Sappho, whose surviving writing lyrically describes erotic love and attraction between women.[184]

Gay

Gay can be used on either men or women who are attracted to people of the same sex. It is generally preferred over the term homosexual because of the latter's derogatory coloring. Exceptions can apply to clinical terms or sexual activities.

Bisexual

A bisexual is a person, man or woman attracted to people from more than one gender group. It denotes the increased range of attraction and is not directly tied to having multiple partners.

Transgender

Transgender refers to people who do not identify as the sex they were assigned to at birth. Their gender identity is separate and not a function of their physical, sexual features. A person can be transgender without having sex reassignment. The term "transgender" was forwarded and popularized by activists such as Kate Bornstein, Holly Boswell, Leslie Feinberg, and Riki Wilchins to create a coalition of persons who did not fit neatly into gender binaries or who defied gender norms and expectations, particularly following the 1993 assault and murder of trans man Brandon Teena in Humboldt, Nebraska.[185]

---

[184] Iovannone, J. J. (2019a, May 30). *A Brief History of the LGBTQ Initialism – Queer History For the People*. Medium. https://medium.com/queer-history-for-the-people/a-brief-history-of-the-lgbtq-initialism-e89db1cf06e3

[185] Iovannone, J. J. (2019a, May 30). *A Brief History of the LGBTQ Initialism – Queer History For the People*. Medium. https://medium.com/queer-history-for-the-people/a-brief-history-of-the-lgbtq-initialism-e89db1cf06e3

Queer or Questioning

Queer was initially used as a word to describe strangeness and was used as a pejorative term for gay people. It has been reclaimed by social activists as an all-encompassing term for those who do not fall within the heteronormative paradigm. Questioning is used for people who are ambivalent about their gender identity, sexual identity, and sexual orientation. For many, it can be a transitionary state with experimentation, where the individual tries to figure out who they are.

Intersex

Intersex is a term used for people with physical characteristics (genitalia, chromosomes, gonads, sex hormones) that do not fit the classical definition of being a male or a female. This means they can display properties on either side of the spectrum. Being intersex is also more common than most people realize. It's hard to know exactly how many people are intersex, but estimates suggest that about 1 in 1000 people born in the world are intersex.

Asexual or Ally

Asexual individuals will not experience or will experience a low level of sexual desire. This does not mean they cannot express or display interest in a romantic relationship. People from all orientations or identities can express asexuality.

Allies are individuals who fall within the traditional heteronormative paradigm but believe in social and legal equality for all others.

(Plus) +

Trying to fit such a diverse community that lives outside of the heteronormative experience with one acronym or label is extremely difficult. Every letter of the LGBTQIA+ acronym comes with a different experience. Each letter receives its own level of support and discrimination. The plus represents self-identifying members of the community who are not included in the LGBTQIA acronym. For example, the plus may represent identities such as pansexual, gender fluid, queer, bi-curious, and so many more. The plus is needed and a signifier of inclusion and acceptance for all experiences.

Respecting All of The Letters

To recognize the importance of respecting each letter, one has to look at the philosophical approach behind the idea.[186] Respect here means not just being courteous and polite; that is just the baseline of expectation. Each term has to be recognized for what it represents, a group of people given an identity through the use of language.

Recognizing these qualities is the first step to humanizing a group that has often been ostracized by society at large throughout history. To give them respect is to recognize their humanity. It acknowledges that they, like everyone else, are a human being that deserves a level of dignity that we afford to all within the heterosexual community.[187]

All terms must be given their due or else it would go against the idea of inclusion and universal love. For example, if only one letter were respected, it would represent a scant change from the exclusion mindset that we are trying to depart from in the first place.

As we move towards an atmosphere of love and acceptance, it is my hope that the hate of the past will become a distant memory. However, until such a time that the LGBTQIA+ can become something that is as common as heteronormative paradigms, there will be a need to

---

[186] Sailes, J. Honoring, Respecting, and Supporting LGBTQ Students.
[187] Brown, C., Frohard-Dourlent, H., Wood, B. A., Saewyc, E., Eisenberg, M. E., & Porta, C. M. (2020). "It makes such a difference": An examination of how LGBTQ youth talk about personal gender pronouns. *Journal of the American Association of Nurse Practitioners*, 32(1), 70-80.

continue our efforts to build a truly equitable society.

To that end, it is important that we recognize the humanity in each other and give what is due to those who have been the victims of discrimination.[188] Such an approach realizes and dignifies all peoples and all groups. It is not meant to exclude anyone or even marginalize those who have enjoyed the privilege of acceptance until this point.

Learn More About Lgbtqia+

Learning is a dynamic process; it's not static and will not occur within a vacuum. One has to consider the dynamics of what we know, what we have known, and what will be known in the future. While work might have been done in the past on different sexual and gender identities and gender orientations, there is no time like the present. Developments in modern scientific fields have enabled us to study and learn more about ourselves than ever before.

Published literature from reputable sources is one of the best and easiest ways to reach for pertinent information.[189] However, journals and articles can be quite dry and academic in their tone, something that might be difficult for an average person to read, understand, and then articulate. To that end, a more comfortable way would be to listen to the LGBTQIA+ people in your community.[190]

Social media has given us access to information and spaces that are outside of our normal day to days. Short stories, novels, documentaries, movies, and podcasts by the LGBTQIA+ community also give great insight into unfamiliar spaces. It is vital to give communities you don't understand the space they need to express

---

[188] Sherriff, N. S., Hamilton, W. E., Wigmore, S., & Giambrone, B. L. (2011). "What do you say to them?" investigating and supporting the needs of lesbian, gay, bisexual, trans, and questioning (LGBTQ) young people. *Journal of Community Psychology*, 39(8), 939-955.

[189] Landi, D., Flory, S. B., Safron, C., & Marttinen, R. (2020). LGBTQ Research in physical education: a rising tide?. *Physical Education and Sport Pedagogy*, 25(3), 259-273.

[190] Fox, J., & Ralston, R. (2016). Queer identity online: Informal learning and teaching experiences of LGBTQ individuals on social media. *Computers in Human Behavior*, 65, 635-642.

themselves freely.

Only by understanding the historical context and the personal perspective of the people can you come to terms with who they are. There are several websites that have been built by the community to help newcomers learn the terminologies and definitions. Aside from this, the most direct course of action is to take a course that provides critical insight into the subject.[191]

What Does It Mean to Be Sexually Fluid?

Sexual fluidity is much like the behavior of water; it is not fixed and can change its shape to match that of the container. Similarly, the sexual orientation of a person can grow and mature over time, transitioning from one state to another. For many people, it can also mean they start questioning the reality of who they are, what attracts them in a person, and how this information has a change on their outlook on themselves and their potential partners.[192]

To be sexually fluid is different from being bisexual, where a person affirms their position and is secure in their mindset. A fluid person, on the other hand, is unsure and displays ambivalence. They may display the characteristics of one orientation but then change at a later point in life. This migration from one state to another is at the core of sexual fluidity, something that sets the person in question apart from other letters.

It is entirely possible for anyone to be sexually fluid, as there are no hard and fast rules to how a person can feel about themselves and other people. As we learn more about sexual orientation and further research is carried out, it is likely that more definite concepts about

---

[191] Snapp, S. D., Burdge, H., Licona, A. C., Moody, R. L., & Russell, S. T. (2015). Students' perspectives on LGBTQ-inclusive curriculum. *Equity & Excellence in Education*, 48(2), 249-265.
[192] Garvey, J. C., Matsumura, J. L., Silvis, J. A., Kiemele, R., Eagan, H., & Chowdhury, P. (2018). Sexual borderlands: Exploring outness among bisexual, pansexual, and sexually fluid undergraduate students. *Journal of College Student Development*, 59(6), 666-680.

sexual fluidity will emerge.

Is "Masc" Harming the Gay Community?

Masculinity is a series of qualities that are commonly associated with the traditional aspect of being a man. This means showing resilience, being tough, competitive, suppressing emotions, and not asking for help. It is a sign of the predominantly heteronormative indoctrination that occurs when children are groomed into a specific role based on their cisgender.[193]

Within a homosexual environment, a gay man has to find a reconciliation between what they were taught from birth and the expression of their sexual identity. The desire to be gay but to also be driven to a traditional route of masculinity can place pressures on individuals to be who they are not. In a sense, it ties back to the suppression of the inner self in an attempt to appear as something that society deems to be acceptable.[194]

I think it would be much more beneficial and help the healing process if we were to drop the idea of masculinity as it is drilled into us from birth. The traditional model of thinking is undergoing an evolution, but the influence of the past still casts a shadow on the future. We have to understand the danger that comes with outlining one certain and specific "approved" way to behave and live.

People are not static objects; they cannot be contained by simple stagnant ideas that try to turn into things. When a person limits themselves to be what they think the community wants them to be, they kill a little part of themselves just to fit in.[195]

---

[193] Fleming, P. J., Lee, J. G., & Dworkin, S. L. (2014). "Real Men Don't": constructions of masculinity and inadvertent harm in public health interventions. American journal of public health, 104(6), 1029-1035.

[194] Mankowski, E. S., & Maton, K. I. (2010). A community psychology of men and masculinity: Historical and conceptual review. American Journal of Community Psychology, 45(1), 73-86.

[195] Dunn, P. (2012). Men as Victims: "Victim" Identities, Gay Identities, and Masculinities. Journal of interpersonal violence, 27(17), 3442-3467.

I get it, you like what you like, and there is nothing wrong with that. The issue is how we project what we like. I hear this, and I have said it plenty of times, "I'm gay because I like men, and I want a man who acts like a man." The problem in that statement is not what I liked; it's what I projected. The more and more I get comfortable being gay, the more and more I am shedding toxic thinking. You have to remember that just because I'm out doesn't mean I've stepped into the fullness of what that means. I spent more time as an undercover gay than I have as a loud and proud gay.

I have to actively confront what I was taught about being a man with what it actually means to be a man in my queerness. I had several people tell me when I came out that it was ok that I was gay as long as I didn't start dressing and acting like a girl. At the time, it made sense, and I even accepted it as a statement of endearment. Today, I would confront that notion and challenge the idea of manliness and masculinity. I meet so many guys who proclaim such a strong sense of masculinity but inwardly or secretly want to explore their feminine side. Some let that side out of them through comedy (dressing as a woman), in private with their partner, or just around close friends. Nothing wrong with any of that. But I think the more we normalize the femininity of our masculinity; we'd decrease the hatred and discrimination against feminine men.

I truly applaud the trailblazers who are taking the heat as they work to redefine masculinity. This work will not be accomplished overnight. We've been governed for thousands of years by toxic masculinity. It will take us some time to overcome.

Why Is "Fem" A Bad Word in Many Spaces?

Femininity, like its masculine counterpart, is connected with the traditional ideas of what it means to be a female. Here the qualities in question are sensitivity, gentleness, expression of emotion, warmth, and passivity, to name a few. Since it does not display the sense of domination and competition, it is often perceived as being weaker or inferior to the heteronormative paradigm.[196]

This makes sense if one realizes the historical context of heteronormative spaces that placed importance on the polarity of the genders. People were expected to be different, to think, and fall within the respective circles under which they were categorized. So, it makes sense that leftovers from that backward time have made it into the present. Men have enjoyed a position of domination and superiority over women for the majority of history. While certain exclusions may apply, in general, men have held power, and women have acted in subservient roles. Over time, the qualities of each sex and their position of power become synonymous.[197] There is an erroneous idea that a masculine person cannot be weak or that a feminine person cannot be strong. The real problem lies in the imbalance of power that existed between the genders, something that oppressive structures have desperately tried to maintain.

In this way of thinking, we can also see that power structures within society have the potential to damage more than just the physical well-being of the individual. Over time, an imbalance within the system can warp the minds of the people into hating themselves because of what they are taught.

Since the beginning of human relations, being feminine has been seen as being weaker or inferior. This isn't something the gays started. We have to work extremely hard to overcome the bad behavior and ill-conceived mindsets of our forefathers. The more we normalize the feminine experience, the more we'll be able to decrease the harm that faces people of the fem experience.

---

[196] Lemish, D. (2003). Spice world: Constructing femininity the popular way. *Popular Music & Society*, 26(1), 17-29.
[197] Lips, H. M. (1991). *Women, men, and power*. Mayfield Publishing Co.

Embracing Both Our Masculine and Feminine Nature

The answer to this polarizing concept presented earlier is to embrace and accept the values of both ends of the spectrum. Harmony can only come when a synthesis arises, removing the problematic dual thinking, which gives rise to imbalanced power structures in the first place. We do not say that one type of value is superior to the other. Instead, we say that both have something to offer and should be embraced for what they are instead of what we want them to be.

A man should be able to express sensitivity and communicate his emotions. A woman should be able to stand strong and be competitive without being looked down on as a person. This way, each person would be free to be themselves without having to bend to the expectations from a bygone era.[198]

As we move forward towards an era of progressiveness and tolerance, I think we can take this a step further. Instead of using the binary approach of defining qualities, we should instead use a spectrum. Qualities for the individual would fall on a scale between masculinity or femininity. On this scale, each term can be placed according to the closeness or value system associated with either side.

To remove the association with the older system, it might be better to eliminate the traditional words used entirely. This would provide the benefit of removing the implicit bias that can exist when trying to learn or judge the different values people hold. It is my hope that we will eventually move onto a system that is so divorced from the heteronormative narrative of the past that the problems associated with masculine and feminine qualities will cease to exist.

---

[198] Anderson, E. (2010). *Inclusive masculinity: The changing nature of masculinities.* Routledge.

Do You Need to Know If I'm A Top or Bottom?

I think the only people that need to know if you are top, bottom, or verse are the people you go to bed with. And if you have no idea what those terms are, try a quick google search.

I used to get offended when the straights would ask, are you 'the man or the woman' or are you 'the giver or the taker'? I now chuckle and roll my eyes. To ask what someone does in their bedroom is so rude and uncouth, stop that. And to associate that position with whether I'm the 'man' or 'woman' in the relationship is simply ignorant. I'm a man who is in a relationship with another man. Neither of us is a woman. That's my case. In other people's cases, things may be different. But the overall point is to break the traditional heteronormative structure of relationships, roles, and identities.

The traditional heteronormative ideas of sex and romance have given rise to the idea of power being involved. In older paradigms, the man would be the actor who would establish his sexual will and prowess onto the woman, who would be the subject of his advances.

This has carried forth into sexual positions and the way people engage with each other physically. In many ways, it can highlight the nature of the relationship without being a case of power imbalance; it all depends on the individual and their partner.[199] Some people like to be dominated by a more powerful partner; they like to go with the flow. Others might want to take the steering wheel a few times but want to be taken along for the ride in other instances. None of that has to do with your sexual position.

Sexual positions within a relationship can have as much impact as the partners within the relationship allow. Some might prefer a fixed term or structure, while others would want to periodically switch

---

[199] Ravenhill, J. P., & de Visser, R. O. (2018). "It takes a man to put me on the bottom": Gay men's experiences of masculinity and anal intercourse. *The Journal of Sex Research*, 55(8), 1033-1047.

things up. Much like how personal preference for a partner can vary, so too can the sexual position in a relationship.[200]

As long as the people involved are comfortable with expressing themselves in a way that does not compromise their identity, their versatility, or lack thereof, it should not be a problem. The greater concern should be respect and love for each other. Sexual positions do not define sexual orientation. Those who think in such a manner only place themselves in a self-constructed sexual prison. Instead of focusing on the labels, you should try and focus on who you and your partner are as human beings.

Yes, We Need Labels

Labels are important, but they don't define who we are in totality. They give way to how we are perceived in the world and how the world should interact with us. As much as we don't like it, we can't stop our brains from finding patterns, labeling 'likes,' or categorizing life. It is essential to our survival and making it through our everyday lives. There is simply too much information to process each day. To fight this urge would be akin to saying, 'I don't see color.' You can deny seeing color all you want. Your brain sees color very well. Oppressive systems see color very well. So instead of resisting what is natural, let's embrace it, get ahead of it, and create spaces where our differences are celebrated.

---

[200] Reilly, A. (2016). Top or bottom: a position paper. *Psychology & sexuality*, 7(3), 167-176.

> "Be who you are and say what you feel because those who mind don't matter and those who matter don't mind."
>
> ~ *DR. SEUSS*

Chapter 17: The Journey to Gender

There is still so much about gender that I know nothing about. The difference between me now and me six years ago is that I am willing and open to educate myself. I never fully understood the transgender experience, and because their journey didn't impact me, I was never willing to try and understand. That was until I started down the path of facing my own ignorance and bias.

In 2016, I volunteered at TransCon in Miami, a free conference for the transgender community put on by Aqua Foundation for Women. The conference serves as a space to educate and empower the transgender community as well as allies. While there, I met some of the most amazing people and learned about the harsh struggles of their journey. What impacted me the most was sitting in a session listening to parents of transitioned teens testify about the pain their child endured being in the wrong body.

We cried the entire session. I walked away with a better sense of what it means to be transgender and a greater appreciation for the courage it takes to defy all odds and walk in your truth. It is so important that we try to look at life through as many lenses as possible. The social construct of just male and female must be destroyed to make way for the lived experiences of millions of people.

The Difference Between Gender and Sexuality

Historically, humans have, for the most part, operated on a dualistic or heteronormative approach, which means straight male and female culture only. There was an established paradigm where sex and the circumstances of one's birth defined an individual's fate. Discounting the personal efforts that a person might have employed or used to diverge from the dominant power structure, people's lives were relatively out of their control.[201]

There were exceptions, as always, for queer individuals who managed to do well, but most queer people were forced to conform to the norm or suffer negative consequences. This oppressive power structure was partly due to ignorance and partly an outcome associated with strict traditionalists and conservatives who saw divergence as a threat to their existence.[202] For this reason, research into human sexuality and identity was mostly sparse until modernity, when the shackles of old-world oppression were cast off in favor of individual-focused experimentation and research.[203]

Gender and sex have been used interchangeably for the most part until the 1950s, where each term was given a distinction that set it apart. Sex refers to the physiological features of a human that define them as either male, female, or intersex.[204] These physical features include primary and secondary sexual characteristics, which are used to assign sex at birth. They can be from both internal and external features. However, around 1 in 1000 people are born with features from both sexes, hence the term intersex. Some believe that sex should exist on a spectrum instead of two extremes and a compromise in between.[205]

Gender is a function of cultural and social characteristics assigned to a person that can fall between male, female, and intersex. In essence, it is the norms, roles, and relationships, with differentiation existing between societies. It is subject to change and evolution and can dramatically alter in the right situations.

---

[201] James, R. (2013). Oppression, Privilege, & Aesthetics: The use of the aesthetic in theories of race, gender, and sexuality, and the role of race, gender, and sexuality in philosophical aesthetics. *Philosophy Compass, 8*(2), 101-116.
[202] Smith, B. (1998). The gender of history. *Cambridge/Mass*, 124, 129.
[203] Schwartz, P., & Rutter, V. (1998). *The gender of sexuality*. Rowman & Littlefield Publishers.
[204] Valocchi, S. (2005). Not yet queer enough: The lessons of queer theory for the sociology of gender and sexuality. *Gender & Society, 19*(6), 750-770.
[205] *How common is intersex? | Intersex Society of North America*. (n.d.). Intersex Society of North America. https://isna.org/faq/frequency

For instance, we automatically assign boy's blue and girl's pink. Any divergence from that social construct breeds contempt. Traditional gender roles see men as the breadwinner of the family, while women are assigned the role of the homemaker. Men wear pants and women wear skirts. What I find most fascinating, and I love to use when dismantling gender norms, is that these norms change based on where you are in the world. For example, high heels were initially worn by men belonging to the upper class; they were used while hunting on horseback. Eventually, females started wearing high heels, and their variation became long and thin, while males wore short and flat heels. Today, high heels are predominantly associated with females. In western culture, specifically America, skirts and dresses are associated with females. However, in some Middle Eastern and Asian cultures, men wear dresses or skirts and consider it a part of their masculinity.[206]

From the examples above, we can ascertain that gender is largely a function of how and what people think. The same subject or practice can be interpreted in vastly different ways if one changes the perspective (time, people, culture, and context). Given the subjective nature of the concept, it would be folly to suggest that one perspective is superior to the other. Instead, it would be much more accurate to articulate the variation and the individual meaning derived from such an act.

The Spectrum of Genders

Given the extensive range of derivatives that can exist for gender identities, a spectrum acts as a much more suitable tool to model and label each one instead of a binary paradigm. Each end of the spectrum represents male and female, masculine and feminine. Within this

---

[206] Little, W. (2014, November 6). *Chapter 12. Gender, Sex, and Sexuality – Introduction to Sociology – 1st Canadian Edition*. Pressbooks. https://opentextbc.ca/introductiontosociology/chapter/chapter12-gender-sex-and-sexuality/

range lies an unlimited potential of identities for everyone and every variation. Initially, one might get the expression that such a model is a ridiculous example of pandering to a supposed "progressive agenda." However, given that we know the culture and personal values are highly subject, it would be an injustice to everyone to declare their ideas superior to the other.[207]

A social model has to consider the different types of people that exist, as well as their thinking patterns. In a spectrum, even the tiniest variations in identities can be illustrated. This is an important development because it humanizes people that have largely been ignored or oppressed throughout history.

Additionally, the incorporation of a wider, more inclusive system to model people helps us better understand society and how it functions as a whole. For one, it abandons the restricted and limited model that employed the perspective of one group over the other, decreasing the chances of a bias.[208]

Under a spectrum, a person can mark themselves depending on what they feel best describes them and how they feel about themselves. For example, instead of being masculine or feminine, one can possess traits from both ends of the spectrum. While they may seem quite strange to many people, they already experience this in one way or another without realizing it. Consider the modern working woman with a family. She may wear dresses and be a breadwinner of the family; she may even wear trousers or a suit. In both instances, she defies the gender identity that is traditionally associated with her sex.[209] Such an example illustrates a gender spectrum already exists and applies to most situations. Many people go around seeing others, or even themselves, express their gender on a spectrum without

---

[207] Barker, M. J., & Richards, C. (2015). Further genders. In *The Palgrave handbook of the psychology of sexuality and gender* (pp. 166-182). Palgrave Macmillan, London.
[208] Goulimari, P. (2020). Genders. In *Oxford Research Encyclopedia of Literature*.
[209] Zacarias, M. (2016). Celebrating the full spectrum of genders and abilities. *Guardian (Sydney)*, (1749), 11.

realizing it. The only difference is that now we have a model and a means of giving a name to something that might previously have been ambivalent. For many, it is a chance to finally have specific words they can use to describe their identity in a way that considers their uniqueness. We are no longer limited to using broad non-descriptive terms for people. It liberates people from having to fall into groups they do not belong to by allowing them greater freedom for self-expression.

Gender Identities

The spectrum provides a chance for an endless number of variations to be derived, but it also brings with it several challenges. For one, the increased variation means the dimensions that have to be considered when modeling and studying people have gotten more complex. People cannot fit into boxes and circles - that much is true in nature, but past models did not reflect on this quality.[210] While the previous approach may have offered a simple and easier way of thinking, it represented an injustice to those who were ignored or cast aside because they were not straight identifying.

The march towards a progressive understanding of who a person is might change significantly as more research is conducted. As more people adopt the diversity that comes with the gender identity spectrum, it is likely we will see further development of novel identities that have never been seen in history. The freedom and chance to express individual qualities of the future may render the current ideas and models outdated. Therefore, the current approach should be seen as a transition towards a more holistic model, not an end-all be-all tool.

The following is a list of gender identities with a brief description and insight into each one. These do not represent the full range of

---

[210] Jones, L. (2016). Language and gender identities. *The Routledge handbook of language and identity*, 210-224.

variations. However, an attempt has been made to ensure that the widest range of differentiation is presented to give you an idea of just how diverse gender identity can be.

From this, you can develop an understanding of the thought process that goes behind defining an identity. For this section, you should take notes from the terms and see if you can identify your gender identity. Your identity may not necessarily fall within the given terms. So, before you get started, try to define your core features, traits, and mannerisms and then try to compare them to the information below. For those who are comfortable with their identity, this information may help broaden your horizons by giving you insight into identities you may not have previously known.[211][212] I have been known to influence people to adopt new gender identities by simply introducing them to all the possibilities. This should be fun for you.

Transgender

Transgender is an umbrella term that applies to anyone whose gender identity does not match what sex they were assigned at birth. Transgender people may be uncomfortable with their physical bodies not matching what they think and feel of themselves on the inside.

A baby assigned a female at birth may identify as a male or vice versa. The expression of this inner turmoil can manifest in a number of ways. For example, in a western setting, the male who is trans-female may start wearing dresses or skirts, something that is usually associated with females. Or in many cases, the individual may wish to alter their bodies through surgery or hormone treatment to match better what they think and feel. Transgender does not have to undergo surgery or hormone therapy; they can remain as they are while

---

[211] *Gender Identity.* (n.d.). Teen Talk. https://teentalk.ca/learn-about/gender-identity/
[212] Abrams, M. (2019, December 20). *64 Terms That Describe Gender Identity and Expression.* Healthline. https://www.healthline.com/health/different-genders

identifying as something different from their sex assigned at birth.

Two-Spirit

A two-spirited individual is an idea that is used by the indigenous Native Americans to describe people who manifest qualities that are both masculine and feminine. This means they can take on a role within society that is unrestricted by traditional structure. In line with their mixed traits, their style of dressing may include a mixture of traditionally masculine and feminine articles. Some dress as a male sometimes, and a female as others.

The distinction here lies in focus on the spirit instead of the material body. Native Americans identify more with the immaterial spirit as opposed to the physical traits as the defining feature of a person. The body is seen as a tool that is occupied by spiritual energy. It would be more accurate to state that a two-spirit person adopts a gender identity that is neither male nor female.

Cisgender

Cisgender, also commonly shortened to cis, refers to a person whose sexual identity matches their gender identity. A biological male would identify as a male in terms of gender and would follow the same values, culture, and mindset that are connected to their variation of what a male is supposed to be. In such a case, a cisgender would be following values that might be perceived as being feminine in another culture. Due to this reason, it would be more appropriate to define their masculinity based on what they consider to be masculine. For instance, a man wearing a dress would be considered feminine in American culture while a man wearing a dress in the Middle East or skirt in Scotland is not. Such a case may provide the precedent for an argument that such variations present the case for removing the distinction that creates this confusion in the first place. Recognizing the difference in gender norms and identities between different cultures as masculine leads to substantial confusion. If the same value can be perceived as a complete opposite across different groups, it may be a sign that the original terms are inherently limiting. Therefore, we should seriously start considering the validity of the masculine and feminine labels that we use for different gender roles.

Non-Binary

Non-binary refers to gender identities that are not masculine, feminine, or anywhere in between. The term is used as a way to identify people who do not fall within the paradigm of normally recognized models within society. A non-binary individual may identify as two or more genders, or none at all, depending on how they see, feel, and think about themselves. Non-binary people may represent the next evolution in gender identity that is free from the biases that come with an approach that is heavily focused on sex. In part, a non-binary approach to thinking may lead to the development of identities where sex is just another trait instead of a central defining feature as is commonly used in society today.

Genderqueer

Genderqueer applies to people who can fall within any diverse range between male or female and those that identify as neither. While genderqueer people can be transgender, they may not identify as such. Therefore, a genderqueer identity is different from being transgender. The mentality behind this approach is to challenge the traditional ideas and mindsets that are associated with the spectrum. They rejected the idea of extreme ends being male and female or a variation between the two.

Instead, they employ a completely different variation, one where sex does not play a significant role in defining who they are. In addition, they may use pronouns that are unorthodox and specific to their identity. This is a migration from the usually gendered language that is used on an everyday basis. The pronouns may be gender-neutral or may express an identity that is entirely unique to that one person.

Gender Fluid

Gender fluid is an identity that matches its namesake, that of a liquid that can take the shape of the container that it is put in. A gender fluid person does not restrict themselves to one identity and will change their disposition based on time, setting, context, or other approaches they deem fit. Change is the only constant in how they define themselves; thus, such people can be stated to have two identities. One would be a meta-identity, and the others would be sub-identities adopted over the course of a lifetime. It can act as a way to manage the roles and responsibilities within the variable circumstances of life. Due to their shifting nature, a gender-fluid person may prefer using neutral nouns to address every variation instead of defining themselves as just one identity i.e., they and them versus he or she.

Gender-Neutral

A gender-neutral person may either define themselves as male or female or lacking any bias or disposition towards one side. Such a person does not consider themselves to be masculine or feminine. The term can also apply to all cases where gender is not applicable or is nullified.

God-given right

When we respect the individual, we acknowledge and accept their choices as a function of who they are. We may not see eye to eye on everything, but we should at least have the decency to leave others be to their pursuits.

Normally, this is a difficult concept to grasp for many people. There is this idea that acceptance and respect only apply to certain, specific individuals who fall within the lines of what is allowed. Those who are not within this arbitrary circle are either beaten into submission or are ostracized and shamed.[213] The only problem, in this case, is that those who fall within the acceptance circle also require acceptance and respect to do what they want. Respect and freedom go both ways. We have to start recognizing that people can hold different views without stepping on each other's toes. Respect does not mean giving undue privilege or bowing down at the feet of another individual. It can be as simple as acknowledging their humanity and recognizing their right to express their own values. We are all just different people trying to make our way in the world. Despite our apparent differences, we should see that our own existence hinges on the freedom that some of us are ready to deny others. Acceptance and dignity are essential.

It always amazes me how people are never able to lay out how someone else's gender choices impact their life. What harm does the transgender community pose to you? What harm does the nonbinary community pose to you?

Supporting Those Who Have Transitioned

A part of respecting others is being considerate to their needs. Those who are trying to find or discover who they are often come under intense pressure, both by themselves and society in general. This may not be the case everywhere, but most people are still not adequately educated on gender identity and expression.[214]

When people are belittled, teased, and attacked for the choices they make, it encourages them to suppress their true emotions. To move forward, we have to support and accept that people will try to move in a direction that is more in line with how they think and feel about

---

[213] Riggle, E. D., & Rostosky, S. S. (2011). *A positive view of LGBTQ: Embracing identity and cultivating well-being*. Rowman & Littlefield Publishers.
[214] Koyama, E. (2003). The transfeminist manifesto. *Catching a wave: Reclaiming feminism for the 21st century*, 244-259.

themselves.[215]

Consider the example of your own thoughts and feelings. Think about how you define yourself as a person, and now imagine what it would be like to come under attack. You would certainly not want your thoughts and expressions to be suppressed, censored, or attacked just because some people do not like the way you look and think. Transgender people have a significantly higher rate of suicide than the general population.[216] This happens because they are consistently attacked in the public sphere or are rejected from joining society. As a result, many develop feelings of guilt, shame, and self-loathing.[217]

Accommodating the needs of those who transition is not a novel concept as most people might think. We, as humans, have different needs and desires and want to ensure that they are met. Think about the different mindsets there are for each aspect of life. Some people avoid meat entirely; others abstain from all animal products. This could be for religious purposes or health reasons. You cannot expect to force a vegetarian to eat meat without being called out as a rude and toxic person. In the same regard, we can try to accommodate those who have transitioned by tending to their needs just as we expect others to do the same.

Gender Expression Revolution (He/She/They/Ze/X)

Gender expression within American culture has stirred up quite a shock, especially from conservative communities.[218] There is an idea of communication being a complicated issue because of the

---

[215] Winter, S., Diamond, M., Green, J., Karasic, D., Reed, T., Whittle, S., & Wylie, K. (2016). Transgender people: health at the margins of society. *The Lancet, 388*(10042), 390-400.
[216] McNeil, J., Ellis, S. J., & Eccles, F. J. (2017). Suicide in trans populations: A systematic review of prevalence and correlates. *Psychology of Sexual Orientation and Gender Diversity, 4*(3), 341.
[217] Tebbe, E. A., & Moradi, B. (2016). Suicide risk in trans populations: An application of minority stress theory. *Journal of Counseling Psychology, 63*(5), 520.
[218] Drescher, J. (2014). Gender identity diagnoses: History and controversies. In *Gender dysphoria and disorders of sex development* (pp. 137-150). Springer, Boston, MA.

potentially enormous amounts of words that may be involved in the conversation. People might say that using the "he/she" traditional paradigm is pragmatic and should not be changed.[219] The argument presented is that they will be unable to talk to other people without first having to check their pronouns; that it would be impractical in daily life.

However, this point is countered with the concept of names. There are literally thousands upon thousands of names in the world, some more common than others. Yet, we still take the time to ask each other what our names are and then use those terms to refer to the individual in question. No one seems to raise an objection that we should simply do away with names because it would mean asking people what they want to be called. Names are an important part of the identity people hold, they define who they are, yet the same standard is not applied to pronouns. The debate on pronouns is something that has just started, and there is a long way to go. Still, starting a conversation has initiated the process, and we will learn more as we go along.[220]

---

[219] Snedecor, R. (2021). Gender Expression. *Encyclopedia of Sex and Sexuality: Understanding Biology, Psychology, and Culture*, 45(2-4), 271.

[220] Borza, N. (2021). Why shall I call you ze?. *Linguistik online*, 106(1), 19-45.

I'M BLACK, I'M A MINISTER, AND I'M GAY

"I am proud, that I found the courage to deal the initial blow to the hydra of public contempt."

~ KARL HEINRICH ULRICHS

Chapter 18: Black Rights is Gay Rights

The Fight for Freedom and Black Rights

We have been fighting for freedom and struggling to attain an equal standing with those in power ever since we were forcefully brought to the continent. As expounded on earlier in the chapter, my ancestors were seen as primitive people, a piece of property much like machinery. Our bodies were forcefully bound and then made to work in different positions. Most of my people labored on farms and were treated no better than tools to be used and disposed of. In fact, I might argue that even tools were given better treatment than my people. A tool receives regular maintenance and care; it is oiled to protect it from rust and is sharpened when dull. My people had no such luxury. We were given just as much food as necessary to keep us alive and slaving away in the cotton fields.

We had to struggle to survive. Still, even within that rough and Hellish climate, my people managed to create a sense of solidarity; the pain bonded us together. We were united in our suffering, and that only gave us the strength we needed to break away from our bonds and cry out for freedom.[221] Black people were fighting for their liberty long before American mainstream politics got involved and started tackling the issue. Long before the civil war, my people stood united against the tyranny of those in privileged positions of power. It wasn't that long ago that we were seen as nothing more than cattle for the industrial complex.[222] When President Abraham Lincoln brought forth the idea of a united America where everyone would be a citizen, we flocked to support the movement. The tree of freedom and liberty that modern Americans enjoy has been watered by the blood of my

---

[221] Morris, A. D. (1986). *The origins of the civil rights movement*. Simon and Schuster.
[222] Hall, J. D. (2007). The long civil rights movement and the political uses of the past. In *The Best American History Essays 2007* (pp. 235-271). Palgrave Macmillan, New York.

ancestors. An untold amount of my people gave their lives to ensure that future generations would not face the same horrors.[223] The war ended, and America was finally united. However, we were stabbed in the back and were still treated as inferior people. In the end, we were used for the goals of a united America, but our needs were tossed aside the minute our usefulness ended.

It was only people like Harriet Tubman, W.E.B. Dubois, Malcolm X, Ida B. Wells, and Dr. Martin Luther King Jr. who saw that we needed to roll up our sleeves and get things done for ourselves. We marched on the streets that we died for and were pelted as enemies of the people.[224] The land and the people we fought for were hostile to us. My ancestors were in danger of getting lynched by the very people they died to protect; talk about gratitude.

That's all in the past, though, right? Wrong, my people are still under attack today and live in fear for their lives. We represent the group that has the highest incarceration rates. We die quicker and suffer from more health complications than the white majority population. Being Black in America comes with the privilege of being shot like an animal in the street. The police see us as inherent criminals.[225] What's more, many of us have been so brainwashed that we start believing all the negative garbage and start to behave in the same manner. The fight for freedom and Black rights is a present struggle that still has a long way to go.

The Fight for Gay Rights in America

The fight for gay rights in America is an even more recent story than that of slavery. As early back as the previous century, homosexuality was seen as gross indecency and a violation of natural

---

[223] McPherson, J. M. (1992). *Abraham Lincoln and the second American revolution.* Oxford University Press.
[224] Jackson, T. F. (2013). *From civil rights to human rights: Martin Luther King, Jr., and the struggle for economic justice.* University of Pennsylvania Press.
[225] Cunneen, C. (2006). Racism, discrimination and the over-representation of Indigenous people in the criminal justice system: Some conceptual and explanatory issues. *Current issues in criminal justice, 17*(3), 329-346.

law. You can go on YouTube right now and search for material from as recently as the 50s that condemns gay people. These campaigns portrayed gay behavior as a mental illness, a disorder of the mind that had to be corrected and fixed.

Gay people were seen as a blight in the community at worst or a sick group who needed to be fixed at best.[226] In fact, many insults and derogatory terms were derived from accusing someone of being gay. Even in modern America, it is common to hear people use words like faggot, homo, and queer to refer to things they find unsavory. It shows that we have still not moved past seeing gayness as something bad and inherently evil.[227]

Gay rights and the fight to secure a future for those who were queer in America began in the early parts of the 20th century. The Society for Human Rights, created by Henry Gerber, is the oldest recorded institute that was made to represent the interests of the gay community. However, attitudes at the time were so intolerant that even having a discussion on the subject was tantamount to endorsing the lifestyle.[228] People seemed to view gayness as a disease, something that could be caught, or something that human rights organizations were trying to peddle to the masses. Unfortunately, the institute was closed due to social pressure.

The work Sexual Behavior in the Human Male by Alfred Kinsey (1948) illustrated the presence of homosexual behavior in men aside from those who identified as being gay. This offered the notion that one could demonstrate attraction to or an inclination for same-sex

---

[226] Clendinen, D., & Nagourney, A. (2001). *Out for good: The struggle to build a gay rights movement in America.* Simon and Schuster.
[227] Carnaghi, A., & Maass, A. (2008). Derogatory language in intergroup context: Are "gay" and "fag" synonymous. *Stereotype Dynamics: Language-based approaches to the formation, maintenance, and transformation of stereotypes*, 117-134.
[228] Kepner, J., Murray, S. O., & Bullough, V. (2002). Henry Gerber (1895-1972): Grandfather of the American gay movement. *Before Stonewall: activists for gay and lesbian rights in historical context*, 24-34.

relations without being inherently homosexual.[229] Think back to the gender identities presented in the previous chapter; literature like this supported the modern concepts that we might take for granted today. In the 50s, Harry Hay founded the next organization that would advocate for gay rights. The aim was to change the attitude and perceptions of the majority into accepting homosexuality as part of everyday society. It is quite telling that there needed to be an effort by a group of people just to have the population see gay individuals as human beings with dignity and thus deserving of respect.

However, in 1952, the American Psychiatric Association would classify homosexuality as a mental illness in their publication of the Diagnostic and Statistical Manual of Mental Disorders. Still, the effect of this move was quite dampened because of changing progressive attitudes that began to question the basis of seeing homosexuality as an illness. It marked a change in public perception but showed officially; homosexuality was still seen as a wrong to be corrected.[230]

The next year, Eisenhower would use his power to pass Executive Order 10450.[231] Homosexuals were barred from working in the federal government and were considered as having a mental affliction that increased the security risk they posed. Homosexuality was compared to being an alcoholic or a mentally disturbed individual.

The first time the American government voted in favor of homosexuals was in the 1958 case of One, Inc. v. Olesen.[232] Here, the publication was granted the protection of the first amendment in its right to publish material that was deemed as being obscene and immoral by the postal service. The next year, Illinois would become the first state to decriminalize homosexuality.

---

[229] Sorenson, G. (1948). Sexual Behavior in the Human Male by Alfred Kinsey, Wardell E. Pomeroy, Clyde E. Martin (Book Review). *Humanist, 8*, 128.
[230] Drescher, J. (2015). Out of DSM: Depathologizing homosexuality. *Behavioral Sciences, 5(4)*, 565-575.
[231] Eisenhower, D. D. (1953). Executive Order 10450. *Security Requirements for Government Employment.*
[232] Hermann, D. H. BOOK REVIEW HOMOSEXUALITY AND THE HIGH COURT.

The fight and awareness of gay rights took off in the 70s and 80s. People were becoming increasingly aware of the bigoted nature of the perception that was previously employed on homosexual individuals.[233] As the AIDS epidemic raged, there was a dramatic shift in culture. Instead of blaming gay people, there was increased pressure on the government to recognize the impact it was having on the gay community. Groups like ACT UP (The AIDS Coalition to Unleash power) played an important part in pushing for public education of AIDS, which was previously seen as a disease confined to the gay community.[234]

In 1993, the Department of Defense issued a directive that turned a blind eye to the homosexual individual in service so long as they abstained from revealing their sexual orientation. The Don't Ask, Don't Tell policy was a sign that the government was willing to overlook gay people so long as they were willing to serve their country. Still, this repression of sexuality showed that open acceptance was still seen as a major issue. It wasn't until 2015 that this act would be repealed,[235] and individuals would be free to express their identity without fear of reprisal. In the same year, in a decision on Obergefell v. Hodges, gay marriage would become legalized in all 50 states in America.[236]

The struggle for gay rights is not a distant memory. It was only six years ago that gay marriage was legalized in all states. This is not a wartime story that old people tell their grandchildren, it's recent, and the wounds are still raw; the process of healing is still underway. So, when people tell me that the fight for gay rights is over in America, I wanted to remind them that gay people only recently got the right to

---

[233] Reif, S. S., Whetten, K., Wilson, E. R., McAllaster, C., Pence, B. W., Legrand, S., & Gong, W. (2014). HIV/AIDS in the Southern USA: a disproportionate epidemic. *AIDS care*, 26(3), 351-359.
[234] Stockdill, B. C. (2013). ACT UP (AIDS Coalition to Unleash Power). *The Wiley-Blackwell Encyclopedia of Social and Political Movements*.
[235] Goldbach, J. T., & Castro, C. A. (2016). Lesbian, gay, bisexual, and transgender (LGBT) service members: Life after don't ask, don't tell. *Current Psychiatry Reports*, 18(6), 56.
[236] Yoshino, K. (2015). A New Birth of Freedom?: Obergefell v. Hodges. *Harv. L. Rev.*, 129, 147.

a civil union that was enjoyed by heterosexuals for most of human history.

People suffered and had their souls stripped in an effort to fight for the rights that we enjoy today. Marsha P. Johnson was a Black transwoman who was a prominent figure in the gay revolution in the Stonewall uprising in New York.[237] Police raids were still common at the time, but the queer community fought back and demanded equal rights in the face of persecution, jail time, and possible chance of being killed in the process. Even today, trans-Black people are killed and abused at disproportionate rates. The mental stress of living in such a world also causes a spike in the suicide rating, which is significantly higher than average against other groups.[238]

The Unique Challenges People Like Me Face

As a proud gay Black American, I have been subject to a lot of problems and hurdles in my effort to gain an equal standing to society. I suffered on multiple levels or layers of oppression brought upon me due to the way my status is seen by society. I am Black, which puts me in a bracket lower than the white majority. I am gay, which pushes me further down the line. The only level missing would be if I were to become transgender. They are at the bottom of the poll. People like me experience life in a completely different way. A typical heterosexual person is never going to know the pain and suffering that people like me go through. I'm discriminated against by white people for being Black and discriminated against by Black people for being gay.

My people, meaning queer Black people, have been so oppressed in the past that the wounds still linger in those who are born today. While there has been much progress and change the impact of systemic

---

[237] Jenkins, A. (2019). Power to the People: The Stonewall Revolution. *QED: A Journal in GLBTQ Worldmaking*, 6(2), 63-68.
[238] Narang, P., Sarai, S. K., Aldrin, S., & Lippmann, S. (2018). Suicide Among Transgender and Gender-Nonconforming People. *The primary care companion for CNS disorders*, 20(3).

actions against my people still exists. While tolerance is rising, there is still a mindset of bigotry and exclusion in society, even if they may not be aware of these biases. As a masculine identifying Black gay man, I can most times go out in public and be fine. But my transgender or extremely queer friends and family still must be extremely guarded in public places. Our challenge lies in getting people to see past our sexual identity, orientation, gender, and the color of our skin to the person underneath. Most don't realize that there is more to queer people than appears on the surface; we are not only who we look like or who we find attractive. Inside us, there is a huge and complex web of interests, thoughts, feelings, hope, and aspirations, just like any other person.

Fighting For Rights as A Black Man and A Gay Man

I have to clarify that being Black and being gay are parts of my identity that are as closely tied together as my skin and its color. Gay rights are human rights, and Black rights are human rights. When we fight for equality, we do not want one side to have an advantage over the other. Instead, we want a playing field where individuals can exercise their liberty without being burdened by bias and prejudice. The fights for Black rights, gay rights, and Trans rights all translate into fighting for the rights of humanity. It does not mean that we are giving preference to one over the other; we want everyone to enjoy the freedom to be themselves.

There has been a debate going on between #Blacklivesmatter and #allBlacklivesmatter. The point is that even in the Black community, there is discrimination against queer Black people. Remember when I talked about the layers of oppression? The same concept applies here. Sadly, many Black people fail to realize they are only perpetuating the violence that was done on them by a group of weaker people. They cannot punch up because they fear retaliation, so they choose to punch down. I'm not saying they are as bad as the original instigators, but they are playing into the process that also entraps them into the cycle of suffering and pain.

Queer people, especially queer Black people, have to stand up to all communities, and yes, even the Black community, and declare that we have just as much a right to liberty as anyone else. We have bled and died for this country, and we are not anymore lower than the Black or white majority. This is a fight for justice and equality, and it cannot succeed unless we pull our heads out of the sand and become united as a people. Black or gay, it does not matter; we are all human beings who deserve dignity and respect.

My Hopes for The Future

It is my sincere hope that we can pave a path for a brighter future where our children will not have to face the same sufferings as we do in the present. Just as my ancestors laid down their lives to pave the way for us, we must continue to struggle and fight for our descendants. The efforts of the people in the past have shown just how much society can change if one is willing to act and bring about that change. By acting now, we will be influencing the future and creating the history of tomorrow.

I just want my people and the queer community to be part of the circle, where people accept you for who you are instead of punishing you. I want people to live in a society where differences between us are embraced, accepted, and celebrated instead of being a cause for polarity and fighting. The violence has to stop, and unless we can find a way to stand united, the cycle of violence and oppression will continue.

Black Queer Pioneers

I would like to dedicate this section to a notable list of Black queer pioneers who deserve some recognition for the work they have done. They all play or have played a part in the struggle for the freedoms and liberties that we enjoy today. This list does not nearly represent all Black queer pioneers, and neither is it my job to teach you about all of them. Online search engines and libraries are available for further discovery. It is my hope that this will help you understand and realize the importance of doing your part. Maybe some of you will become inspired and will have a place in the history books of the future.

Gladys Bentley (1907-1960)

Bentley started out defying the gender norms of her time by wearing her brother's clothes. She would eventually be ostracized by society at large, being the target of bullying for acting unladylike. Her parents would try to fix her supposed via a doctor. She would end up running away at the age of 16. She started her career as a popular musician, still faced hurdles because of being openly lesbian. She would be forced to act as if she was treated during the McCarthy era of Communist fears. Despite the continual opposition, she stood proudly breaking barriers paving the way for the lesbian community. She later developed pneumonia and died at the age of 52.

Bayard Rustin (1912-1987)

Rustin is one of the less well-known Black rights activists. He played an important part in the movement of Dr. Martin Luther King Jr. by helping him develop his idea of non-violent resistance. He mentored Dr. King and so many others. He was a gay man who initially tried to keep his sexuality from the public but made no effort to hide it once he was outed. Many people didn't like that a gay man was so close to Dr. King. Rustin's sexuality was weaponized many times.

Rustin's esteemed mentor A. Phillip Randolph, King, and Rustin had begun arrangements to march at the Democratic National

Convention of presidential candidate John F. Kennedy and his running mate Lyndon B. Johnson in Los Angeles, protesting the party's weak position on civil rights. The Democratic leadership sent a Black Congressman, Adam Clayton Powell, to stop the march before it happened.

Powell sent an intermediary to threaten King, telling him that if they proceeded with the march, he would accuse King of having an affair with Rustin, not only killing the march but also dealing a possibly fatal blow to the movement as a whole.

After consulting with his colleagues and advisors, King decided to distance himself from Rustin. Rustin's reluctant resignation from the Southern Christian Leadership Conference marked one of few times that King lost a battle to fear. The politics of the movement and the weaponization of Rustin's sexuality would not stop him. He was a big player in the civil rights movement, helping anyone who was facing oppression, including the Japanese Americans. His involvement would play a large part in victory through non-violent means. He died at the age of 75.

Stormé DeLarverie (1920-2014)

DeLarveire was a masculine identifying lesbian, something that was uncommon in her day. Like many others of her disposition, she was involved in the entertainment industry and worked as a host and a performer in the Radio City Music Hall and the Apollo Theater. Aside from this, her career also included working as a protective hen mother of the lesbians. She was part of the Stonewall riots, fighting for the rights of people who had no one else standing up for them; it was about solidarity. Wearing masculine clothes, she often came across as being androgynous. She passed away in her sleep at the age of 93.

James Baldwin (1924-1987)

Baldwin was a writer and used his novels, essays, and poems to express ideas that so many people could not digest. His eloquence with words helped bridge the gap between the majority of the queer community. Baldwin could present ideas and develop a sense of empathy in the readers, making them see the blight that was upon the queer community. He also used his works to express his own confusion and struggles with his spiritual, sexual, and racial identities. He would pass away in France at the age of 63.

Alvin Ailey (1931-1989)

Ailey was a dancer and a choreographer who used rhythm and movement to give expression to his thoughts and feelings. He founded the Alvin Ailey American Dance Theater (AAADT), a body meant to help Black people express their identity and thoughts through the art of dance. His work in the ballet circles is recognized as being revolutionary, being some of the best in the world. However, he was harassed by government agencies for being a "sexual deviant" that defied normal social convention. His company was threatened with bankruptcy if he ever displayed signs of being gay, or in other words, himself. He passed away in 1989 at the age of 58.

Audre Lorde (1934-1992)

Lorde was a writer and a feminist that fought to ensure that women had equal standing to men in society. In her words, she was a "Black, lesbian, mother, warrior, poet." Her work, both personal and professional, was meant to tackle the racism and injustice that existed in society. She did not shy away from sensitive issues and talked through her poems and prose. Her flowery language portrayed the hatred and hardship that were a part of the life of oppressed groups. She also provided possible solutions to most of the problems she wrote about. She passed away at 58.

Ernestine Eckstein (1941-1992)

Eckstein was a notable figure who was the head of a branch of Daughters of Bilitis (DOB). She helped the oppressed take their voices to the streets and make the public hear what they had to say through the power of protests. She used a pseudonym in her works to remain incognito in circles where her life could be in danger due to her deviation from the norm. She helped many people give voice to their feelings and contributed to the empowerment of the oppressed by pushing them to demand their right to be heard. To her, demonstrations and the people within them were critical to changing the status quo. She died in 1992 at the age of 51.

Archbishop Carl Bean (1944 -2021)

Archbishop Bean was an American singer and activist who was the founding prelate of the Unity Fellowship Church Movement, a liberal protestant denomination that is particularly welcoming of LGBTQ African Americans. Before founding the first church of the denomination in 1975, Archbishop Bean was a Motown and disco singer, noted particularly for his version of the early gay liberation song "I Was Born This Way". In 1982, Bean became an activist, working on behalf of people with AIDS. Under Bean's leadership, Minority AIDS Project was born as the main outreach ministry of Unity Fellowship of Christ Church. MAP remains the first non-profit, community service agency founded and managed by people of color to educate and serve communities of color who continue to be disproportionately infected and affected by the HIV/AIDS virus. Bean's autobiography, I Was Born This Way, came out in 2010. He was the inspiration for Lady Gaga's "Born This Way". He died at the age of 77.

Miss Major Griffin-Gracy (1940)

Griffin is a trans woman leading the fight for the rights of the transgender community. Her work highlighted the biased treatment of transgender individuals, showing that they were disproportionately imprisoned compared to other groups. She has faced a lot of cruelty and discrimination from peers because she deviated from the norm. She continues her work to this day, despite facing strong opposition.

Phill Wilson (1956)

Wilson is a big part of the movement to address the problem of HIV/AIDS. He founded the Black HIV AIDS institute in 1999 when moved by the death of his partner from the disease and his own diagnosis of HIV. His efforts have led to increased awareness about the disease; it is no longer thought of as being exclusive to the gay community. President Obama would appoint him as part of the advisory council on HIV/AIDS. His work promotes HIV testing, prevention, and treatment so that people can be saved from the same fate as his partner.

Willi Ninja (1961-2006)

Ninja is best known for his part in the *Paris is Burning* documentary. Like so many other people, he used to dance and rhythm to express himself and the queer community. He developed his own unique approach, helping develop the idea of voguing and other unique performance styles. His work and dance style would go on to influence people like Michael Jackson and Madonna. He passed at the age of 45.

Ru Paul (1960)

Paul is a multitalented drag queen who is a songwriter, singer, actor, model, and television personality. He is, by most accounts, one of the most popular and successful drag queens in the entire world. He has used his exposure and position within the media to introduce queer material. This serves to normalize concepts that the public might see as being deviant or off-putting. He is an activist working through media and entertainment to bring his message to the people.

Bishop Yvette A. Flunder (1955)

Bishop Flunder is a womanist, pastor, activist, and singer from San Francisco, CA. She is the senior pastor of the City of Refuge United Church of Christ in Oakland, California, and Presiding Bishop of The Fellowship of Affirming Ministries. In 1986, Flunder was moved to minister to people with HIV/AIDS in response to the epidemic of the 1980s. She founded several not-for-profits providing services for people affected by HIV: Hazard-Ashley House, Walker House, and Restoration House, through the Ark of Refuge, Inc., which later became the Y. A. Flunder Foundation.

Alphonso David (1970)

David is an attorney by profession and works within the queer community as a civil rights leader. His increased familiarity with the law allows him to legally represent and fight for those who are in a vulnerable position in society from the start. He has represented queer clients in cases that deal with specific issues that are unique to their circles. Through the power of law, he has ensured that no one goes without a legal representative, even those who have been rejected by the majority.

Darnell Moore (1976)

I met Darnell on a Summit cruise ship conference headed to the Bahamas just after Trump was elected president. I was distraught and overwhelmed by the election results. Being in Darnell's company was what I needed. I had been an admirer from the sidelines for a minute and had no clue I'd get to spend the weekend with him and so many other phenomenal freedom fighters. My mentor sent me an article written by Darnell that outlined his faith and sexuality. It was that article and watching its impact that gave me the courage to continue telling my story.

Darnell is a writer and an activist working on presenting pieces and social commentary meant to combat racism, sexism, and colonialism. He has appeared in different renowned publications and has used the power of written language to communicate complex ideas in an easy-to-understand manner. He was a part of the LGBT Concerns Advisory Commission in Newark. He has worked both within public and private circles to ensure the message of peace and tolerance regarding Black and LGBTQIA+ struggle is something on everyone's mind.

David J. Johns

David is executive director of the National Black Justice Coalition. He is the former executive director of the Obama White House Initiative on Educational Excellence for African Americans. David is known for his passion, public policy acumen and fierce advocacy for youth. He is an enthusiast about equity—leveraging his time, talent and treasures to address the needs of individuals and communities often neglected and ignored. A recognized thought leader and social justice champion, David's career has focused on improving life outcomes and opportunities for Black people.

Zaya Wade (2007)

Wade is a Black transgender youth who is only 13 at the time of this writing. She is the daughter of Dwayne Wade, a successful NBA player and media personality. She came out as transgender at the age of 11 and has been strongly supported by her family, especially her stepmom accomplished actress Gabriel Union. She represents the progress that we have made in our struggle to let people be who they are instead of letting others mold their personalities. She is the voice of young queer people and I hope she continues to influence the masses to love and accept themselves.

Tiq Milan

After I came out in 2015, I was invited to a JUST Faith conference put on by the National LGBTQ Taskforce. It was there that I would be introduced to the powerhouse advocate Tiq Milan. Tiq would be the first Black trans-male I'd ever meet and build a connection with. It was so refreshing to learn about his experience. Tiq is currently a spokesperson for GLAAD (Gay & Lesbian Alliance Against Defamation), is a public speaker, writer, activist, and media consultant. He acts as a mentor and teacher to the LGBTQIA+ community, helping young people find their way in life. His national campaign Live Out Loud's Homecoming Project has helped countless individuals in the last ten years. He helped others educate themselves on HIV prevention, the practice of safe sex, and the promotion of building healthy relationships.

Brian Michael Smith (1983)

Smith is a Black trans actor best known for the outstanding performances of television shows and the work he has done for trans representation in the media. His major work in Queen Sugar made him popular and gave him a post to broadcast his view onto the world. Like others before him, he passes on the knowledge and experience of his art by teaching and mentoring the next generation of youths. He has extensively participated in talks and conversations to bring key elements about the trans and queer experience into mainstream dialogue.

Big Freedia (1978)

Freedia is a rapper and focuses on hip-hop, creating her own blend of bounce music. She identifies as a gay man but prefers to use she/her nouns. She has appeared in films and has an accomplished discography. Using the power of music and motion, she reaches out to young people, especially those who have been ostracized by society at large.

Michael Sam (1990)

Sam is a professional football player who has publicly come out as gay. Since coming out, he has faced problems with his career and even discrimination from his fellow players who refused to shower with him. This shows that even in the modern world, there are intolerant people willing to ruin the career of a young man just because he's different. Sam has worked with and supported activists fighting for queer rights.

Jason Collins (1978)

Collins is a former basketball player who also came out as being openly gay. He received widespread support and praise for coming out from the public, including Barack Obama, Michelle Obama, and even Hillary Clinton. He presents a slow trend of famous personalities coming out of their shell and showing themselves without the mask of PR.

Billy Porter (1969)

My friend invited me to a GLAAD event in New York City. All the big names in the LGBTQIA+ space generally attend these events and this one was no different, except I didn't pack any gala attire. Did I mention my friend invited me 30 minutes after the event started? One of her table guests cancelled at the last minute and I was next on her list. Not wanting to miss the event I put on the best shirt I had in my suitcase, some slacks, and sneakers. I was so insecure but was happy to be in the space. Throughout the night I was self-conscious and kept mentioning why I was there in sneakers every time I met a new person. Sitting in proximity was thee Billy Porter and I guess he got tired of hearing my story and said, "baby you are here, and you look fine, and no one is paying attention to your damn shoes anyway, let that go and enjoy yourself." I turned to my friend and said isn't that the guy from

Kinky Boots, she laughed and said boy give me your gay card. This was before he starred in the hit series Pose on FX, so cut me a little slack.

Porter is an award-winning actor, Broadway star, and a singer. He has dedicated his time to using this craft to express the perspectives of the downtrodden and misunderstood. He continues to work in film and song, acting as a representation and inspiration for all the queer people out there like myself. In 2021, Porter came out as HIV+ and works to normalize the HIV experience and debunk myths associated with the disease.

Lil Naz X (1999)

Lil Nas X is an American rapper, singer, songwriter, and media personality who I met at the 2019 BET Awards. I was on the red carpet doing an interview and this tall young man walks by me in a lime green country suit that was sparkled down. I immediately said to myself, he's going to be trouble. And boy was I right, like the late John Lewis would say, Lil Nas X is getting in good trouble.

This young Black man rose to prominence in the country music world, with the release of his country rap single "Old Town Road," which first achieved viral popularity in early 2019 before climbing music charts internationally and becoming diamond certified. On June 30, 2019, the last day of Pride Month, Lil Nas X came out publicly as gay, tweeting: "some of y'all already know, some of y'all don't care, some of y'all not gone fwm no more. but before this month ends i want y'all to listen closely to c7osure." Rolling Stone noted the song "touches on themes such as coming clean, growing up and embracing oneself." Since coming out, Lil Naz X has been shattering glass ceilings, making ways for young gay Black entertainers who are unapologetic about who they are. He also uses his platform to challenge the status quo and religious discrimination.

In the spring of 2021, Lil Naz X launched a controversial pair of

"Satan Shoes" featuring a bronze pentagram, an inverted cross, and a drop of real human blood -- and they sold out almost immediately. The shoes sparked outrage and attracted criticism from many political and religious leaders. In response, Lil Nas X posted a video to his official YouTube account titled "Lil Nas X Apologizes for Satan Shoe," but after a few seconds, the apology cuts to a scene from his music video, "Montero (Call Me by Your Name)," showing him dancing provocatively with Satan.

The day after Lil Nas X released the music video, he responded to the backlash over its rebellious religious imagery. "I spent my entire teenage years hating myself because of the shit y'all preached would happen to me because i was gay, so i hope u are mad, stay mad, feel the same anger you teach us to have towards ourselves."

Angelica Ross (1980)

Ross is a businesswoman, actress, and transgender rights advocate. A self-taught computer programmer, she went on to become founder and CEO of TransTech Social Enterprises, a firm that helps employ transgender people in the tech industry.

Ross began her acting career in the web series Her Story (2016), after which she received further recognition and critical acclaim for her starring roles in the FX drama series Pose and the FX anthology horror series American Horror Story. On September 20, 2019, Ross hosted the 2020 Presidential Candidate Forum on LGBTQIA+ Issues. This made her the first openly transgender person to host an American presidential forum. She is still continuing to make strides.

"Wherever you identify yourself sexually along God's rainbow of sexuality, know that you are not in error. Homosexual, Lesbian, Bisexual, Heterosexual, Transsexual...you are not a mistake. God made you the way you are and God loves you just the way you are. So love yourself and know that you are very special!"

~ ARCHBISHOP CARL BEAN

Chapter 19: The Real Gay Agenda

The Beginning

The gay rights movement, as we know it today, is not as recent as we might believe. Individuals have fought for the freedom to be themselves and maintain their sense of identity long before written texts even existed. In fact, clashes between humans have existed since the creation of mankind, each one trying to establish dominance over the other. From a biblical standpoint, Adam and Eve clashed over the tree in the Garden of Life, and not too long after, their children clashed, with one killing the other (Cain and Able).

In this regard, I think it is safe to assume that gay rights are as old as conflict itself in human history. Especially considering that gay humans have always been around. As societies evolved, so too did the records of their daily lives. For one, we know that homosexuality was widely practiced and accepted within the ancient Greek world.[239] Spartans were known to have male lovers as they would spend a significant part of their lives training and being deployed for combat.[240] The Romans were also accepting of homosexuality, and many instances of this can be found in the graffiti they have left behind.[241][242] And most recently, let's consider how the Native Americans were ahead of the times in regards to valuing all the elements of mankind. They honored the spectrum of gender and sexuality. They were so in touch with the human experience that it superseded basic understanding. Colonial powers miss that entirely and saw them as a primitive people.[243]

---

[239] Bynum, B. (2002). Homosexuality. *The Lancet, 359*(9325), 2284.
[240] Crompton, L. (2009). *Homosexuality and civilization.* Harvard University Press.
[241] Williams, C. A. (2010). *Roman homosexuality.* Oxford University Press.
[242] Levin-Richardson, S. (2013). Fututa sum hic: female subjectivity and agency in Pompeian sexual graffiti. *Classical Journal, The, 108*(3), 319-345.
[243] Tan, A., Fujioka, Y., & Lucht, N. (1997). Native American stereotypes, TV portrayals, and personal contact. *Journalism & Mass Communication Quarterly, 74*(2), 265-284.

This shows us that for one, being gay isn't a new phenomenon, and two, all the silly reasons people make up why people "turn gay" are just that, silly. Each era carries with it its own relationship to the LGBTQIA+ community. Each era has its own rules, beliefs, and stories. The question is, when do we get to the era where all humans are accepted for who they are and who they love? And what does getting there look like? There is no definite answer that can show us where the fight for gay rights began, but we know it wasn't in our lifetime. We can only refer to the people and the era and their respective fight for gay freedoms.

We, as a human race, still have a lot of progress to make. We all can join the fight in our own way using our own levels of influence. For instance, not all fights have been violent; some have been small-scale movements or protests. For example, Oscar Wilde, an 18th-century poet, used his position to subtly jab at the intolerances that existed within society.[244] Art and literature have often been at the forefront of expressing the opinions of those who are marginalized.[245] What can you bring to the fight? What special skill or talent do you have that can be used to push the needle forward? How can you use what God has given you to create a more equitable mankind?

Today, the fight for freedom and gay liberty has grown into a movement that perhaps the framers of the fight could not have imagined. Initially, people wanted the freedom to express their sexuality and live their lives without threat from others. However, the public only viewed the homosexual aspect of the fight and didn't consider the aspect of gender, identity, and biological sex, as I have explained in this book.

The gay movement has become something much larger; it is being

---

[244] Adut, A. (2005). A theory of scandal: Victorians, homosexuality, and the fall of Oscar Wilde. *American journal of sociology*, 111(1), 213-248.
[245] Crompton, L. (2009). *Homosexuality and civilization*. Harvard University Press.

led by young people. And not just young adults but youth and teens. People are coming into themselves at much earlier ages and rejecting the notion that who they are is wrong. At every level, anti-queerness is being challenged and rejected. In church, in school, at work, in athletic spaces, people are stepping up and speaking out. What also makes the movement different is the support from mainstream and corporate America. Hate speech is rejected, not tolerated, and comes with severe consequences. Advertisers have even embraced the diversity of mankind and have made space for LGBTQIA+ voices.

As we celebrate these amazing feats, we should also continue to consider and ponder on what the future might hold for this movement. There might still be different ways we oppress each other, sometimes without even knowing that we are doing harm.[246] As we become more educated about the human condition, it is likely that we will uncover more areas of oppression and bigotry. The queer and gay movement of the future will likely be quite a departure from what we can think of today. I like to think that we are leaving a positive legacy for future generations to follow.

Debunking Myths About the Gay Agenda

Those who oppose gay rights often come up with absurd conspiracy theories that vilify an already marginalized group as a blight on society. In their eyes, queer and gay people stand against their beliefs or values and thus are evil by default. You are either with us or against us, as the saying goes in those circles. To help fuel their hatred and generate an excuse for bigotry, they make claims of queer people being involved in the far-reaching conspiracy.[247]

These imagined plots consist of queer people spreading out into positions of power and then using their influence to change things in

---
[246] Engel, S. M., & Engel, S. M. (2001). *The unfinished revolution: Social movement theory and the gay and lesbian movement.* Cambridge University Press.
[247] Knight, P. (2000). *Conspiracy Culture: From the Kennedy assassination to the X-Files.* Psychology Press.

their favor. There is this idea that gay people are using nepotism and favoritism to attack any individual who does not toe the line to the progressive agenda.[248] Opponents will state that queer people are using the blanket of hate speech accusations to attack people, get them fired from their jobs, and publicly shaming to harass and intimidate those who would stand against them.[249] One merely has to look at the media to see how these claims are false. How could such an agenda exist, and there be no shred of proof that could verify it? It is quite clear that there those who oppose the gay rights movement do so because they are intolerant of other people being different from them. The gay agenda, if it even exists, is not to spread hate or violence. The gay agenda is about spreading peace, love, and tolerance within the community.

People like me know what it is like to be cornered and outnumbered. We know what it's like to be attacked simply for being true to yourself. Why would a movement led by us seek to instill the same punishment on others that we have received on our person? In many ways, the violent reactions by those opposing the gay agenda are more a reflection of their insecurities and violent tendencies. If they actually took the time to look at what we preach and promote, they would realize that our movement stands up for even their rights, not just our own. We want to support everyone. We are humanitarians, not tyrants bent out, forcing others to accept our views.

The Benefits of Queer Storytelling and Queer Characters in Media

Stories are a way of sharing information and passing on knowledge between the generations. For as long as we have had spoken communication and language, we have told stories. We have used this

---

[248] Sherry, M. S. (2007). *Gay artists in modern American culture: An imagined conspiracy.* Univ of North Carolina Press.
[249] Livers, K. A. (2020). Conspiracy Culture. In *Conspiracy Culture.* University of Toronto Press

narrative tool to convey ideas, express our thoughts and feelings, our hopes, our desires, our fears; it is a deep dive into the mind of the person speaking.[250]

Storytelling is something that is indicative of the person and the societal group from which the narrative emerges. It is for this reason that we find that each region or people within the world carry their own myths and legends. Some themes are universal, while others are more unique and particular. For instance, the fear of the dark is something that is universal amongst humans as an evolutionary outcome of avoiding predation.[251]

Having gay characters in gay stories is merely an acknowledgment of those elements within society that have existed alongside the normative group. Just because we refuse to name something does not mean it stops existing. Gay storytelling can help us explore the mindset of those who were normally shunned in society.[252] Think of the way average people relate to stories and use them as a tool of character exploration. Now, apply the same logic to gay storytelling and gay characters. Think of how much perspective the average straight person could gain by reading a story focusing on a gay protagonist.[253]

Aside from helping straight people empathize with the gay characters, it can lead to the slow but persistent development of solidarity. People fear what they don't understand or what they cannot relate to; stories are a perfect tool for creating that anchor. Furthermore, it helps as a morale boost to the rest of the queer community. It shows that their existence is not ignored and that they are not mere props in a play that are ignored in favor of the majority.[254]

---

[250] Yoder-Wise, P. S., & Kowalski, K. (2003). The power of storytelling. *Nursing Outlook, 51*(1), 37–42.
[251] Heerwagen, J. H., & Orians, G. H. (1995). Humans, habitats. *Biophilia hypothesis, 138,* 138–172.
[252] Gross, L. (2001). *Up from invisibility: Lesbians, gay men, and the media in America.* Columbia University Press.
[253] Christian, A. J. (2011). Gay Identity, New Storytelling, and the Media.
[254] Boon, R., & Plastow, J. (Eds.). (2004). *Theatre and empowerment: Community drama on the world stage.* Cambridge University Press.

This is especially beneficial for those who are stigmatized and might feel that they are all alone.

The Benefits of Telling the Stories of Black Queer Leaders Around the Country

Expounding on the previous point, we can improve our stories by having them positively influence people and change their views to be more tolerant and loving. Storytelling as a medium to raise awareness is a basic good that we can all hope to try and achieve with effort. However, the mere representation of a person is only the first step in moving towards a better future.[255]

Surely, if we can acknowledge the presence of a person, then we push the bar farther along the way. This might seem a bit biased, but it's really a reflection of the privilege that straight people have been enjoying for an untold amount of time.[256] This is not meant to be an insult or a jab. It is merely an attempt to point out something that most people might have taken for granted. Think back to your childhood and the stories and media that you grew up with and loved. Think about all the positive role models and heroic figures that were present in the media and stories that you consumed. Those things were not there by accident; they were there to push you in a certain direction. The human mind seeks inspirations and people on which it can model its own identity. How many of us have wanted to be superheroes in the past and continue to have the same aspirations even today?[257]

In fact, if you look at the recent media releases, you will find the hero narrative to be selling like hotcakes. People are in love with the idea of an individual taking charge of their life by embracing who they

---

[255] Zaidi, R., Freihofer, I., & Townsend, G. C. (2017, March). Using Scratch and Female Role Models while Storytelling Improves Fifth-Grade Students' Attitudes toward Computing. In *Proceedings of the 2017 ACM SIGCSE Technical Symposium on Computer Science Education* (pp. 791-792).
[256] Boatwright, T. (2019). Flux zine: Black queer storytelling. *Equity & Excellence in Education*, 52(4), 383-395.
[257] Fajer, M. A. (1991). Can Two Real Men Eat Quiche Together-Storytelling, Gender-Role Stereotypes, and Legal Protection for Lesbians and Gay Men. *U. Miami L. Rev.*, 46, 511.

are and not falling to the pressures of the world. That's all well and good, but what about the people who have been historically marginalized? They, too, were told to conform to a mold in which they did not fit, to give up their identity for a supposed "greater good."[258]

Through the power of positive role models and leaders within the stories that people consume, we can bring about a change. It can be as simple as placing marginalized groups into a position of power, authority, and leadership as a way to inspire other people. A gay Black man seeing another person like them acting in a role that is both desirable and admirable can go a long way. Think of how many minds we can uplift by showing them just how great a potential they can be through positive encouragement. It's not about pushing an agenda or bullying people into submission; it's about empowerment, encouragement, and giving people hope.

If you remember, this is how God answered my prayers. He began to show me who I could be as an out and proud gay Black leader through examples of powerful Black gay leaders. People are complaining that there's too many random gay characters for no reason. I say there's not enough. The fact that people are complaining about queerness on TV is all the more reason to give us more. We need to normalize queerness.

Gay Liberation Around the World

It is a sad reality of a modern world that not all countries embrace all people despite their differences. There are still many areas in the world where gay people face discrimination, and somewhere, they face a threat to their very existence.[259] In general, most western countries demonstrate a high level of tolerance for queer people. Not all of these countries are equal in their standing, but they demonstrate

---

[258] Allen, J. S. (2012). Black/queer/diaspora at the current conjuncture. *GLQ: A Journal of Lesbian and Gay Studies*, 18(2-3), 211-248.
[259] Walter, A. (2018). *Come Together: Years of Gay Liberation*. Verso Books.

a level of care that is beyond what is found in the east, particularly in Asia, the Middle East, and Africa.[260][261][262]

Canada, Netherlands, and Spain demonstrate some of the highest levels of tolerance and support for the queer community. In fact, the Canadian Prime Minister Justin Trudeau has been seen on multiple occasions going out of his way to take part in pride marches as a demonstration of his support to the queer community. In most western countries, gay marriage is seen as a default right that citizens should have. Take note of this notion; it is a right and not a privilege. This shows just how far we have come in making historically excluded people feel like a part of society. However, not everything is sunshine and roses. [263]

In some countries in Africa and the Middle East, queer and gay people face serious dangers. They can be imprisoned and sentenced to death under the allegations of being impure or spreading supposed degeneracy. These areas practice a system where their faith-based values are an inherent part of the government instead of being a private matter like most developed countries. For this reason, personal expression is much more limited, as one can end up offending or acting against a government simply by expressing who they are as a person. For example, in Iraq, one can be sentenced to death if they are proven or even suspected of being a homosexual. Even in Russia, queer people and their ability to express themselves are greatly limited by the authoritarian government.

It is sad to say that the United States, a country founded on the idea of life, liberty, and the pursuit of happiness, is not on the top of the tolerance list. In fact, in many ways, we may have regressed into a

---

[260] Mole, R. C. (2016). Nationalism and homophobia in Central and Eastern Europe. In *The EU enlargement and gay politics* (pp. 99-121). Palgrave Macmillan, London.
[261] Clobert, M. (2020). East vs. West: Psychology of religion in East Asian cultures. *Current Opinion in Psychology*.
[262] Whitaker, B. (2011). *Unspeakable Love: Gay and lesbian life in the Middle East*. Saqi.
[263] Arestis, S. (2020, December 16). *Our top 25 most gay-friendly countries in the world*. Nomadic Boys. https://nomadicboys.com/most-gay-friendly-countries-in-the-world/

more primitive state as our society has dug into trenches to defend its positions. However, it is still important to consider the size of the country. Each state can represent its own nation, owing to the considerable real estate America occupies. As such, moving across the United States is akin to moving between different nations.

The more liberal and developed parts of the country demonstrate strong support for the queer community. For example, California is widely proclaimed as being the most tolerant state in the entire country. Where queer people face increased resistance and aggression is in the rural and less developed parts of the country that identify as conservatives. I'm not saying that all conservatives are bad, nor that all liberals are good. Still, we cannot deny that there is a heavy bias against queer people in the conservative community.[264][265][266]

While they may not express this animosity outright due to federal laws, they can still undermine other people in a multitude of ways. For example, communities can isolate a queer person or group by refusing to let them participate in events and be a part of a larger collective. Queer folks may be ignored or face a bias when seeking employment. No one will explicitly state their reasons or display outright hostility, but the implicit shade is there. In this case, the queer person is tolerated at best and silently hated at worst. They are prodded and nudged to get them to leave and be with their "own kind." Queer or Black, it does not matter, only that they belong to the "other."

---

[264] Tilcsik, A. (2011). Pride and prejudice: employment discrimination against openly gay men in the United States. *American Journal of Sociology*, 117(2), 586-626.
[265] Martos, A. J., Wilson, P. A., & Meyer, I. H. (2017). Lesbian, gay, bisexual, and transgender (LGBT) health services in the United States: Origins, evolution, and contemporary landscape. *PloS one*, 12(7), e0180544.
[266] Casey, L. S., Reisner, S. L., Findling, M. G., Blendon, R. J., Benson, J. M., Sayde, J. M., & Miller, C. (2019). Discrimination in the United States: Experiences of lesbian, gay, bisexual, transgender, and queer Americans. *Health services research*, 54, 1454-1466.

I'M BLACK, I'M A MINISTER, AND I'M GAY

"I believe that telling our stories, first to ourselves and then to one another and the world, is a revolutionary act."

~ JANET MOCK

Chapter 20: Love Wins; How to Live Free

Love

One night while bored, scrolling through the thousands of channels that are now available on internet TV, I stumbled upon a very interesting movie called Ex Machina (2014). In the movie, the protagonist talks about the idea of a robot truly understanding what it means to be alive. He uses a thought experiment to explore the idea. Think about an individual who lives in a sealed chamber where everything is Black and white, including themselves. For their entire lives, they have never seen color. However, they have been fed a consistent and progressive stream of knowledge on colors.

This includes everything from light interaction, the emotional response from humans, and all manner of physical properties. Still, despite all of their knowledge, they have never actually seen a color. It is only after being released into the world of color, free from their Black and white prison, can they truly know what it is like to see color.

That is what Love is. You can be given all the definitions and descriptions of love in the world, but it doesn't become real until you experience it.

Love is such a universal concept that no matter where you are in the world, you can experience it. Pure love is the acceptance of oneself and everyone else around you. To love another unconditionally is the greatest gift you can give to them. When one realizes this reality of love, they begin to express an inherent need to ensure that the well-being of other people is sustained and secured. Love can exist in different forms. Think about the love between a parent and a child, a pet and its owner, the love between friends, the love between siblings, and the love between a teacher and their students. Love exists all around us; we only need to recognize it.

Love Is the Answer

How is love the answer to the extensive problem of intolerance and hate? Love is a position that brings empathy and understanding in a way that words or technical explanations can never achieve. It is one thing to be told of the pain of another individual, but another to live through the experiences. It is why movies and media that allow us to "see" through the eyes of a person are so effective in their message.

We learn the context and setting from the perspective of another and come to understand many of the questions we may have had regarding their lives or actions. Ever watch a movie, and you doubt the actions of a character until a scene reveals the full picture? Suddenly the suspicion becomes clear, and we may even stand by them as they make questionable decisions.

When people learn to love, they also learn to impart a piece of themselves to others and vice versa. It is this exchange of commonality and the establishment of humanity between people that allows us to become a better collective. Think about how human civilization came into existence. We moved away from our tribal state, recognizing the humanity in others, putting our differences aside for a common goal. As we advance as a humanity, we are becoming more intertwined. People will even begin to shy away from national or citizenship-based intolerance. It is predicted that white people's grandchildren will not look like their white grandparents as more races begin to intermingle.

We are all people, and we are all inwardly, whether recognized or not, striving to be our true selves. It is only by accepting others and our true identity we can live authentic versions of our lives, free from the superficial layer that use to be presentable to a supposed ideal. Love is the key that allows people to truly appreciate themselves and others around them, no matter how different they are. If you have pure love for yourself, you have pure love for others.

When one does not love themselves, they end up projecting that hatred toward themselves at another human. If they operated in pure love, they would instead project their love on another person, and harmony would prevail. We don't have to agree with the choices that other people make, but we can certainly stand up for their right to make those choices.

Love Is an Inside Job

Self-love is an important issue that should be handled with the utmost care. The identity of a person is very much the core of their being and is, in large parts, the defining feature they use to connect and contextualize their existence. If you don't love who you are, it is impossible to love others. I can't teach you tolerance if you can't even tolerate yourself. From birth, many people are taught to find love externally and never taught to find love internally first. We prepare ourselves to be loved and liked by others but never prepare ourselves to love ourselves. But it's never too late to start.

There are a certain number of things that we cannot change about ourselves or our upbringing. But that doesn't mean we can't work to change the things we do have control over. And most times we can't get there on our own. It takes the love of another to guide us to that place. Sometimes we have to go through a make-over to get in touch with the real us. When a person knows who they are, they have a sense of direction in their life; a purpose that grounds them.

What's the harm in getting to know the real you? What are you afraid of? Why not just explore you? After all, no one can know you better than you, right? But sometimes, we need help getting to know the real us. While thinking about yourself and reflecting on your ideals is important, you have to look at the bigger picture that includes outside forces you may be overlooking. You cannot be completely objective when trying to criticize yourself.

To assess yourself accurately, you have to be unbiased and objective. Most times, this is not possible because of our preconceived notions and unconscious biases. It's like trying to measure a problem with a broken scale. You need an outside perspective to help shed light on the issue. A good therapist will help you bring out thoughts and ideas that you might be suppressing or were floating around in your head without you knowing.

A trained therapist is not a magic pill that will solve all your problems, but it's a start. You may have to shop around for a professional who is the best fit for you and your needs. Remember, therapists are people too; you will get along with some more than others, it is to be expected.

The idea is to better understand yourself, so you can be free and authentic. Once you are free from the things stopping you from knowing yourself, you can begin to fall in love with the real you. Sometimes these deep-seeded issues cannot be explored on your own. It's an inside job that may require another to dive in with you. It is always a good idea to seek a professional who can help you explore. It was through much therapy that I learned to love the whole me. Do not let the stigma of mental illness cloud your judgment from doing what's best for you.

Becoming Holistic for The Greater Good

Holistic means in context or relation to a greater whole. That is, taking into consideration and thinking about things not just in their local application but the greater conceptual framework that connects everything else. This vast array of the web is akin to the internet.

The devices that we use are like the small parts of a whole that contribute to the creation of a widespread collective that is greater than the sum of the whole. This vast and expansive web has led to the creation of many services that would have seemed right out of science fiction to the early people not aware of these technologies.

Think about what we can do with our smartphones alone. We can order food, book travel tickets, make reservations, play games, talk across vast distances, order taxis, invest in our portfolio, conduct banking transactions, and so much more.

How did all of this happen? How was this even possible in the first place? We made it happen by connecting the different aspects of our daily lives through a series of networks that everyone else is operating on. In this same manner, you can connect yourself on a greater level, bringing parts of yourself together to be more holistic while at the same time connecting with the greater whole.

Being holistic is about seeing all the things that make you you, operating in a world where others are being themselves. We are all a part of the greater whole. We can order our food online at the same time as millions of other people are doing a million other things on that same network.

The same idea applies to sexual orientation and gender identity. We all don't have to be the same. You can live your life as you choose with your significant other or others, and I can live my life as I choose with my man or menz', and we still have enough life to go around.

Becoming holistic is not shrinking so that others can fit, but it's expanding to the fullness of who you are so that we all can harmoniously be looped and tied in together as one human race. Presenting only a piece of yourself to the world leaves so much of life untapped. Being one-minded or close-minded only feeds ignorance, intolerance, and hatred. Furthermore, the presentation of a façade only eats away at the authentic self until you find yourself as a hollow shell, existing only on the surface.

Truly Loving Yourself Takes Time

While reading through this book, some of you might have gotten excited and enthusiastic about becoming a better person. Many of you will think, ok, now it is time to cast off the chains that society has thrown on me and become liberated. I think this is beautiful; you should be motivated to be true to yourself.

Without a doubt freedom and liberty are things that come with struggle and sacrifice. You don't just become liberated; you have to fight for it. But more importantly, you need to maintain your liberty of mind or risk going backwards because you could not handle the increased freedom that you were so desperately seeking. Your journey ahead will not be like some heroic movie plot. There will be many struggles, and there will be many bumps and even boulders along the way. You will have to be truly persistent and dedicated to the task if you want any hopes of achievement.

Freedom is a constant journey. Life, people, and circumstances will always push you to revert to what is familiar, what is most comfortable. This happens naturally and spiritually. If you stop working out, your body will revert to its out-of-shape form. If you stop expanding your mind, it will revert to what was the norm. I've been closeted longer than I have been out. My mindset and patterns always want to revert to that lifestyle. I must work hard to maintain my freedom and mentality. One cannot just love themselves by flipping a switch. Think about all that you have read in the previous chapters. Thoughts and mental concepts are like deep trenches carved out in the fields of our minds; they don't just disappear because of our whims. Think back to the people who were so brainwashed by colonial ideas that they turned from the oppressed into the oppressors. The colonized person started lashing out at his own people, beating them into submission for not falling into the same neat little box as he did.

The ideas you have about yourself and your sense of being may be deeply rooted, with many of them being poisonous. Pulling them out or resolving the conundrums they present will not be easy. The hardest battles are fought in the mind. You won't just wake up one day and start to think, hey, I love myself, and I'm so great. It may feel that way for a while; you may feel elevated and high on energy. This high does not last long; it comes crashing down when confronted with strong opposition. You have to slowly resolve the conflicts and the poisonous thoughts from your mind. Nullify them so that you can operate while being normal, don't rely on the high as a persistent state to get you through life. As with anything that has true value, it takes time and patience, but the rewards are worth the effort.

Don't Let Gender or Sexuality Be Your Only Qualifier

This part may seem to be quite contradictory to the message of the book. Trust me, it is a part of being holistic, and I'm not trying to take away from your sense of sexuality or gender identity. People have, and still do, possess qualities and attributes that exist outside the scope of sexuality and gender identity.

Think about it for a second; it's why we have the entire spectrum trying to represent the endless range of diversities that are possible. Sexual orientation and gender identity are core features of a person; they are very important; no one can deny this argument. However, to make these qualities, the only thing around which your life revolves is akin to ignoring or removing other parts of yourselves that can be equally as important. Think about your passions and your desires; what do you want to achieve in life.

I know this might be a hard line of thought for some who have spent their entire lives dedicated to fighting for justice. Still, think about it for a moment, consider the possibility that your fight, your justice, and your liberty have succeeded. You have won, we are now all equal, the war is over.

Now, what would you do next? Pursue a dream, learn a trade, explore, settle down? Even those who came before us, the ones who started the fight, did so because they wanted the freedom to live their life as they saw fit. They wanted to be free, not just to express their sexuality and identity, but to have the rights and access to the liberty afforded to those in power. You are not just your sexual or gender identity. You are also your dreams, your hopes, your wants, your desires, and your aspirations. Don't fall into the trap that popular media likes to spout; they think that people like us only exist in our sexual and gender identities. Ignorant people try to push the idea of us being beastly creatures, only driven by lust and desire.

Do not let their bigoted mindset shrink your own purpose and sense of true self. Think about who you truly are and what you want to do; do not be brainwashed by the ignorance of people. They don't know you, and they cannot judge you, be free, and be true to yourself.

7 Reasons Why Living in Your Truth Won't Send You to Hell

I can almost bet you are wondering where in the world are the seven reasons. Did he forget to outline them in the book? Nope, I didn't. Throughout the book, I've laid out tons of reasons why living in your truth won't send you to Hell. You may find one reason that works for you or ten reasons that work for you. Everyone is experiencing this book and relating to it in their own way. At the end of life, it is only you and your idea of your creator. I'd be foolish to give you my personal reasons of why you're not going to Hell. How about you tell me why you're not going to Hell. Is Hell even real? Why are humans more focused on Hell in the first place. Shouldn't love be our motivation to treat others right? After reading this book, you should be well equipped with your own answers.

What seven reasons did you pull from the book that made sense for you?

I'd love to read them and post them for others to see. Visit me at www.imfreeforme.com or find me on social media at @ibencarlton.

Let's talk!